DIVE INTO ALGORITHMS

A Pythonic Adventure for the Intrepid Beginner

Bradford Tuckfield

**no starch
press**

DIVE INTO ALGORITHMS. Copyright © 2021 by Bradford Tuckfield

Printed in in the United States of America

First printing

24 23 22 21 20   1 2 3 4 5 6 7 8 9

ISBN-13: 978-1-71850-068-6 (print)
ISBN-13: 978-1-71850-069-3 (ebook)

Publisher: William Pollock
Execuitve Editor: Barbara Yien
Production Editors: Maureen Forys, Happenstance Type-O-Rama and Laurel Chun
Developmental Editor: Alex Freed
Cover Design: Gina Redman
Interior Design: Octopod Studios
Technical Reviewer: Alok Malik
Copyeditor: Scout Festa
Compositor: Jeff Lytle, Happenstance Type-O-Rama
Proofreader: Rachel Monaghan
Illustrator: Jeff Wilson, Happenstance Type-O-Rama
Indexer: Valerie Perry

For information on distribution, translations, or bulk sales, please contact No Starch Press, Inc. directly:
No Starch Press, Inc.
245 8th Street, San Francisco, CA 94103
phone: 1.415.863.9900; info@nostarch.com
www.nostarch.com

Library of Congress Cataloging-in-Publication Data

Names: Tuckfield, Bradford, author.
Title: Dive into algorithms / Bradford Tuckfield.
Description: San Francisco : No Starch Press, [2020] | Includes index.
Identifiers: LCCN 2020026327 (print) | LCCN 2020026328 (ebook) | ISBN
    9781718500686 (paperback) | ISBN 1718500688 (paperback) | ISBN
    9781718500693 (ebook)
Subjects: LCSH: Computer algorithms. | Computer programming.
Classification: LCC QA76.9.A43 T83 2020 (print) | LCC QA76.9.A43 (ebook)
    | DDC 005.13--dc23
LC record available at https://lccn.loc.gov/2020026327
LC ebook record available at https://lccn.loc.gov/2020026328

Dedicated to my parents, David and Becky
Tuckfield, for believing in me and for
teaching me *la pipopipette.*

About the Author

Bradford Tuckfield is a data scientist and writer. He runs a data science consulting firm called Kmbara (*https://kmbara.com/*) and a fiction website called Dreamtigers (*http://thedreamtigers.com/*).

About the Technical Reviewer

Alok Malik is a data scientist based in New Delhi, India. He works on developing deep learning models in both natural language processing and computer vision with Python. He has developed and deployed solutions such as language models, image and text classifiers, language translators, speech-to-text models, named entity recognizers, and object detectors. He has also co-authored a book on machine learning. In his free time he likes to read about finance, do MOOCs, and play video games on his console.

BRIEF CONTENTS

CONTENTS IN DETAIL

ACKNOWLEDGMENTS

"A word is not the same with one writer as it is with another. One tears it from his guts. The other pulls it out of his overcoat pocket." This is how Charles Peguy described writing individual words. The same thing is true of chapters and whole books. At times, it felt like I was pulling this book out of my overcoat pocket. At other times, it felt like I was tearing it from my guts. It seems appropriate to acknowledge everyone who contributed to the long process, either by loaning me an overcoat or by helping me clean up my spilled guts.

Many kind people helped me on the long path I took to gain the experience and skills required to write this book. My parents, David and Becky Tuckfield, gave me so many gifts, starting with life and education, and continued to believe in me, encourage me, and help me in many other ways too numerous to list here. Scott Robertson gave me my first job writing code, even though I was unqualified and not very good. Randy Jenson gave me my first data science job, again despite my inexperience and limitations. Kumar Kashyap gave me my first chance to lead a development team to implement algorithms. David Zou was the first person to pay me for writing an article ($10 minus PayPal fees for 10 short movie reviews), and that felt so good, it put me on a path to writing more. Aditya Date was the first person to suggest that I write a book and gave me my first chance to do so.

I also received encouragement from many teachers and mentors. David Cardon gave me my first chance to collaborate on academic research, and taught me many things during that process. Bryan Skelton and

Leonard Woo showed me examples of what I wanted to grow up to be. Wes Hutchinson taught me crucial algorithms, like k-means clustering, and helped me better understand how algorithms work. Chad Emmett taught me how to think about history and culture, and Chapter 2 is dedicated to him. Uri Simonsohn showed me how to think about data.

Some people helped to make the process of writing this book a joy. Seshu Edala helped me adjust my work schedule to be able to write, and provided constant encouragement. Alex Freed was a joy to work with during the editing process. Jennifer Eagar, via Venmo transfer months before initial publication, unofficially became the first person to buy a copy of the book; that was appreciated during a difficult time. Hlaing Hlaing Tun was supportive, helpful, sweet, and encouraging at every step.

I cannot repay all of these debts of gratitude, but at least I can say thank you. Thank you!

INTRODUCTION

Algorithms are everywhere. You have probably executed a few already today. In this book, you will read about dozens of algorithms: some simple, some complex, some famous, some unknown, all interesting, and all worth learning. The first algorithm of the book is also the most delicious—it generates a berry granola parfait, and it's shown in its entirety in Figure 1. You may be accustomed to calling this type of algorithm a "recipe," but it fits Donald Knuth's definition of an *algorithm*: a finite set of rules that gives a sequence of operations for solving a specific type of problem.

Berry Granola Parfaits

Directions

1. Place one-sixth of one cup of blueberries at the bottom of a large serving glass.
2. Cover the blueberries with a half cup of plain Turkish yogurt.
3. Place one-third of one cup of granola on top of the yogurt.
4. Cover the granola with a half cup of plain Turkish yogurt.
5. Place strawberries on top of everything in the glass so far.
6. Top it all off with your favorite whipped cream.

Figure 1: An algorithm: a finite set of rules that gives a sequence of operations for solving a specific type of problem

Parfait-making is not the only domain of life governed by algorithms. Every year, the US government requires each adult citizen to execute an algorithm, and strives to imprison those who fail to do so correctly. In 2017, millions of Americans fulfilled this duty by completing the algorithm shown in Figure 2, which is taken from a form called 1040-EZ.

1	Wages, salaries, and tips. This should be shown in box 1 of your Form(s) W-2. Attach your Form(s) W-2.	1
2	Taxable interest. If the total is over $1,500, you cannot use Form 1040EZ.	2
3	Unemployment compensation and Alaska Permanent Fund dividends (see instructions).	3
4	Add lines 1, 2, and 3. This is your **adjusted gross income.**	4
5	If someone can claim you (or your spouse if a joint return) as a dependent, check the applicable box(es) below and enter the amount from the worksheet on back. ☐ **You** ☐ **Spouse** If no one can claim you (or your spouse if a joint return), enter $10,400 if **single;** $20,800 if **married filing jointly.** See back for explanation.	5
6	Subtract line 5 from line 4. If line 5 is larger than line 4, enter -0-. This is your **taxable income.** ▶	6
7	Federal income tax withheld from Form(s) W-2 and 1099.	7
8a	**Earned income credit (EIC)** (see instructions)	8a
b	Nontaxable combat pay election. 8b	
9	Add lines 7 and 8a. These are your **total payments and credits.** ▶	9
10	**Tax.** Use the amount on **line 6 above** to find your tax in the tax table in the instructions. Then, enter the tax from the table on this line.	10
11	Health care: individual responsibility (see instructions) Full-year coverage ☐	11
12	Add lines 10 and 11. This is your **total tax.**	12

Figure 2: The instructions for filing taxes fit the definition of an algorithm.

How is it that taxes and parfaits can have anything in common? Taxes are inevitable, numeric, difficult, and universally disliked. Parfaits are infrequent, artistic, effortless, and adored without exception. The only trait they share is that people prepare both by following algorithms.

In addition to defining *algorithm*, the great computer scientist Donald Knuth noted that it is nearly synonymous with *recipe*, *procedure*, and *rigmarole*. In the case of filing taxes via the pictured 1040-EZ form, we have 12 steps (a finite list) that specify operations (like addition in step 4 and subtraction in step 6) to solve a specific type of problem: wanting to avoid being imprisoned for tax evasion. In the case of making a parfait, we have six finite steps that specify operations (like placing in step 1 and covering in step 2) to solve a specific type of problem: wanting to have a parfait in your hand or mouth.

As you learn more about algorithms, you will begin to see them everywhere and come to appreciate just how powerful they can be. In Chapter 1, we will discuss the remarkable human ability to catch a ball, and find out the details of the algorithm in the human subconscious that enables us to do so. Later, we will talk about algorithms for debugging code, deciding how much to eat at a buffet, maximizing revenue, sorting lists, scheduling tasks, proofreading text, delivering mail, and winning games like chess and sudoku. Along the way, we will learn to judge algorithms according to several attributes that professionals believe are important for them to possess. And we will begin to get a sense of the craftsmanship or even, dare we say, the *art* of algorithms, which provides scope for creativity and personality in an otherwise precise and quantitative endeavor.

Who Is This Book For?

This book provides a friendly introduction to algorithms, with accompanying Python code. To get the greatest possible benefit from it, you should have some experience with the following:

Programming/coding. Every major example in the book is illustrated with Python code. We strive to provide walkthroughs and explanations of every code snippet to make the book digestible for someone with no Python experience and not much programming experience. Nevertheless, someone who has at least some basic understanding of the fundamentals of programming—such as variable assignment, for loops, if/then statements, and function calls—will be the most prepared to benefit.

High school math. Algorithms are often used to accomplish many of the same goals as math, like solving equations, optimizing, and calculating values. Algorithms also apply many of the same principles that are associated with mathematical thinking, like logic and the need for precise definitions. Some of our discussions veer into mathematical territory, including algebra, the Pythagorean theorem, pi, and the teensiest bit of very basic calculus. We strive to avoid abstruseness and we don't venture beyond the math taught in American high schools.

Anyone who feels comfortable with these prerequisites should be able to master all the content in this book. It was written with the following groups in mind:

Students. This book is suitable for an introductory class on algorithms, computer science, or programming at the high school or undergraduate level.

Professionals.   Several types of professionals could gain valuable skills from this book, including developers or engineers who want to gain familiarity with Python, and developers who want to learn more about the foundations of computer science and how to improve code by thinking algorithmically.

Interested amateurs.   The true target audience of this book is interested amateurs. Algorithms touch nearly every part of life, so everyone should be able to find at least something in this book that enhances their appreciation of the world around them.

About This Book

This book does not cover every aspect of every extant algorithm; it's meant only as an introduction. After reading it, you will have a solid grasp of what an algorithm is, know how to write code to implement important algorithms, and understand how to judge and optimize algorithms' performance. You will also be familiar with many of the most popular algorithms professionals use today. The chapters are organized as follows:

Chapter 1: Problem-Solving with Algorithms, in which we tackle the problem of how to catch a ball, find evidence for a subconscious algorithm governing human behavior, and discuss what that teaches us about the utility of algorithms and how to design them.

Chapter 2: Algorithms in History, in which we travel around the world and through history to find out how ancient Egyptians and Russian peasants multiplied numbers, how the ancient Greeks found greatest common divisors, and how medieval Japanese scholars created magic squares.

Chapter 3: Maximizing and Minimizing, in which we introduce gradient ascent and gradient descent. These simple methods for finding the maxima and minima of functions are used for optimization, an important goal of many algorithms.

Chapter 4: Sorting and Searching, in which we present fundamental algorithms for sorting lists and searching for elements within them. We also introduce how to measure the efficiency and speed of algorithms.

Chapter 5: Pure Math, in which we concern ourselves with purely mathematical algorithms, including those for generating continued fractions, calculating square roots, and generating pseudorandom numbers.

Chapter 6: Advanced Optimization, in which we cover an advanced method for finding optimal solutions: simulated annealing. We also introduce the traveling salesman problem, a standard problem in advanced computer science.

Chapter 7: Geometry, in which we go over how to generate Voronoi diagrams, which can be useful in a variety of geometric applications.

Chapter 8: Language, in which we discuss how to intelligently add spaces to a text that's missing them, and how to intelligently suggest the next words in phrases.

Chapter 9: Machine Learning, in which we discuss decision trees, a fundamental machine learning method.

Chapter 10: Artificial Intelligence, in which we jump to an ambitious project: implementing an algorithm that can play games against us—and maybe even win. We start with a simple game, dots and boxes, and discuss how we could improve performance.

Chapter 11: Forging Ahead, in which talk about how to progress to more advanced work related to algorithms. We discuss how to build a chatbot, and how to win a million dollars by creating a sudoku algorithm.

Setting Up the Environment

We'll implement the algorithms described in this book by using the Python language. Python is free and open source, and it runs on every major platform. You can use the following steps to install Python on Windows, macOS, and Linux.

Install Python on Windows

To install Python on Windows, follow these steps:

1. Open the page dedicated to the latest version of Python for Windows (make sure you include the final slash): *https://www.python.org/downloads/windows/*.

2. Click the link for the Python release you want to download. To download the most recent release, click the link **Latest Python 3 Release - 3.X.Y**, where *3.X.Y* is the latest version number, like 3.8.3. The code in this book was tested on both Python 3.6 and Python 3.8. If you're interested in downloading an older version, scroll down on this page to the Stable Releases section to find a release you prefer.

3. The link you clicked in step 2 takes you to a page dedicated to your chosen Python release. In the Files section, click the **Windows x86-64 executable installer** link.

4. The link in step 3 downloads a *.exe* file to your computer. This is an installer file; double-click it to open it. It will execute the installation process automatically. Check the box **Add Python 3.X to PATH** where *X* is the release number of the installer you downloaded, like 8. After that, click **Install Now** and choose the default options.

5. When you see the "Setup was successful" message, click **Close** to complete the installation process.

There is now a new application on your computer. Its name is Python 3.*X*, where *X* is the version of Python 3 that you installed. In the Windows search bar, type `Python`. When the application appears, click it to open a Python console. You can enter Python commands in this console, and they'll run there.

Install Python on macOS

To install Python on macOS follow these steps:

1. Open the page dedicated to the latest version of Python for macOS (make sure you include the final slash): *https://www.python.org/downloads/ mac-osx/*.

2. Click the link for the Python release you want to download. To download the most recent release, click the link **Latest Python 3 Release - 3.X.Y**, where *3.X.Y* is the latest version number, like 3.8.3. The code in this book was tested on both Python 3.6 and Python 3.8. If you're interested in downloading an older version, scroll down on this page to the Stable Releases section to find a release you prefer.

3. The link you clicked in step 2 takes you to a page dedicated to the latest Python release. In the Files section, click the **macOS 64-bit installer** link.

4. The link in step 3 downloads a *.pkg* file to your computer. This is an installer file; double-click it to open it. It will execute the installation process automatically. Choose the default options.

5. The installer will create a folder on your computer called *Python 3*.X, where *X* is the number of the Python release you installed. In this folder, double-click the icon labeled IDLE. This will open the Python 3.*X.Y* Shell, where *3.X.Y* is the latest version number. This is a Python console where you can run any Python commands.

Install Python on Linux

To install Python on Linux follow these steps:

1. Determine which package manager your version of Linux uses. Two common examples of package managers are `yum` and `apt-get`.

2. Open the Linux console (also called the terminal), and execute the following two commands:

```
> sudo apt-get update
> sudo apt-get install python3.8
```

If you are using `yum` or some other package manager, replace both instances of `apt-get` in these two lines with `yum` or the name of your package manager. Likewise, if you want to install an older version of Python, replace `3.8` (the latest version number at the time of this writing) with any other release number, like 3.6, one of the versions used to test the code in this book. To see what the latest version of Python is, go to *https://www.python.org/downloads/source/*. There, you will see a **Latest Python 3 Release - Python 3.***X.Y* link, where *3.X.Y* is a release number; use the first two digits in the installation command just shown.

3. Run Python by executing the following command in the Linux console:

```
python3
```

The Python console opens in the Linux console window. You can enter Python commands here.

Installing Third-Party Modules

Some of the code we'll introduce in this book will rely on Python modules that are not part of the core Python software that you downloaded from Python's official website. To install third-party modules on your computer, follow the instructions at *http://automatetheboringstuff.com/2e/appendixa/*.

Summary

Our study of algorithms will take us around the world and many centuries back through history. We'll explore innovations from ancient Egypt, Babylon, Periclean Athens, Baghdad, medieval Europe, Edo Japan, and the British Raj, all the way up to our remarkable present day and its breathtaking technology. We'll be pushed to find new ways around problems and through constraints that initially seem impossible to confront. In doing so, we'll connect not only to the pioneers of ancient science but also to anyone today who uses a computer or catches a ball, to generations of algorithm users and creators yet unborn who will build on what we leave to them in faraway times. This book is the beginning of your adventure with algorithms.

1

PROBLEM-SOLVING WITH ALGORITHMS

The act of catching a ball is remarkable. A ball may start so far away that it seems only a speck on the horizon. It may be in the air for only a few short seconds or less. The ball will meet air resistance, wind, and of course, gravity, moving in something like a parabolic arc. And each time a ball is thrown, it is sent with a different force, at a different angle, and in a different environment with different conditions. So how is it that the moment a batter hits a baseball, an outfielder 300 feet away seems to immediately know where to run in order to catch it before it hits the ground?

This question is called *the outfielder problem*, and it's still being discussed in scholarly journals today. We're starting with the outfielder problem because it has two very different solutions: an analytic solution and an algorithmic solution. Comparing these solutions will provide a vivid illustration of what an algorithm is and how it's different from other approaches to problem-solving. Additionally, the outfielder problem will help us visualize a field that is occasionally abstract—you probably have some experience throwing and catching something, and this experience can help you understand the theory behind your practice.

Before we can really understand how a human knows exactly where a ball will land, it will help to understand how a machine does it. We'll start by looking at an analytic solution to the outfielder problem. This solution is mathematically precise and easy for computers to execute instantaneously, and some version of it is usually taught in introductory physics classes. It would enable a sufficiently agile robot to play outfield for a baseball team.

However, humans can't easily run analytic equations in their heads, and certainly not as quickly as computers can. A solution that's better suited to human brains is an algorithmic solution, which we'll use to explore what an algorithm is and what its strengths are compared to other problem-solving solutions. Moreover, the algorithmic solution will show us that algorithms are natural to human thought processes and don't need to be intimidating. The outfielder problem is meant to introduce a new way to solve problems: the algorithmic approach.

The Analytic Approach

To solve this problem analytically, we have to go back a few centuries to an early model of motion.

The Galilean Model

The equations most commonly used to model a ball's movement date back to Galileo, who centuries ago formulated polynomials that capture acceleration, speed, and distance. If we ignore wind and air resistance and assume the ball starts at ground level, Galileo's model says that the horizontal position of a thrown ball at time t will be given by the formula

$$x = v_1 t$$

where v_1 represents the starting speed of the ball in the x (horizontal) direction. Moreover, the height of a thrown ball (y), according to Galileo, can be calculated at time t as

$$y = v_2 t + \frac{at^2}{2}$$

where v_2 represents the starting speed of the ball in the y (vertical) direction, and a represents the constant downward acceleration due to gravity (which will be about −9.81 if we are working in metric units). When we substitute the first equation into the second equation, we find that the height of a thrown ball (y) relates to the horizontal position of the ball (x) as follows:

$$y = \frac{v_2}{v_1}x + \frac{ax^2}{2v_1^2}$$

We can use Galileo's equations to model a hypothetical ball's trajectory in Python using the function in Listing 1-1. The specific polynomial in Listing 1-1 is appropriate for a ball whose initial horizontal speed is about 0.99 meters per second, and whose initial vertical speed is about 9.9 meters per second. You can feel free to try other values for v_1 and v_2 to model any type of throw that interests you.

```
def ball_trajectory(x):
    location = 10*x - 5*(x**2)
    return(location)
```

Listing 1-1: A function for calculating the trajectory of a ball

We can plot the function in Listing 1-1 in Python to see what, approximately, a ball's trajectory should look like (ignoring air resistance and other negligible factors). We'll import some plotting capabilities from a module called matplotlib in the first line. The matplotlib module is one of many third-party modules we'll import in code throughout this book. Before you use a third-party module, you'll have to install it. You can install matplotlib and any other third-party modules by following the instructions at *http:// automatetheboringstuff.com/2e/appendixa/*.

```
import matplotlib.pyplot as plt
xs = [x/100 for x in list(range(201))]
ys = [ball_trajectory(x) for x in xs]
plt.plot(xs,ys)
plt.title('The Trajectory of a Thrown Ball')
plt.xlabel('Horizontal Position of Ball')
plt.ylabel('Vertical Position of Ball')
plt.axhline(y = 0)
plt.show()
```

Listing 1-2: Plotting a hypothetical ball trajectory between the moment it is thrown (at x = 0) and when it hits the ground again (at x = 2)

The output (Figure 1-1) is a nice plot that shows the path our hypothetical ball is expected to follow through space. This pretty curved path is similar for every moving projectile that's influenced by gravity and has been poetically called *Gravity's Rainbow* by the novelist Thomas Pynchon.

Not all balls will follow this exact path, but this is one possible path that a ball could follow. The ball starts at 0, and it goes up and then down exactly like we are used to seeing balls go up and down, from the left of our field of view to the right.

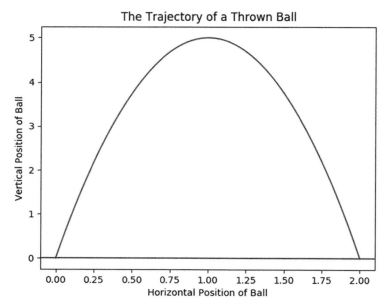

Figure 1-1: The trajectory of a hypothetical thrown ball

The Solve-for-x Strategy

Now that we have an equation for the ball's position, we can solve that equation for anything that interests us: where the ball will reach its highest point, for example, or where it will get to ground level again, which is the one thing that an outfielder needs to know in order to catch it. Students in physics classes all over the world are taught how to find these solutions, and if we wanted to teach a robot to play outfield, it would be very natural to teach the robot these equations as well. The method for solving for the ball's final location is as simple as taking the ball_trajectory() function we started with and setting it equal to 0:

$$0 = 10x - 5x^2$$

Then, we can solve this for x, using the quadratic formula taught to teenagers everywhere:

$$x = \frac{-b \pm \sqrt{b^2 - 4ac}}{2a}$$

In this case, we find that $x = 0$ and $x = 2$ are the solutions. The first solution, $x = 0$, is where the ball started, where it was thrown by the pitcher or hit by the batter. The second solution, $x = 2$, is where the ball returns to the ground again after its flight.

The strategy we just used is a relatively simple one. Let's call it the *solve-for-x strategy*. We write down an equation that describes a situation, and then solve that equation for the variable we're interested in. The solve-for-*x* strategy is extremely common in the hard sciences, at both the high school and college levels. Students are asked to solve for: a ball's expected destination, the ideal level of economic production, the proportion of a chemical that should be used in an experiment, or any number of other things.

The solve-for-x strategy is extremely powerful. If, for example, an army observed an enemy force fire a projectile weapon (say, a missile), they could quickly plug Galileo's equation into their calculators and nearly instantaneously find where the missile was expected to land, and evade it or intercept it accordingly. It could be done for free on a consumer-level laptop running Python. If a robot were playing outfield in a baseball game, it could do the same to catch a ball without breaking a sweat.

The solve-for-x strategy is easy in this case because we already know the equation that needs to be solved and the method to solve it. We owe the equation for a thrown ball to Galileo, as mentioned. We owe the quadratic formula to the great Muhammad ibn Musa al-Khwarizmi, who was the first to specify a fully general solution of the quadratic equation.

Al-Khwarizmi was a ninth-century polymath who contributed to astronomy, cartography, and trigonometry, besides giving us the word *algebra* and the method it refers to. He's one of the important figures who has enabled us to take the journey of this book. Since we live after giants like Galileo and al-Khwarizmi, we don't need to suffer through the difficult part of deriving their equations—we just have to memorize them and use them appropriately.

The Inner Physicist

Using Galileo's and al-Khwarizmi's equations and a solve-for-x strategy, a sophisticated machine can catch a ball or intercept a missile. But it seems reasonable to assume that most baseball players don't start writing out equations as soon as they see a ball go into the air. Reliable observers have reported that professional baseball spring training programs consist of a great deal of time running around and playing, and considerably less time gathered around a whiteboard deriving the Navier-Stokes equations. Solving the mystery of where a ball will land doesn't provide a clear-cut answer to the outfielder problem—that is, how a *human* can instinctively know where a ball will land without plugging it into a computer program.

Or maybe it does. The glibbest possible solution to the outfielder problem is to assert that if computers are solving Galilean quadratics to determine where balls will land, then so are humans. We'll call this solution the *inner physicist theory*. According to this theory, the "wetware" of our brains is able to set up and solve quadratic equations, or else draw plots and extrapolate their lines, all far beneath the level of our consciousness. Each of us, in other words, has an "inner physicist" deep in our brains who can calculate exact solutions to difficult math problems in seconds and deliver the solutions to our muscles, which can then find their way to the ball, bringing our bodies and mitts along. Our subconscious might be able to do this even if we've never taken a physics class or solved for x.

The inner physicist theory is not without its proponents. Notably, the well-known mathematician Keith Devlin published a book in 2006 called *The Math Instinct: Why You're a Mathematical Genius (Along with Lobsters, Birds,*

Cats, and Dogs). The book's cover shows a dog jumping to catch a Frisbee, with arrows tracing the respective trajectory vectors of the Frisbee and the dog, implying that the dog is able to perform the intricate calculations that would be required to make those vectors meet.

The manifest ability of dogs to catch Frisbees and humans to catch baseballs seems to be a point in favor of the inner physicist theory. The subconscious is a mysterious and powerful thing, whose depths we have yet to fully plumb. So why couldn't it solve some high school–level equations now and then? More pressingly, the inner physicist theory is difficult to refute because it's hard to think of alternatives to it: if dogs can't solve partial differential equations to catch Frisbees, then how do they catch them anyway? They take great leaps into the air and catch erratically moving Frisbees in their jaws like it's nothing. If they aren't solving some physics problem in their brains, then how else could they (and we) possibly know how to precisely intercept a ball?

As recently as 1967, no one had a good answer. That year, the engineer Vannevar Bush wrote a book in which he described the scientific features of baseball as he understood them, and he was unable to provide any explanation for how outfielders know where to run to catch fly balls. Luckily for us, the physicist Seville Chapman read Bush's book and was inspired to propose a theory of his own the very next year.

The Algorithmic Approach

Chapman, true scientist that he was, was not satisfied with a mystical and unverified trust in the human subconscious, and he wanted a more concrete explanation for outfielders' powers. This is what he discovered.

Thinking with Your Neck

Chapman began to tackle the outfielder problem by noting the information available to someone catching a ball. Though it's difficult for humans to estimate an exact velocity or the trajectory of a parabolic arc, he thought we would have an easier time observing angles. If someone throws or hits a ball from the ground and the ground is flat and even, then the outfielder will see the ball start at close to eye level. Imagine an angle formed by two lines: the ground, and the line between the outfielder's eyes and the ball. The moment the ball is hit by the batter, this angle will be (roughly) 0 degrees. After the ball has been in flight for a brief moment, it will be higher than the ground, so the angle between the ground and the outfielder's line of sight with the ball will have increased. Even if the outfielder has not studied geometry, they will have a "feel" for this angle—for example, by feeling how far back they have to tilt their neck to see the ball.

If we suppose that the outfielder is standing where the ball will eventually land, at $x = 2$, we can get a sense of the way the angle of the outfielder's line of sight with the ball increases by plotting a line of sight from early in the ball's trajectory. The following line of code creates a line segment for the plot we drew in Listing 1-2, and it is meant to be run in the same Python session. This line segment represents the line between the outfielder's eyes and the ball after the ball has traveled 0.1 meters horizontally.

```
xs2 = [0.1,2]
ys2 = [ball_trajectory(0.1),0]
```

We can plot this line of sight along with other lines of sight to see how the angle continues to increase over the course of the ball's trajectory. The following lines of code add more line segments to the same plot we drew in Listing 1-2. These line segments represent the line between the outfielder's eyes and the ball at two more points in the ball's journey: the points when the ball has traveled 0.1, 0.2, and 0.3 meters horizontally. After creating all of these line segments, we will plot them all together.

```
xs3 = [0.2,2]
ys3 = [ball_trajectory(0.2),0]
xs4 = [0.3,2]
ys4 = [ball_trajectory(0.3),0]
plt.title('The Trajectory of a Thrown Ball - with Lines of Sight')
plt.xlabel('Horizontal Position of Ball')
plt.ylabel('Vertical Position of Ball')
plt.plot(xs,ys,xs2,ys2,xs3,ys3,xs4,ys4)
plt.show()
```

The resulting plot shows several lines of sight that form continuously increasing angles with the ground (Figure 1-2).

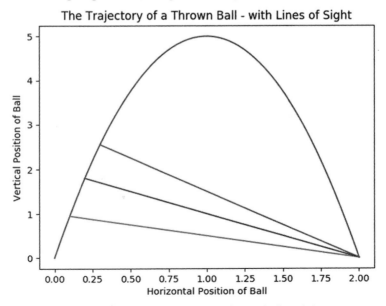

Figure 1-2: The trajectory of a hypothetical thrown ball, with line segments representing the outfielder looking at the ball as it travels

As the ball progresses through its flight, the angle of the outfielder's line of sight continues to increase, and the outfielder has to keep tipping their head back until they make the catch. Let's call the angle between the ground and the outfielder's line of sight with the ball *theta*. We assume that the outfielder is standing at the ball's eventual destination ($x = 2$). Recall from high school geometry class that the tangent of an angle in a right triangle is the ratio of the length of the side that's opposite the angle and the length of the side that's adjacent to the angle (and is not the hypotenuse). In this case, the tangent of theta is the ratio of the height of the ball to its horizontal distance from the outfielder. We can plot the sides whose ratio constitutes the tangent with the following Python code:

```
xs5 = [0.3,0.3]
ys5 = [0,ball_trajectory(0.3)]
xs6 = [0.3,2]
ys6 = [0,0]
plt.title('The Trajectory of a Thrown Ball - Tangent Calculation')
plt.xlabel('Horizontal Position of Ball')
plt.ylabel('Vertical Position of Ball')
plt.plot(xs,ys,xs4,ys4,xs5,ys5,xs6,ys6)
plt.text(0.31,ball_trajectory(0.3)/2,'A',fontsize = 16)
plt.text((0.3 + 2)/2,0.05,'B',fontsize = 16)
plt.show()
```

The resulting plot is shown in Figure 1-3.

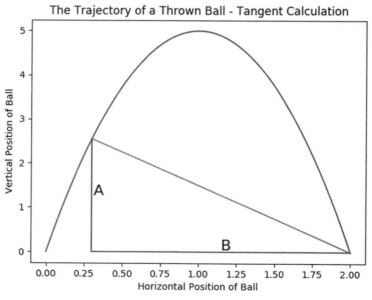

Figure 1-3: The trajectory of a hypothetical thrown ball, with a line segment representing the outfielder looking at the ball as it travels, and line segments A and B showing the lengths whose ratio constitutes the tangent we are interested in

We calculate the tangent by taking the ratio of the length of the side labeled A and the length of the side labeled B. The equation for the height A will be $10x - 5x^2$, while the equation for the length of B will be $2 - x$. So the following equation implicitly describes the ball's angle *theta* at each moment of its flight:

$$tan(\theta) = \frac{10x - 5x^2}{2 - x} = 5x$$

The overall situation is complex: a ball is hit far away and quickly shoots through a parabolic curve whose end is hard to immediately estimate. But in this complex situation, Chapman has found this simple relationship: that *when the outfielder is standing in the right location*, the tangent of theta grows at a simple, constant rate. The kernel of Chapman's breakthrough is that the tangent of theta, the ball's angle with the ground, grows linearly over time. Since Chapman found that simple relationship in the weeds of the outfielder problem, he was able to develop an elegant algorithmic solution to it.

His solution depends on the fact that if something—in this case, the tangent of theta—grows at a constant rate, it has zero acceleration. So if you are standing exactly where a ball is headed, you'll observe an angle whose tangent experiences zero acceleration. By contrast, if you are standing too close to the ball's initial position, you'll observe positive acceleration. If you are standing too far from the ball's initial position, you'll observe negative acceleration. (You are encouraged to verify the messy calculus behind these truths if you so desire.) This means that an outfielder can know where they need to go by feeling how steadily they have to tilt back their head as they look at the ball rising—thinking, so to speak, with their neck.

Applying Chapman's Algorithm

Robots don't necessarily have necks, and so a method for "thinking with one's neck" may not be helpful for a robot outfielder. Remember that they can solve quadratic equations directly and instantaneously to find where to go to catch a ball, without worrying about the acceleration of the tangent of theta. But for humans, Chapman's neck-thinking method could be extremely useful. In order to get to the ball's eventual destination, a human outfielder could follow this relatively simple process:

1. Observe the acceleration of the tangent of the angle between the ground and your line of sight with the ball.
2. If the acceleration is positive, step backward.
3. If the acceleration is negative, step forward.
4. Repeat steps 1–3 until the ball is directly in front of your face.
5. Catch it.

One serious objection to Chapman's five-step method is that outfielders following this process seem to have to calculate the tangents of angles on the fly, meaning we're replacing an inner physicist theory with an "inner geometer theory" in which baseball players can instantaneously, and subconsciously, take tangents.

One potential resolution to this objection is that for many angles, tan(theta) is approximately equal to theta, so rather than observing the acceleration of a tangent, outfielders can merely observe the acceleration of an angle. If the acceleration of an angle can be estimated by the felt acceleration of the neck joints that crick as the neck moves back to observe the ball, and if an angle is a reasonable approximation for its tangent, then we don't need to assume any great subconscious mathematical or geometrical powers on the part of outfielders—only the physical skill of being accurately attuned to subtle sensory inputs.

By making an acceleration estimate the only difficult part of the process, we have obtained a potential solution to the outfielder problem that has much more psychological plausibility than the inner physicist's theory of subconsciously extrapolated parabolas. Of course, the psychological appeal of the solution doesn't mean that it can be used only by humans. A robot outfielder could also be programmed to follow Chapman's five-step process, and it might even perform better at catching the ball if it did so, because, for example, Chapman's process enables those who use it to dynamically respond to changes due to wind or bounces.

Besides psychological plausibility, there's one more crucial feature that the five-step process implied by Chapman's insight possesses: it doesn't rely on a solve-for-*x* strategy or any explicit equation at all. Instead, it proposes successive iterations of easy observations and small, gradual steps to reach a well-defined goal. In other words, the process that we have inferred from Chapman's theory is an algorithm.

Solving Problems with Algorithms

The word *algorithm* came from the name of the great al-Khwarizmi, mentioned earlier. It's not an easy word to define, not least because its accepted definition has changed over time. Stated simply, an algorithm is just a set of instructions that produce a well-defined outcome. This is a broad definition; as we saw in the Introduction, tax forms and recipes for parfaits could rightly be considered algorithms.

Chapman's ball-catching process, or Chapman's algorithm as we may want to call it, is arguably even more algorithm-like than a recipe for a parfait, because it contains a looping structure in which small steps are taken repeatedly until a definite condition is reached. This is a common algorithmic structure you'll see throughout this book.

Chapman proposed an algorithmic solution to the outfielder problem because a solve-for-*x* solution was not plausible (outfielders often don't know the relevant equations). In general, algorithms are most useful when the solve-for-*x* strategy fails. Sometimes we don't know the right equations to use, but more often there is no equation that could fully describe a situation, the equation is impossible to solve, or we face time or space constraints. Algorithms exist at the edge of what is possible, and every time an algorithm is created or improved, we push the frontier of efficiency and knowledge out a little further.

Today, there is a common perception that algorithms are difficult, esoteric, mysterious, and strictly mathematical and that they require years of study to understand. The way our education system is structured today, we begin teaching children the solve-for-x strategy as early as possible, and we explicitly teach algorithms only at the college or graduate school levels, if at all. For many students, it takes years to master the solve-for-x strategy, and it always feels unnatural to them. People who have had this experience may assume that algorithms will feel just as unnatural, and will also be more difficult to understand because they are more "advanced."

However, the lesson I take from Chapman's algorithm is that we have gotten it all exactly backward. During recess, students learn and perfect their performance of dozens of algorithms, for catching, throwing, kicking, running, and moving. There are probably also much more complex algorithms, which have not been fully delineated, that govern the operation of the social world of recess: the talking, status seeking, gossiping, alliance formation, and friendship cultivation. When we end recess time and start math class, we take students out of a world of algorithm exploration and push them to learn an unnatural and mechanistic process of solving for x, a process that is not a natural part of human development and is not even the most powerful method for solving analytical problems. Only if students progress to advanced math and computer science do they return to the natural world of algorithms and the powerful processes that they were unconsciously and joyfully mastering at recess.

This book is meant to be an intellectual recess for the curious—a recess in the sense that a young student means it: the beginning of all important activity, the end of all drudgery, and the continuation of cheerful exploration with friends. If you have any feeling of trepidation about algorithms, remind yourself that we humans are naturally algorithmic, and if you can catch a ball or bake a cake, you can master an algorithm.

In the remainder of this book, we explore many different algorithms. Some will sort lists or calculate numbers. Others will enable natural language processing and artificial intelligence. I encourage you to bear in mind that algorithms don't grow on trees. Each algorithm, before it became mainstream and was packaged for general consumption in this book, was discovered or created by someone like Chapman, who woke up one day in a world in which his algorithm didn't exist and went to sleep at the end of that day in a world in which it did. I encourage you to try to get in the mindset of these heroic discoverers. That is, I encourage you to approach an algorithm not only as a tool to be used but also as a formidable problem that was solved. The world of algorithms is not yet close to being fully mapped—many remain to be discovered and perfected, and I earnestly hope that you can be a part of that discovery process.

Summary

In this chapter, you saw two approaches to solving a problem: the analytic one and the algorithmic one. By solving the outfield problem two ways, we explored the differences between these approaches, ultimately arriving at Chapman's algorithm. Chapman found a simple pattern in a complex situation (the constant acceleration of the tangent of theta) and used it to develop the idea of an iterative, looping process that requires only one simple input (the feeling of acceleration in a craning neck) and leads to a definite goal (catching a ball). When you seek to develop and use algorithms in your own work, you can try to emulate Chapman's example.

In the next chapter, we look at some examples of algorithms in history. These examples should deepen your appreciation of algorithms, including what they are and how they work. We'll talk about algorithms from ancient Egypt, ancient Greece, and Imperial Japan. Every new algorithm you learn can be an addition to the "toolbox" of algorithms that you can rely on when you eventually advance to the point at which you can design and perfect your own.

2

ALGORITHMS IN HISTORY

Most people associate algorithms with computers. This is not unreasonable; computer operating systems use many sophisticated algorithms, and programming is well suited to implementing all sorts of algorithms precisely. But algorithms are more fundamental than the computer architecture we implement them on. As mentioned in Chapter 1, the word *algorithm* dates back about a millennium, and algorithms have been described in ancient records going back much further than that. Even outside of written records, there is abundant evidence for the use of complex algorithms in the ancient world—in, for example, their construction methods.

This chapter presents several algorithms of antique provenance. They show great ingenuity and insight, especially considering that they had to be invented and verified without the aid of computers. We start by discussing

Russian peasant multiplication, a method for arithmetic that, despite the name, might be Egyptian and might not actually be associated with peasants. We continue by covering Euclid's algorithm, an important "classic" algorithm for finding greatest common divisors. Finally, we cover an algorithm from Japan that generates magic squares.

Russian Peasant Multiplication

Many people remember learning the multiplication table as a particularly painful part of their education. Young children ask their parents why learning the multiplication table is necessary, and parents usually respond that they can't multiply without knowing it. How wrong they are. *Russian peasant multiplication (RPM)* is a method that enables people to multiply large numbers without knowing most of the multiplication table.

RPM's origins are unclear. An ancient Egyptian scroll called the Rhind papyrus contains a version of this algorithm, and some historians have proposed (mostly unconvincing) conjectures about how the method could have spread from ancient Egyptian scholars to the peasants of the vast Russian hinterlands. Regardless of the details of its history, RPM is an interesting algorithm.

Doing RPM by Hand

Consider the task of multiplying 89 by 18. Russian peasant multiplication proceeds as follows. First, create two columns next to each other. The first column is called the *halving* column and starts with 89. The second column is the *doubling* column and starts with 18 (Table 2-1).

Table 2-1: Halving/Doubling Table, Part 1

Halving	Doubling
89	18

We'll fill out the halving column first. Each row of the halving column takes the previous entry and divides it by 2, ignoring the remainder. For example, 89 divided by 2 is 44 remainder 1, so we write 44 in the second row of the halving column (Table 2-2).

Table 2-2: Halving/Doubling Table, Part 2

Halving	Doubling
89	18
44	

We continue dividing by 2 until we reach 1, dropping the remainder every time and writing the result in the next row. As we continue, we find that 44 divided by 2 is 22, then half of that is 11, then half of that (dropping the remainder) is 5, then 2, then 1. After writing these in the halving column, we have Table 2-3.

Table 2-3: Halving/Doubling Table, Part 3

Halving	Doubling
89	18
44	
22	
11	
5	
2	
1	

We've completed the halving column. As the name suggests, each entry in the doubling column will be double the previous entry. So since 18 × 2 is 36, 36 is the second entry in the doubling column (Table 2-4).

Table 2-4: Halving/Doubling Table, Part 4

Halving	Doubling
89	18
44	36
22	
11	
5	
2	
1	

We continue to add entries to the doubling column by following the same rule: just double the previous entry. We do this until the doubling column has as many entries as the halving column (Table 2-5).

Table 2-5: Halving/Doubling Table, Part 5

Halving	Doubling
89	18
44	36
22	72
11	144
5	288
2	576
1	1,152

The next step is to cross out or remove every row in which the halving column contains an even number. The result is shown in Table 2-6.

Table 2-6: Halving/Doubling Table, Part 6

Halving	Doubling
89	18
11	144
5	288
1	1,152

The final step is to take the sum of the remaining entries in the doubling column. The result is 18 + 144 + 288 + 1,152 = 1,602. You can check with a calculator that this is correct: 89 × 18 = 1,602. We have accomplished multiplication through halving, doubling, and addition, all without needing to memorize most of the tedious multiplication table that young children so despise.

To see why this method works, try rewriting the doubling column in terms of 18, the number we are trying to multiply (Table 2-7).

Table 2-7: Halving/Doubling Table, Part 7

Halving	Doubling
89	18 × 1
44	18 × 2
22	18 × 4
11	18 × 8
5	18 × 16
2	18 × 32
1	18 × 64

The doubling column is now written in terms of 1, 2, 4, 8, and so on to 64. These are powers of 2, and we can also write them as 2^0, 2^1, 2^2, and so on. When we take our final sum (adding together the doubling rows with odd entries in the halving column), we're really finding this sum:

$$18 \times 2^0 + 18 \times 2^3 + 18 \times 2^4 + 18 \times 2^6 = 18 \times (2^0 + 2^3 + 2^4 + 2^6) = 18 \times 89$$

The fact that RPM works hinges on the fact that

$$(2^0 + 2^3 + 2^4 + 2^6) = 89$$

If you look closely enough at the halving column, you can get a sense for why the preceding equation is true. We can also write this column in terms of powers of 2 (Table 2-8). When we do so, it's easier to start at the lowest entry and work upward. Remember that 2^0 is 1 and 2^1 is 2. In every row, we multiply by 2^1, and in the rows where the halving number is odd, we also add 2^0. You can see the expression start to resemble our equation more and more as you rise through the rows. By the time we reach the top of the table, we have an expression that simplifies to exactly $2^6 + 2^4 + 2^3 + 2^0$.

Table 2-8: Halving/Doubling Table, Part 8

Halving	Doubling
$(2^5 + 2^3 + 2^2) \times 2^1 + 2^0 = 2^6 + 2^4 + 2^3 + 2^0$	18×2^0
$(2^4 + 2^2 + 2^1) \times 2^1 = 2^5 + 2^3 + 2^2$	18×2^1
$(2^3 + 2^1 + 2^0) \times 2^1 = 2^4 + 2^2 + 2^1$	18×2^2
$(2^2 + 2^0) \times 2^1 + 2^0 = 2^3 + 2^1 + 2^0$	18×2^3
$2^1 \times 2^1 + 2^0 = 2^2 + 2^0$	18×2^4
$2^0 \times 2^1 = 2^1$	18×2^5
2^0	18×2^6

If you number the rows of the halving column starting with the top row as row 0, then 1, 2, and all the way to the bottom row as row 6, you can see that the rows with odd values in the halving column are rows 0, 3, 4, and 6. Now notice the crucial pattern: those row numbers are exactly the exponents in the expression for 89 that we found: $2^6 + 2^4 + 2^3 + 2^0$. This is not a coincidence; the way we constructed the halving column means that the odd entries will always have row numbers that are the exponents in a sum of powers of 2 equaling our original number. When we take a sum of the doubling entries with those indices, we're summing up 18 multiplied by powers of 2 that sum to exactly 89, so we'll get 89 × 18 as our result.

The reason this works is that really, RPM is an algorithm within an algorithm. The halving column itself is an implementation of an algorithm that finds the sum of powers of 2 that equals the number at the top of the column. This sum of powers of 2 is also called the *binary expansion* of 89. Binary is an alternative way to write numbers using only 0s and 1s, and it has become extremely important in recent decades because computers store information in binary. We can write 89 in binary as 1011001, with 1s in the zeroth, third, fourth, and sixth places (counting from the right), the same as the odd rows of the halving column, and also the same as the exponents in our equation. We can interpret the 1s and 0s in a binary representation as coefficients in a sum of powers of 2. For example, if we write 100, we interpret it in binary as

$$1 \times 2^2 + 0 \times 2^1 + 0 \times 2^0$$

or what we would usually write as 4. If we write 1001, we interpret it in binary as

$$1 \times 2^3 + 0 \times 2^2 + 0 \times 2^1 + 1 \times 2^0$$

or what we would usually write as 9. After running this mini-algorithm to get the binary expansion of 89, we are poised to easily run the full algorithm and complete the multiplication process.

Implementing RPM in Python

It's relatively simple to implement RPM in Python. Let's say that we want to multiply two numbers that we will call n_1 and n_2. First, let's open a Python script and define these variables:

```
n1 = 89
n2 = 18
```

Next, we'll start our halving column. Just as described, the halving column begins with one of the numbers we want to multiply:

```
halving = [n1]
```

The next entry will be `halving[0]/2`, ignoring the remainder. In Python, we can use the `math.floor()` function to accomplish this. This function just takes the closest integer less than a given number. For example, the second row of the halving column can be calculated as follows:

```
import math
print(math.floor(halving[0]/2))
```

If you run this in Python, you'll see that the answer is 44.

We can loop through each row of the halving column, and in each iteration of our loop, we will find the next entry in the halving column in the same way, stopping when we reach 1:

```
while(min(halving) > 1):
    halving.append(math.floor(min(halving)/2))
```

This loop uses the `append()` method for concatenation. At each iteration of the `while` loop, it concatenates the `halving` vector with half of its last value, using the `math.floor()` function to ignore the remainder.

For the doubling column, we can do the same: start with 18, and then continue through a loop. In each iteration of the loop, we'll add double the previous entry to the doubling column, and we'll stop after this column is the same length as the halving column:

```
doubling = [n2]
while(len(doubling) < len(halving)):
    doubling.append(max(doubling) * 2)
```

Finally, let's put these two columns together in a dataframe called `half_double`:

```
import pandas as pd
half_double = pd.DataFrame(zip(halving,doubling))
```

We imported the Python module called `pandas` here. This module enables us to work with tables easily. In this case, we used the `zip` command, which, as suggested by its name, joins `halving` and `doubling` together like a zipper joins two sides of a garment together. The two sets of numbers, `halving` and `doubling`, start as independent lists, and after being zipped together and converted into a `pandas` dataframe, are stored in a table as two aligned columns, as shown in Table 2-5. Since they're aligned and zipped together, we can refer to any row of Table 2-5, such as the third row, and get the full row, including the elements from both `halving` and `doubling` (22 and 72). Being able to refer to and work with these rows will make it easy to remove the rows we don't want, like we did to Table 2-5 to convert it to Table 2-6.

Now we need to remove the rows whose entries in the halving column are even. We can test for evenness using the % (modulo) operator in Python, which returns a remainder after division. If a number x is odd, then x%2 will be 1. The following line will keep only the rows of the table whose entry in the halving column is odd:

```
half_double = half_double.loc[half_double[0]%2 == 1,:]
```

In this case, we use the `loc` functionality in the `pandas` module to select only the rows we want. When we use `loc`, we specify which rows and columns we want to select in the square brackets ([]) that follow it. Inside the square brackets, we specify which rows and columns we want in order, separated by a comma: the format is [*row, column*]. For example, if we wanted the row with index 4 and the column with index 1, we could write `half_double.loc[4,1]`. In this case, we will do more than just specify indices. We will express a logical pattern for which rows we want: we want all rows where `halving` is odd. We specify the `halving` column in our logic with `half_double[0]`, since it's the column with index 0. We specify oddness with `%2 == 1`. Finally, we specify that we want all columns after the comma by writing a colon, which is a shortcut indicating that we want every column.

Finally, we simply take the sum of the remaining doubling entries:

```
answer = sum(half_double.loc[:,1])
```

Here, we are using `loc` again. We specify inside the square brackets that we want every row by using the colon shortcut. We specify that we want `doubling`, the column with index 1, after the comma. Note that the 89 × 18 example we worked through could be done more quickly and easily if we instead calculated 18 × 89—that is, if we put 18 in the halving column and 89 in the doubling column. I encourage you to try this to see the improvement. In general, RPM is faster if the smaller multiplicand is placed in the halving column and the larger one in the doubling column.

To someone who has already memorized the multiplication table, RPM may seem pointless. But besides its historical charm, RPM is worth learning for a few reasons. First, it shows that even something as dry as multiplying numbers can be done in multiple ways and is amenable to creative approaches. Just because you've learned one algorithm for something doesn't mean that it's the only, or the best, algorithm for the purpose—keep your mind open to new and potentially better ways of doing things.

RPM may be slow, but it requires less memorization up front because it doesn't require knowledge of most of the multiplication table. Sometimes it can be very useful to sacrifice a little speed for the sake of low memory requirements, and this speed/memory tradeoff is an important consideration in many situations where we're designing and implementing algorithms.

Like many of the best algorithms, RPM also brings into focus relationships between apparently disparate ideas. Binary expansions may seem like just a curiosity, of interest to transistor engineers but not useful to a layperson or even a professional programmer. But RPM shows a deep connection between the binary expansion of a number and a convenient way to multiply with only minimal knowledge of the multiplication table. This is another reason to always keep learning: you never know when some apparently useless factoid may form the basis for a powerful algorithm.

Euclid's Algorithm

The ancient Greeks gave many gifts to humanity. One of their greatest was theoretical geometry, which was rigorously compiled by the great Euclid in his 13 books called the *Elements*. Most of Euclid's mathematical writing is in a theorem/proof style, in which a proposition is deduced logically from simpler assumptions. Some of his work is also *constructive*, meaning that it provides a method for using simple tools to draw or create a useful figure, like a square with a particular area or a tangent to a curve. Though the word had not been coined yet, Euclid's constructive methods were algorithms, and some of the ideas behind his algorithms can still be useful today.

Doing Euclid's Algorithm by Hand

Euclid's most famous algorithm is commonly known as *Euclid's algorithm*, though it is only one of many that he wrote about. Euclid's algorithm is a method for finding the greatest common divisor of two numbers. It is simple and elegant and takes only a few lines to implement in Python.

We begin with two natural (whole) numbers: let's call them a and b. Let's say that a is larger than b (if it's not, just rename a to b and rename b to a, and then a will be larger). If we divide a/b, we'll get an integer quotient and an integer remainder. Let's call the quotient q_1, and the remainder c. We can write this as follows:

$$a = q_1 \times b + c$$

For example, if we say that $a = 105$ and $b = 33$, we find that $105/33$ is 3, remainder 6. Notice that the remainder c will always be smaller than both a and b—that's how remainders work. The next step of the process is to forget about *a*, and focus on *b* and *c*. Just like before, we say that *b* is larger than *c*. We then find the quotient and remainder when dividing *b/c*. If we say that *b/c* is q_2, with remainder *d*, we can write our result as follows:

$$b = q_2 \times c + d$$

Again, *d* will be smaller than both *b* and *c*, since it's a remainder. If you look at our two equations here, you can start to see a pattern: we're working our way through the alphabet, shifting terms to the left every time. We started with *a*, *b*, and *c*, and then we had *b*, *c*, and *d*. You can see this pattern continue in our next step, in which we divide *c/d*, and call the quotient q_3 and the remainder *e*.

$$c = q_3 \times d + e$$

We can continue this process, proceeding as far as we need through the alphabet, until the remainder is equal to zero. Remember that remainders are always smaller than the numbers that were divided to get them, so *c* is smaller than *a* and *b*, *d* is smaller than *b* and *c*, *e* is smaller than *c* and *d*, and so on. This means that at every step, we're working with smaller and smaller integers, so we must eventually get to zero. When we get a zero remainder, we stop the process, and we know that the last nonzero remainder is the greatest common divisor. For example, if we find that *e* is zero, then *d* is the greatest common divisor of our original two numbers.

Implementing Euclid's Algorithm in Python

We can implement this algorithm in Python quite easily, as shown in Listing 2-1.

```
def gcd(x,y):
    larger = max(x,y)
    smaller = min(x,y)

    remainder = larger % smaller

    if(remainder == 0):
        return(smaller)

    if(remainder != 0):
❶        return(gcd(smaller,remainder))
```

Listing 2-1: Implementing Euclid's algorithm using recursion

The first thing to notice is that we don't need any of the q_1, q_2, q_3 . . . quotients. We need only the remainders, the successive letters of the alphabet. Remainders are easy to get in Python: we can use the % operator from the previous section. We can write a function that takes the remainder after division for any two numbers. If the remainder is zero, then the greatest common divisor is the smaller of the two inputs. If the remainder is not zero, we use the smaller of the two inputs and the remainder as inputs into the same function.

Notice that this function calls itself if the remainder is nonzero ❶. The act of a function calling itself is known as *recursion*. Recursion can seem intimidating or confusing at first; a function that calls itself may seem paradoxical, like a snake that can eat itself or a person trying to fly by pulling on their own bootstraps. But don't be scared. If you're unfamiliar with recursion, one of the best things to do is start with a concrete example, like finding the greatest common divisor of 105 and 33, and follow each step of the code as if you are the computer. You will see that in this example, recursion is just a concise way to express the steps we listed in "Doing Euclid's Algorithm by Hand" on page 20. There is always a danger with recursion that you create an infinite recursion—that a function calls itself, and while calling itself, calls itself again, and nothing ever causes the function to end, so it attempts to call itself endlessly, which is a problem because we need the program to terminate in order to get the final answer. In this case, we can feel safe because at each step we are getting smaller and smaller remainders that will eventually go down to zero and enable us to exit the function.

Euclid's algorithm is short and sweet and useful. I encourage you to create an even more concise implementation of it in Python.

Japanese Magic Squares

The history of Japanese mathematics is particularly fascinating. In *A History of Japanese Mathematics*, originally published in 1914, the historians David Eugene Smith and Yoshio Mikami wrote that Japanese math had historically possessed a "genius for taking infinite pains" and "ingenuity in untangling minute knots and thousands of them." On the one hand, mathematics uncovers absolute truths that should not vary between times and cultures. On the other hand, the types of problems that distinct groups tend to focus on and their idiosyncratic approaches to them, not to mention differences in notation and communication, provide great scope for noteworthy cultural differences, even in a field as austere as math.

Creating the Luo Shu Square in Python

Japanese mathematicians had a fondness for geometry, and many of their ancient manuscripts pose and solve problems related to finding the areas of exotic shapes like circles inscribed within ellipses and Japanese hand fans. Another steady area of focus for Japanese mathematicians throughout several centuries was the study of magic squares.

A *magic square* is an array of unique, consecutive natural numbers such that all rows, all columns, and both of the main diagonals have the same sum. Magic squares can be any size. Table 2-9 shows an example of a 3×3 magic square.

Table 2-9: The Luo Shu Square

4	9	2
3	5	7
8	1	6

In this square, each row, each column, and both main diagonals sum to 15. This is more than just a random example—it's the famous *Luo Shu square*. According to an ancient Chinese legend, this magic square was first seen inscribed on the back of a magical turtle who came out of a river in response to the prayers and sacrifices of a suffering people. In addition to the definitional pattern that each row, column, and diagonal sums to 15, there are a few other patterns. For example, the outer ring of numbers alternates between even and odd numbers, and the consecutive numbers 4, 5, and 6 appear in the main diagonal.

The legend of the sudden appearance of this simple but fascinating square as a gift from the gods is fitting for the study of algorithms. Algorithms are often easy to verify and use, but they can be difficult to design from scratch. Especially elegant algorithms, when we have the good luck to invent one, seem revelatory, as if they have come out of nowhere as a gift from the gods inscribed on the back of a magical turtle. If you doubt this, try to create an 11×11 magic square from scratch, or try to discover a general-purpose algorithm for generating new magic squares.

Knowledge of this and other magic squares apparently passed from China to Japan at least as early as 1673, when a mathematician named Sanenobu published a 20×20 magic square in Japan. We can create the Luo Shu square in Python with the following command:

```
luoshu = [[4,9,2],[3,5,7],[8,1,6]]
```

It will come in handy to have a function that verifies whether a given matrix is a magic square. The following function does this by verifying the sums across all rows, columns, and diagonals and then checking whether they are all the same:

```
def verifysquare(square):
    sums = []
    rowsums = [sum(square[i]) for i in range(0,len(square))]
    sums.append(rowsums)
    colsums = [sum([row[i] for row in square]) for i in range(0,len(square))]
    sums.append(colsums)
    maindiag = sum([square[i][i] for i in range(0,len(square))])
    sums.append([maindiag])
    antidiag = sum([square[i][len(square) - 1 - i] for i in \
range(0,len(square))])
    sums.append([antidiag])
    flattened = [j for i in sums for j in i]
    return(len(list(set(flattened))) == 1)
```

Implementing Kurushima's Algorithm in Python

In the previous sections, we discussed how to perform our algorithms of interest "by hand" before providing details of the implementation of the code. In the case of Kurushima's algorithm, we'll outline the steps and introduce the code simultaneously. The reason for this change is the relative complexity of the algorithm, and especially the length of the code required to implement it.

One of the most elegant algorithms for generating magic squares, *Kurushima's algorithm* is named for Kurushima Yoshita, who lived during the Edo period. Kurushima's algorithm works only for magic squares of *odd dimension*, meaning that it works for any *n×n* square if *n* is an odd number. It begins by filling out the center of the square in a way that matches the Luo Shu square. In particular, the central five squares are given by the following expressions, with *n* here referring to the dimension of the square (Table 2-10).

Table 2-10: The Center of Kurushima's Square

	n^2	
n	$(n^2 + 1)/2$	$n^2 + 1 - n$
	1	

Kurushima's algorithm for generating an *n×n* magic square for odd *n* can be described simply as follows:

1. Fill in the five central squares according to Table 2-10.
2. Beginning with any entry whose value is known, determine the value of an unknown neighboring entry by following one of the three rules (described next).
3. Repeat step 2 until every entry in the full magic square is filled in.

Filling in the Central Squares

We can begin the process of creating a magic square by creating an empty square matrix that we'll fill up. For example, if we want to create a 7×7 matrix, we can define n=7 and then create a matrix with n rows and n columns:

```
n = 7
square = [[float('nan') for i in range(0,n)] for j in range(0,n)]
```

In this case, we don't know what numbers to put in the square, so we fill it entirely with entries equal to float('nan'). Here, nan stands for *not a number*, which we can use as a placeholder in Python when we want to fill up a list before we know what numbers to use. If we run print(square), we find that this matrix by default is filled with nan entries:

```
[[nan, nan, nan, nan, nan, nan, nan], [nan, nan, nan, nan, nan, nan, nan],
[nan, nan, nan, nan, nan, nan, nan], [nan, nan, nan, nan, nan, nan, nan],
[nan, nan, nan, nan, nan, nan, nan], [nan, nan, nan, nan, nan, nan, nan],
[nan, nan, nan, nan, nan, nan, nan]]
```

This square is not too pretty as it is output in the Python console, so we can write a function that will print it in a more readable way:

```
def printsquare(square):
    labels = ['['+str(x)+']' for x in range(0,len(square))]
    format_row = "{:>6}" * (len(labels) + 1)
    print(format_row.format("", *labels))
    for label, row in zip(labels, square):
        print(format_row.format(label, *row))
```

Don't worry about the details of the printsquare() function, since it's only for pretty printing and not part of our algorithm. We can fill in the central five squares with simple commands. First, we can get the indices of the central entry as follows:

```
import math
center_i = math.floor(n/2)
center_j = math.floor(n/2)
```

The central five squares can be populated according to the expressions in Table 2-10 as follows:

```
square[center_i][center_j] = int((n**2 +1)/2)
square[center_i + 1][center_j] = 1
square[center_i - 1][center_j] = n**2
square[center_i][center_j + 1] = n**2 + 1 - n
square[center_i][center_j - 1] = n
```

Specifying the Three Rules

The purpose of Kurushima's algorithm is to fill in the rest of the nan entries according to simple rules. We can specify three simple rules that enable us to fill out every other entry, no matter how big the magic square is. The first rule is expressed in Figure 2-1.

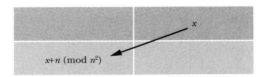

Figure 2-1: Rule 1 of Kurushima's algorithm

So for any x in the magic square, we can determine the entry that is situated in this diagonal relationship to x by simply adding n and taking the result mod n^2 (mod refers to the modulo operation). Of course, we can also go in the opposite direction by reversing the operation: subtracting n and taking the result mod n^2.

The second rule is even simpler, and is expressed in Figure 2-2.

Figure 2-2: Rule 2 of Kurushima's algorithm

For any x in the magic square, the entry below and to the right of x is 1 greater than x, mod n^2. This is a simple rule, but it has one important exception: this rule is not followed when we cross from the upper-left half of the magic square to the lower-right half of the square. Another way to say this is that we do not follow the second rule if we are crossing the magic square's *antidiagonal*, the bottom-left-to-top-right line shown in Figure 2-3.

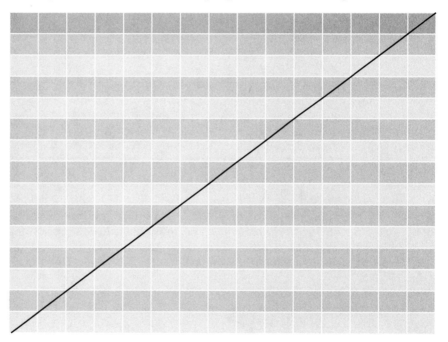

Figure 2-3: The antidiagonal of a square matrix

You can see the cells that are on the antidiagonal. The antidiagonal line passes fully through them. We can follow our normal two rules when we are dealing with these cells. We need the exceptional third rule only when starting in a cell that is fully above the antidiagonal and crossing to a cell that is fully below it, or vice versa. That final rule is expressed in Figure 2-4, which shows an antidiagonal and two cells that would need to follow this rule when crossing it.

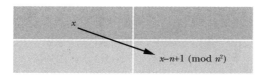

Figure 2-4: Rule 3 of Kurushima's algorithm

This rule is followed when we are crossing the antidiagonal. If we cross from the bottom right to the top left, we can follow the inverse of this rule, in which x is transformed to $x + n - 1$, mod n^2.

We can write a simple implementation of Rule 1 in Python by defining a function that takes x and n as its arguments and returns (x+n)%n**2:

```
def rule1(x,n):
    return((x + n)%n**2)
```

We can try this out with the central entry in the Luo Shu square. Remember, the Luo Shu square is a 3×3 square matrix, so $n = 3$. The central entry of the Luo Shu square is 5. The entry below and to the left of this entry is 8, and if we have implemented our rule1() function correctly we'll get an 8 when we run the following line:

```
print(rule1(5,3))
```

You should see an 8 in the Python console. Our rule1() function seems to work as intended. However, we could improve it by enabling it to go "in reverse," determining not only the entry on the bottom left of a given entry, but also the entry to the top right (that is, being able to go from 8 to 5 in addition to going from 5 to 8). We can make this improvement by adding one more argument to the function. We'll call our new argument upright, and it will be a True/False indicator of whether we're looking for the entry up and to the right of x. If not, we will by default look for the entry to the bottom left of x:

```
def rule1(x,n,upright):
    return((x + ((-1)**upright) * n)%n**2)
```

In a mathematical expression, Python will interpret True as 1 and False as 0. If upright is False, our function will return the same value as before, since $(-1)^0 = 1$. If upright is True, then it will subtract n instead of adding n, which will enable us to go in the other direction. Let's check whether it can determine the entry above and to the right of 1 in the Luo Shu square:

```
print(rule1(1,3,True))
```

It should print 7, the correct value in the Luo Shu square.

For Rule 2, we can create an analogous function. Our Rule 2 function will take x and n as arguments, just like Rule 1. But Rule 2 is by default finding the entry below and to the right of x. So we will add an `upleft` argument that will be `True` if we want to reverse the rule. The final rule is as follows:

```
def rule2(x,n,upleft):
    return((x + ((-1)**upleft))%n**2)
```

You can test this on the Luo Shu square, though there are only two pairs of entries for which this doesn't run into the exception to Rule 2. For this exception, we can write the following function:

```
def rule3(x,n,upleft):
    return((x + ((-1)**upleft * (-n + 1)))%n**2)
```

This rule needs to be followed only when we're crossing the magic square's antidiagonal. We'll see later how to determine whether or not we are crossing the antidiagonal.

Now that we know how to fill the five central squares, and we have a rule to fill out the remaining squares based on knowledge of those central squares, we can fill out the rest of the square.

Filling in the Rest of the Square

One way to fill in the rest of the square is to "walk" randomly through it, using known entries to fill in unknown entries. First, we'll determine the indices of our central entry as follows:

```
center_i = math.floor(n/2)
center_j = math.floor(n/2)
```

Then, we can randomly select a direction to "walk," as follows:

```
import random
entry_i = center_i
entry_j = center_j
where_we_can_go = ['up_left','up_right','down_left','down_right']
where_to_go = random.choice(where_we_can_go)
```

Here, we've used Python's `random.choice()` function, which does random selection from lists. It takes an element from the set we specified (`where_we_can_go`), but it chooses at random (or as close to random as it can get).

After we've decided a direction to travel, we can follow whichever rule corresponds to our direction of travel. If we have chosen to go `down_left` or `up_right`, we'll follow Rule 1, choosing the right arguments and indices as follows:

```
if(where_to_go == 'up_right'):
    new_entry_i = entry_i - 1
    new_entry_j = entry_j + 1
    square[new_entry_i][new_entry_j] = rule1(square[entry_i][entry_j],n,True)
```

```
if(where_to_go == 'down_left'):
    new_entry_i = entry_i + 1
    new_entry_j = entry_j - 1
    square[new_entry_i][new_entry_j] = rule1(square[entry_i][entry_j],n,False)
```

Similarly, we'll follow Rule 2 if we have chosen to travel up_left or down_right:

```
if(where_to_go == 'up_left'):
    new_entry_i = entry_i - 1
    new_entry_j = entry_j - 1
    square[new_entry_i][new_entry_j] = rule2(square[entry_i][entry_j],n,True)

if(where_to_go == 'down_right'):
    new_entry_i = entry_i + 1
    new_entry_j = entry_j + 1
    square[new_entry_i][new_entry_j] = rule2(square[entry_i][entry_j],n,False)
```

This code is for going up-left and down-right, but we should follow it only if we're not crossing the antidiagonal. We'll have to make sure that we follow Rule 3 in the case where we are crossing the antidiagonal. There is a simple way to know if we are in an entry that is near the antidiagonal: the entries just above the antidiagonal will have indices that sum to n-2, and the entries just below the antidiagonal will have indices that sum to n. We'll want to implement Rule 3 in these exceptional cases:

```
if(where_to_go == 'up_left' and (entry_i + entry_j) == (n)):
    new_entry_i = entry_i - 1
    new_entry_j = entry_j - 1
    square[new_entry_i][new_entry_j] = rule3(square[entry_i][entry_j],n,True)


if(where_to_go == 'down_right' and (entry_i + entry_j) == (n-2)):
    new_entry_i = entry_i + 1
    new_entry_j = entry_j + 1
    square[new_entry_i][new_entry_j] = rule3(square[entry_i][entry_j],n,False)
```

Keep in mind that our magic square is finite, so we cannot, for example, travel up/left from the top row or leftmost column. By creating our list of where it's possible to travel based on our current location, we can add some simple logic to ensure that we travel only in allowed directions:

```
where_we_can_go = []

if(entry_i < (n - 1) and entry_j < (n - 1)):
    where_we_can_go.append('down_right')

if(entry_i < (n - 1) and entry_j > 0):
    where_we_can_go.append('down_left')
```

```
        if(entry_i > 0 and entry_j < (n - 1)):
            where_we_can_go.append('up_right')

        if(entry_i > 0 and entry_j > 0):
            where_we_can_go.append('up_left')
```

We have all the elements we need to write Python code that implements Kurushima's algorithm.

Putting It All Together

We can put everything together in a function that takes a starting square with some nan entries and travels through it using our three rules to fill them in. Listing 2-2 contains the whole function.

```
import random
def fillsquare(square,entry_i,entry_j,howfull):
    while(sum(math.isnan(i) for row in square for i in row) > howfull):
        where_we_can_go = []

        if(entry_i < (n - 1) and entry_j < (n - 1)):
            where_we_can_go.append('down_right')
        if(entry_i < (n - 1) and entry_j > 0):
            where_we_can_go.append('down_left')
        if(entry_i > 0 and entry_j < (n - 1)):
            where_we_can_go.append('up_right')
        if(entry_i > 0 and entry_j > 0):
            where_we_can_go.append('up_left')

        where_to_go = random.choice(where_we_can_go)
        if(where_to_go == 'up_right'):
            new_entry_i = entry_i - 1
            new_entry_j = entry_j + 1
            square[new_entry_i][new_entry_j] = rule1(square[entry_i][entry_j],n,True)

        if(where_to_go == 'down_left'):
            new_entry_i = entry_i + 1
            new_entry_j = entry_j - 1
            square[new_entry_i][new_entry_j] = rule1(square[entry_i][entry_j],n,False)

        if(where_to_go == 'up_left' and (entry_i + entry_j) != (n)):
            new_entry_i = entry_i - 1
            new_entry_j = entry_j - 1
            square[new_entry_i][new_entry_j] = rule2(square[entry_i][entry_j],n,True)

        if(where_to_go == 'down_right' and (entry_i + entry_j) != (n-2)):
            new_entry_i = entry_i + 1
            new_entry_j = entry_j + 1
            square[new_entry_i][new_entry_j] = rule2(square[entry_i][entry_j],n,False)

        if(where_to_go == 'up_left' and (entry_i + entry_j) == (n)):
            new_entry_i = entry_i - 1
            new_entry_j = entry_j - 1
            square[new_entry_i][new_entry_j] = rule3(square[entry_i][entry_j],n,True)
```

```
        if(where_to_go == 'down_right' and (entry_i + entry_j) == (n-2)):
            new_entry_i = entry_i + 1
            new_entry_j = entry_j + 1
            square[new_entry_i][new_entry_j] = rule3(square[entry_i][entry_j],n,False)

❶   entry_i = new_entry_i
    entry_j = new_entry_j

return(square)
```

Listing 2-2: A function that enables an implementation of Kurushima's algorithm

This function will take four arguments: first, a starting square that has some nan entries; second and third, the indices of the entry that we want to start with; and fourth, how much we want to fill up the square (measured by the number of nan entries we are willing to tolerate). The function consists of a while loop that writes a number to an entry in the square at every iteration by following one of our three rules. It continues until it has as many nan entries as we have specified in the function's fourth argument. After it writes to a particular entry, it "travels" to that entry by changing its indices ❶, and then it repeats again.

Now that we have this function, all that remains is to call it in the right way.

Using the Right Arguments

Let's start with the central entry and fill up the magic square from there. For our howfull argument, we'll specify (n**2)/2-4. The reason for using this value for howfull will become clear after we see our results:

```
entry_i = math.floor(n/2)
entry_j = math.floor(n/2)

square = fillsquare(square,entry_i,entry_j,(n**2)/2 - 4)
```

In this case, we call the fillsquare() function using the existing square variable that we defined previously. Remember we defined it to be full of nan entries except for five central elements that we specified. After we run the fillsquare() function with that square as its input, the fillsquare() function fills in many of the remaining entries. Let's print out the resulting square and see what it looks like afterward:

```
printsquare(square)
```

The result is as follows:

	[0]	[1]	[2]	[3]	[4]	[5]	[6]
[0]	22	nan	16	nan	10	nan	4
[1]	nan	23	nan	17	nan	11	nan
[2]	30	nan	24	49	18	nan	12
[3]	nan	31	7	25	43	19	nan
[4]	38	nan	32	1	26	nan	20
[5]	nan	39	nan	33	nan	27	nan
[6]	46	nan	40	nan	34	nan	28

You'll notice that the nans occupy alternating entries, like a checkerboard. The reason for this is that the rules we have for moving diagonally give us access to only about half of the total entries, depending on which entry we started with. The valid moves are the same as in checkers: a piece that starts on a dark square can move diagonally to other dark squares, but its diagonal moving pattern will never allow it to move to any of the light squares. The nan entries we see are inaccessible if we start on the central entry. We specified (n**2)/2 - 4 for our howfull argument instead of zero because we know that we wouldn't be able to fill the matrix completely by calling our function only once. But if we start again on one of the central entry's neighbors, we will be able to access the rest of the nan entries in our "checkerboard." Let's call the fillsquare() function again, this time starting on a different entry and specifying our fourth argument as zero, indicating that we want to completely fill our square:

```
entry_i = math.floor(n/2) + 1
entry_j = math.floor(n/2)

square = fillsquare(square,entry_i,entry_j,0)
```

If we print our square now, we can see that it is completely full:

```
>>> printsquare(square)
        [0]  [1]  [2]  [3]  [4]  [5]  [6]
   [0]   22   47   16   41   10   35    4
   [1]    5   23   48   17   42   11   29
   [2]   30    6   24    0   18   36   12
   [3]   13   31    7   25   43   19   37
   [4]   38   14   32    1   26   44   20
   [5]   21   39    8   33    2   27   45
   [6]   46   15   40    9   34    3   28
```

There is just one final change we need to make. Because of the rules of the % operator, our square contains consecutive integers between 0 and 48, but Kurushima's algorithm is meant to fill our square with the integers from 1 to 49. We can add one line that replaces 0 with 49 in our square:

```
square=[[n**2 if x == 0 else x for x in row] for row in square]
```

Now our square is complete. We can verify that it is indeed a magic square by using the verifysquare() function we created earlier:

```
verifysquare(square)
```

This should return True, indicating that we've succeeded.

We just created a 7×7 magic square by following Kurushima's algorithm. Let's test our code and see if it can create a larger magic square. If we change n to 11 or any other odd number, we can run exactly the same code and get a magic square of any size:

```
n = 11
square=[[float('nan') for i in range(0,n)] for j in range(0,n)]


center_i = math.floor(n/2)
center_j = math.floor(n/2)

square[center_i][center_j] = int((n**2 + 1)/2)
square[center_i + 1][center_j] = 1
square[center_i - 1][center_j] = n**2
square[center_i][center_j + 1] = n**2 + 1 - n
square[center_i][center_j - 1] = n


entry_i = center_i
entry_j = center_j

square = fillsquare(square,entry_i,entry_j,(n**2)/2 - 4)

entry_i = math.floor(n/2) + 1
entry_j = math.floor(n/2)

square = fillsquare(square,entry_i,entry_j,0)

square = [[n**2 if x == 0 else x for x in row] for row in square]
```

Our 11×11 square looks as follows:

```
>>> printsquare(square)
        [0]   [1]   [2]   [3]   [4]   [5]   [6]   [7]   [8]   [9]  [10]
  [0]    56   117    46   107    36    97    26    87    16    77     6
  [1]     7    57   118    47   108    37    98    27    88    17    67
  [2]    68     8    58   119    48   109    38    99    28    78    18
  [3]    19    69     9    59   120    49   110    39    89    29    79
  [4]    80    20    70    10    60   121    50   100    40    90    30
  [5]    31    81    21    71    11    61   111    51   101    41    91
  [6]    92    32    82    22    72     1    62   112    52   102    42
  [7]    43    93    33    83    12    73     2    63   113    53   103
  [8]   104    44    94    23    84    13    74     3    64   114    54
  [9]    55   105    34    95    24    85    14    75     4    65   115
 [10]   116    45   106    35    96    25    86    15    76     5    66
```

We can verify, either manually or with our verifysquare() function, that this is indeed a magic square. You can do the same with any odd n and marvel at the results.

Magic squares don't have much practical significance, but it's fun to observe their patterns anyway. If you're interested, you might spend some time thinking about the following questions:

- Do the larger magic squares we created follow the odd/even alternating pattern seen in the outer edge of the Luo Shu square? Do you think every possible magic square follows this pattern? What reason, if any, would there be for this pattern?
- Do you see any other patterns in the magic squares we've created that haven't been mentioned yet?
- Can you find another set of rules that create Kurushima's squares? For example, are there rules that enable one to travel up and down through Kurushima's square instead of diagonally?
- Are there other types of magic squares that satisfy the definition of a magic square but don't follow Kurushima's rules at all?
- Is there a more efficient way to write code to implement Kurushima's algorithm?

Magic squares occupied the attention of great Japanese mathematicians for several centuries, and they've found a significant place in cultures around the world. We can count ourselves lucky that the great mathematicians of the past gave us algorithms for generating and analyzing magic squares that we can easily implement on today's powerful computers. At the same time, we can admire the patience and insight that was required for them to investigate magic squares with only pen, paper, and their wits (and the occasional magical turtle) to guide them.

Summary

In this chapter, we discussed some historical algorithms that range from a few centuries to a few millenia old. Readers who are interested in historical algorithms can find many more to study. These algorithms may not be of great practical utility today, but it can be worthwhile to study them— first because they give us a sense of history, and second because they help broaden our horizons and may provide the inspiration for writing our own innovative algorithms.

The algorithms in the next chapter enable us to do some commonly needed and useful tasks with mathematical functions: maximize and minimize them. Now that we have discussed algorithms in general and algorithms in history, you should be comfortable with what an algorithm is and how one works, and you should be ready to dive into serious algorithms used in the most cutting-edge software being developed today.

3

MAXIMIZING AND MINIMIZING

Goldilocks preferred the middle, but in the world of algorithms we're usually more interested in the extreme highs and lows. Some powerful algorithms enable us to reach maxima (for example, maximum revenue, maximum profits, maximum efficiency, maximum productivity) and minima (for example, minimum cost, minimum error, minimum discomfort, and minimum loss). This chapter covers gradient ascent and gradient descent, two simple but effective methods to efficiently find maxima and minima of functions. We also discuss some of the issues that come with maximization and minimization problems, and how to deal with them. Finally, we discuss how to know whether a particular algorithm is appropriate to use in a given situation. We'll start with a hypothetical scenario—trying to set optimal tax rates to maximize a government's revenues—and we'll see how to use an algorithm to find the right solution.

Setting Tax Rates

Imagine that you're elected prime minister of a small country. You have ambitious goals, but you don't feel like you have the budget to achieve them. So your first order of business after taking office is to maximize the tax revenues your government brings in.

It's not obvious what taxation rate you should choose to maximize revenues. If your tax rate is 0 percent, you will get zero revenue. At 100 percent, it seems likely that taxpayers would avoid productive activity and assiduously seek tax shelters to the point that revenue would be quite close to zero. Optimizing your revenue will require finding the right balance between rates that are so high that they discourage productive activity and rates that are so low that they undercollect. To achieve that balance is, you'll need to know more about the way tax rates relate to revenue.

Steps in the Right Direction

Suppose that you discuss this with your team of economists. They see your point and retire to their research office, where they consult the apparatuses used by top-level research economists everywhere—mostly test tubes, hamsters running on wheels, astrolabes, and dowsing rods—to determine the precise relationship between tax rates and revenues.

After some time thus sequestered, the team tells you that they've determined a function that relates the taxation rate to the revenue collected, and they've been kind enough to write it in Python for you. Maybe the function looks like the following:

```
import math
def revenue(tax):
    return(100 * (math.log(tax+1) - (tax - 0.2)**2 + 0.04))
```

This is a Python function that takes tax as its argument and returns a numeric output. The function itself is stored in a variable called revenue. You fire up Python to generate a simple graph of this curve, entering the following in the console. Just as in Chapter 1, we'll use the matplotlib module for its plotting capabilities.

```
import matplotlib.pyplot as plt
xs = [x/1000 for x in range(1001)]
ys = [revenue(x) for x in xs]
plt.plot(xs,ys)
plt.title('Tax Rates and Revenue')
plt.xlabel('Tax Rate')
plt.ylabel('Revenue')
plt.show()
```

This plot shows the revenues (in billions of your country's currency) that your team of economists expects for each tax rate between 0 and 1 (where 1 represents a 100 percent tax rate). If your country currently has a flat 70 percent tax on all income, we can add two lines to our code to plot that point on the curve as follows:

```
import matplotlib.pyplot as plt
xs = [x/1000 for x in range(1001)]
ys = [revenue(x) for x in xs]
plt.plot(xs,ys)
current_rate = 0.7
plt.plot(current_rate,revenue(current_rate),'ro')
plt.title('Tax Rates and Revenue')
plt.xlabel('Tax Rate')
plt.ylabel('Revenue')
plt.show()
```

The final output is the simple plot in Figure 3-1.

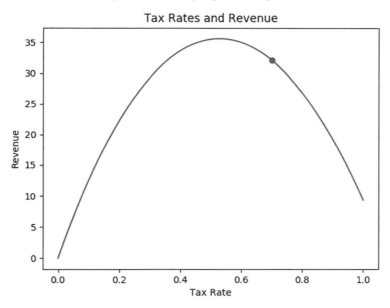

Figure 3-1: The relationship between tax rates and revenue, with a dot representing your country's current situation

Your country's current tax rate, according to the economists' formula, is not quite maximizing the government's revenue. Although a simple visual inspection of the plot will indicate approximately what level corresponds to the maximum revenue, you are not satisfied with loose approximations and you want to find a more precise figure for the optimal tax rate. It's apparent from the plot of the curve that any increase from the current 70 percent rate should decrease total revenues, and some amount of decrease from the current 70 percent rate should increase total revenues, so in this situation, revenue maximization will require a decrease in the overall tax rate.

We can verify whether this is true more formally by taking the derivative of the economists' revenue formula. A *derivative* is a measurement of the slope of a tangent line, with large values denoting steepness and negative values denoting downward motion. You can see an illustration of a derivative in Figure 3-2: it's just a way to measure how quickly a function is growing or shrinking.

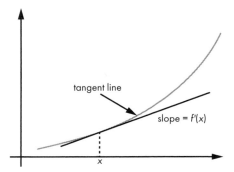

Figure 3-2: To calculate a derivative, we take a tangent line to a curve at a point and find its slope.

We can create a function in Python that specifies this derivative as follows:

```
def revenue_derivative(tax):
    return(100 * (1/(tax + 1) - 2 * (tax - 0.2)))
```

We used four rules of calculus to derive that function. First, we used the rule that the derivative of $log(x)$ is $1/x$. That's why the derivative of $log(tax + 1)$ is $1/(tax + 1)$. Another rule is that the derivative of x^2 is $2x$. That's why the derivative of $(tax - 0.2)^2$ is $2(tax - 0.2)$. Two more rules are that the derivative of a constant number is always 0, and the derivative of $100f(x)$ is 100 times the derivative of $f(x)$. If you combine all these rules, you'll find that our tax-revenue function, $100(log(tax + 1) - (tax - 0.2)^2 + 0.04)$, has a derivative equal to the following, as described in the Python function:

$$100((\frac{1}{tax + 1}) - 2(tax - 0.2))$$

We can check that the derivative is indeed negative at the country's current taxation rate:

```
print(revenue_derivative(0.7))
```

This gives us the output -41.17647.

A negative derivative means that an increase in tax rate leads to a decrease in revenue. By the same token, a decrease in tax rate should lead to an increase in revenue. While we are not yet sure of the precise tax rate corresponding to the maximum of the curve, we can at least be sure that if we take a small step from where are in the direction of decreased taxation, revenue should increase.

To take a step toward the revenue maximum, we should first specify a step size. We can store a prudently small step size in a variable in Python as follows:

```
step_size = 0.001
```

Next, we can take a step in the direction of the maximum by finding a new rate that is proportional to one step size away from our current rate, in the direction of the maximum:

```
current_rate = current_rate + step_size * revenue_derivative(current_rate)
```

Our process so far is that we start at our current tax rate and take a step toward the maximum whose size is proportional to the step_size we chose and whose direction is determined by the derivative of the tax-revenue function at the current rate.

We can verify that after this step, the new current_rate is 0.6588235 (about a 66 percent tax rate), and the revenue corresponding to this new rate is 33.55896. But while we have taken a step toward the maximum and increased the revenue, but we find ourselves in essentially the same situation as before: we are not yet at the maximum, but we know the derivative of the function and the general direction in which we should travel to get there. So we simply need to take another step, exactly as before but with the values representing the new rate. Yet again we set:

```
current_rate = current_rate + step_size * revenue_derivative(current_rate)
```

After running this again, we find that the new current_rate is 0.6273425, and the revenue corresponding to this new rate is 34.43267. We have taken another step in the right direction. But we are still not at the maximum revenue rate, and we will have to take another step to get closer.

Turning the Steps into an Algorithm

You can see the pattern that is emerging. We're following these steps repeatedly:

1. Start with a current_rate and a step_size.
2. Calculate the derivative of the function you are trying to maximize at the current_rate.
3. Add step_size * revenue_derivative(current_rate) to the current rate, to get a new current_rate.
4. Repeat steps 2 and 3.

The only thing that's missing is a rule for when to stop, a rule that triggers when we have reached the maximum. In practice, it's quite likely that we'll be *asymptotically* approaching the maximum: getting closer and closer to it but always remaining microscopically distant. So although we may never reach the maximum, we can get close enough that we match it up to 3 or 4 or 20 decimal places. We will know when we are sufficiently close to the asymptote when the amount by which we change our rate is very small. We can specify a threshold for this in Python:

```
threshold = 0.0001
```

Our plan is to stop our process when we are changing the rate by less than this amount at each iteration of our process. It's possible that our step-taking process will never converge to the maximum we are seeking, so if we set up a loop, we'll get stuck in an infinite loop. To prepare for this possibility, we'll specify a number of "maximum iterations," and if we take a number of steps equal to this maximum, we'll simply give up and stop.

Now, we can put all these steps together (Listing 3-1).

```
threshold = 0.0001
maximum_iterations = 100000

keep_going = True
iterations = 0
while(keep_going):
    rate_change = step_size * revenue_derivative(current_rate)
    current_rate = current_rate + rate_change

    if(abs(rate_change) < threshold):
        keep_going = False

    if(iterations >= maximum_iterations):
        keep_going = False

    iterations = iterations+1
```

Listing 3-1: Implementing gradient ascent

After running this code, you'll find that the revenue-maximizing tax rate is about 0.528. What we've done in Listing 3-1 is something called *gradient ascent*. It's called that because it's used to ascend to a maximum, and it determines the direction of movement by taking the gradient. (In a two-dimensional case like ours, a gradient is simply called a derivative.) We can write out a full list of the steps we followed here, including a description of our stopping criteria:

1. Start with a current_rate and a step_size.
2. Calculate the derivative of the function you are trying to maximize at the current_rate.
3. Add step_size * revenue_derivative(current_rate) to the current rate, to get a new current_rate.
4. Repeat steps 2 and 3 until you are so close to the maximum that your current tax rate is changing less than a very small threshold at each step, or until you have reached a number of iterations that is sufficiently high.

Our process can be written out simply, with only four steps. Though humble in appearance and simple in concept, gradient ascent is an algorithm, just like the algorithms described in previous chapters. Unlike most of those algorithms, though, gradient ascent is in common use today and is a key part of many of the advanced machine learning methods that professionals use daily.

Objections to Gradient Ascent

We've just performed gradient ascent to maximize the revenues of a hypothetical government. Many people who learn gradient ascent have practical if not moral objections to it. Here are some of the arguments that people raise about gradient ascent:

- It's unnecessary because we can do a visual inspection to find the maximum.
- It's unnecessary because we can do repeated guesses, a guess-and-check strategy, to find the maximum.
- It's unnecessary because we can solve the first-order conditions.

Let's consider each of these objections in turn. We discussed visual inspection previously. For our taxation/revenue curve, it's easy to get an approximate idea of the location of a maximum through visual inspection. But visual inspection of a plot does not enable high precision. More importantly, our curve is extremely simple: it can be plotted in two dimensions and obviously has only one maximum on the range that interests us. If you imagine more complex functions, you can start to see why visual inspection is not a satisfactory way to find the maximum value of a function.

For example, consider a multidimensional case. If our economists had concluded that revenue depended not only on tax rates but also on tariff rates, then our curve would have to be drawn in three dimensions, and if it were a complex function, it could be harder to see where the maximum lies. If our economists had created a function that related 10 or 20 or a 100 predictors to expected revenue, it would not be possible to draw a plot of all of them simultaneously given the limitations of our universe, our eyes, and our brains. If we couldn't even draw the tax/revenue curve, then there's no way visual inspection could enable us to find its maximum. Visual inspection works for simple toy examples like the tax/revenue curve, but not for highly complex multidimensional problems. Besides all of that, plotting a curve itself requires calculating the function's value at every single point of interest, so it always takes longer than a well-written algorithm.

It may seem that gradient ascent is overcomplicating the issue, and that a guess-and-check strategy is sufficient for finding the maximum. A guess-and-check strategy would consist of guessing a potential maximum and checking whether it is higher than all previously guessed candidate maxima until we are confident that we have found the maximum. One potential reply to this is to point out that, just as with visual inspections, with high-complexity multidimensional functions, guess-and-check could be prohibitively difficult to successfully implement in practice. But the best reply to the idea of guessing and checking to find maxima is that this is exactly what gradient ascent is *already doing*. Gradient ascent already is a guess-and-check strategy, but one that is "guided" by moving guesses in the direction of the gradient rather than by guessing randomly. Gradient ascent is just a more efficient version of guess-and-check.

Finally, consider the idea of solving the first-order conditions to find a maximum. This is a method that is taught in calculus classes all around the world. It could be called an algorithm, and its steps are:

1. Find the derivative of the function you are trying to maximize.
2. Set that derivative equal to zero.
3. Solve for the point at which the derivative is equal to zero.
4. Make sure that point is a maximum rather than a minimum.

(In multiple dimensions, we can work with a gradient instead of a derivative and perform an analogous process.) This optimization algorithm is fine as far as it goes, but it could be difficult or impossible to find a closed-form solution for which a derivative is equal to zero (step 2), and it could be harder to find that solution than it would be to simply perform gradient ascent. Besides that, it could take huge computing resources, including space, processing power, or time, and not all software has symbolic algebra capabilities. In that sense, gradient ascent is more robust than this algorithm.

The Problem of Local Extrema

Every algorithm that tries to find a maximum or minimum faces a very serious potential problem with local extrema (local maximums and minimums). We may perform gradient ascent perfectly, but realize that the peak we have reached at the end is only a "local" peak—it's higher than every point around it, but not higher than some faraway global maximum. This could happen in real life as well: you try to climb a mountain, you reach a summit where you are higher than all of your immediate surroundings, but you realize that you're only on the foothill and the real summit is far away and much higher. Paradoxically, you may have to walk down a little to eventually get to that higher summit, so the "naive" strategy that gradient ascent follows, always stepping to a slightly higher point in one's immediate neighborhood, fails to get to the global maximum.

Education and Lifetime Income

Local extrema are a very serious problem in gradient ascent. As an example, consider trying to maximize lifelong income by choosing the optimal level of education. In this case, we might suppose that lifelong earnings relate to years of education according to the following formula:

```python
import math
def income(edu_yrs):
    return(math.sin((edu_yrs - 10.6) * (2 * math.pi/4)) + (edu_yrs - 11)/2)
```

Here, edu_yrs is a variable expressing how many years of education one has received, and income is a measurement of one's lifetime income. We can plot this curve as follows, including a point for a person who has 12.5 years of formal education—that is, someone who has graduated from high school (12 years of formal education) and is half a year into a bachelor's degree program:

```
import matplotlib.pyplot as plt
xs = [11 + x/100 for x in list(range(901))]
ys = [income(x) for x in xs]
plt.plot(xs,ys)
current_edu = 12.5
plt.plot(current_edu,income(current_edu),'ro')
plt.title('Education and Income')
plt.xlabel('Years of Education')
plt.ylabel('Lifetime Income')
plt.show()
```

We get the graph in Figure 3-3.

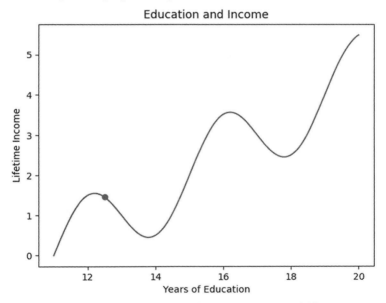

Figure 3-3: The relationship between formal education and lifetime income

This graph, and the income function used to generate it, is not based on empirical research but is used only as an illustrative, purely hypothetical example. It shows what might be intuitive relationships between education and income. Lifetime income is likely to be low for someone who does not graduate from high school (has fewer than 12 years of formal education). Graduation from high school—12 years—is an important milestone and should correspond to higher earnings than dropping out. In other words, it's a maximum, but importantly it's only a local maximum. Getting more than 12 years of education is helpful, but not at first. Someone who has completed only a few months of college education is not likely to get jobs that differ from those available to a high school graduate, but by going to school for extra months, they've missed an opportunity to earn in those months, so their lifetime earnings are actually lower than the earnings of people who enter the workforce directly after high school graduation and remain there.

Only after several years of college education does someone acquire skills that enable them to earn more over a lifetime than a high school graduate after we take into account the lost earning potential of the years spent at school. Then, college graduates (at 16 years of education) are at another earnings peak higher than the local high school peak. Once again, it's only a local one. Getting a little more education after earning a bachelor's degree leads to the same situation as getting a little more education after a high school diploma: you don't immediately acquire enough skills to compensate for the time not spent earning. Eventually, that's reversed, and you reach what looks like another peak after obtaining a postgraduate degree. It's hard to speculate much further beyond that, but this simplistic view of education and earnings will suffice for our purposes.

Climbing the Education Hill—the Right Way

For the individual we've imagined, drawn at 12.5 years of education on our graph, we can perform gradient ascent exactly as outlined previously. Listing 3-2 has a slightly altered version of the gradient ascent code we introduced in Listing 3-1.

```
def income_derivative(edu_yrs):
    return(math.cos((edu_yrs - 10.6) * (2 * math.pi/4)) + 1/2)

threshold = 0.0001
maximum_iterations = 100000

current_education = 12.5
step_size = 0.001

keep_going = True
iterations = 0
while(keep_going):
    education_change = step_size * income_derivative(current_education)
    current_education = current_education + education_change
    if(abs(education_change) < threshold):
        keep_going = False
    if(iterations >= maximum_iterations):
        keep_going=False
    iterations = iterations + 1
```

Listing 3-2: An implementation of gradient ascent that climbs an income hill instead of a revenue hill

The code in Listing 3-2 follows exactly the same gradient ascent algorithm as the revenue-maximization process we implemented previously. The only difference is the curve we are working with. Our taxation/revenue curve had one global maximum value that was also the only local maximum. Our education/income curve, by contrast, is more complicated: it has a global maximum, but also several local maximum values (local peaks or maxima) that are lower than the global maximum. We have to specify the derivative of this education/income curve (in the first lines of Listing 3-2), we have a different initial value (12.5 years of education instead of 70 percent taxation), and we have different names for the variables (current_education instead of current_rate). But these differences are superficial; fundamentally we are doing the same thing: taking small steps in the direction of the gradient toward a maximum until we reach an appropriate stopping point.

The outcome of this gradient ascent process is that we conclude that this person is overeducated, and actually about 12 years is the income-maximizing number of years of education. If we are naive and trust the gradient ascent algorithm too much, we might recommend that college freshmen drop out and join the workforce immediately to maximize earnings at this local maximum. This is a conclusion that some college students have come to in the past, as they see their high school–graduate friends making more money than them as they work toward an uncertain future. Obviously, this is not right: our gradient ascent process has found the top of a local hill, but not the global maximum. The gradient ascent process is depressingly local: it climbs only the hill it's on, and it isn't capable of taking temporary steps downward for the sake of eventually getting to another hill with a higher peak. There are some analogues to this in real life, as with people who fail to complete a university degree because it will prevent them from earning in the near term. They don't consider that their long-term earnings will be improved if they push through a local minimum to another hill to climb (their next, more valuable degree).

The local extrema problem is a serious one, and there's no silver bullet for resolving it. One way to attack the problem is to attempt multiple initial guesses and perform gradient ascent for each of them. For example, if we performed gradient ascent for 12.5, 15.5, and 18.5 years of education, we would get different results each time, and we could compare these results to see that in fact the global maximum comes from maximizing years of education (at least on this scale).

This is a reasonable way to deal with the local extremum problem, but it can take too long to perform gradient ascent enough times to get the right maximum, and we're never guaranteed to get the right answer even after hundreds of attempts. An apparently better way to avoid the problem is to introduce some degree of randomness into the process, so that we can sometimes step in a way that leads to a locally worse solution, but which in the long term can lead us to better maxima. An advanced version of gradient ascent, called *stochastic gradient ascent*, incorporates randomness for this reason, and other algorithms, like simulated annealing, do the same. We'll discuss simulated annealing and the issues related to advanced optimization in Chapter 6. For now, just keep in mind that as powerful as gradient ascent is, it will always face difficulties with the local extrema problem.

From Maximization to Minimization

So far we've sought to maximize revenue: to climb a hill and to ascend. It's reasonable to wonder whether we would ever want to go down a hill, to descend and to minimize something (like cost or error). You might think that a whole new set of techniques is required for minimization or that our existing techniques need to be flipped upside down, turned inside out, or run in reverse.

In fact, moving from maximization to minimization is quite simple. One way to do it is to "flip" our function or, more precisely, to take its negative. Going back to our tax/revenue curve example, it is as simple as defining a new flipped function like so:

```
def revenue_flipped(tax):
    return(0 - revenue(tax))
```

We can then plot the flipped curve as follows:

```
import matplotlib.pyplot as plt
xs = [x/1000 for x in range(1001)]
ys = [revenue_flipped(x) for x in xs]
plt.plot(xs,ys)
plt.title('The Tax/Revenue Curve - Flipped')
plt.xlabel('Current Tax Rate')
plt.ylabel('Revenue - Flipped')
plt.show()
```

Figure 3-4 shows the flipped curve.

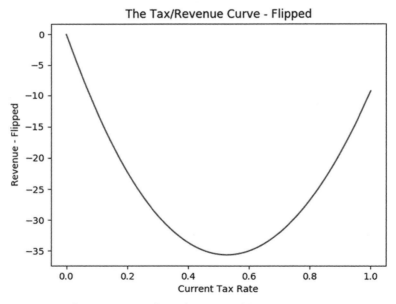

Figure 3-4: The negative or "flipped" version of the tax/revenue curve

So if we want to maximize the tax/revenue curve, one option is to minimize the flipped tax/revenue curve. If we want to minimize the flipped tax/revenue curve, one option is to maximize the flipped flipped curve—in other words, the original curve. Every minimization problem is a maximization problem of a flipped function, and every maximization problem is a minimization of a flipped function. If you can do one, you can do the other (after flipping). Instead of learning to minimize functions, you can just learn to maximize them, and every time you are asked to minimize, maximize the flipped function instead and you'll get the right answer.

Flipping is not the only solution. The actual process of minimization is very similar to the process of maximization: we can use *gradient descent* instead of gradient ascent. The only difference is the direction of movement at each step; in gradient descent, we go down instead of up. Remember that to find the maximum of the tax/revenue curve, we move in the direction of the gradient. In order to minimize, we move in the opposite direction of the gradient. This means we can alter our original gradient ascent code as in Listing 3-3.

```
threshold = 0.0001
maximum_iterations = 10000

def revenue_derivative_flipped(tax):
    return(0-revenue_derivative(tax))

current_rate = 0.7

keep_going = True
iterations = 0
while(keep_going):
    rate_change = step_size * revenue_derivative_flipped(current_rate)
    current_rate = current_rate - rate_change
    if(abs(rate_change) < threshold):
        keep_going = False
    if(iterations >= maximum_iterations):
        keep_going = False
    iterations = iterations + 1
```

Listing 3-3: Implementating gradient descent

Here everything is the same except we have changed a + to a - when we change the current_rate. By making this very small change, we've converted gradient ascent code to gradient descent code. In a way, they're essentially the same thing; they use a gradient to determine a direction, and then they move in that direction toward a definite goal. In fact, the most common convention today is to speak of gradient descent, and to refer to gradient ascent as a slightly altered version of gradient descent, the opposite of how this chapter has introduced it.

Hill Climbing in General

Being elected prime minister is a rare occurrence, and setting taxation rates to maximize government revenue is not an everyday activity even for prime ministers. (For the real-life version of the taxation/revenue discussion at the beginning of the chapter, I encourage you to look up the Laffer curve.) However, the idea of maximizing or minimizing something is extremely common. Businesses attempt to choose prices to maximize profits. Manufacturers attempt to choose practices that maximize efficiency and minimize defects. Engineers attempt to choose design features that maximize performance or minimize drag or cost. Economics is largely structured around maximization and minimization problems: maximizing utility especially, and also maximizing dollar amounts like GDP and revenue, and minimizing estimation error. Machine learning and statistics rely on minimization for the bulk of their methods; they minimize a "loss function" or an error metric. For each of these, there is the potential to use a hill-climbing solution like gradient ascent or descent to get to an optimal solution.

Even in everyday life, we choose how much money to spend to maximize achievement of our financial goals. We strive to maximize happiness and joy and peace and love and minimize pain and discomfort and sadness.

For a vivid and relatable example, think of being at a buffet and seeking, as all of us do, to eat the right amount to maximize satisfaction. If you eat too little, you will walk out hungry and you may feel that by paying the full buffet price for only a little food, you haven't gotten your money's worth. If you eat too much, you will feel uncomfortable and maybe even sick, and maybe you will violate your self-imposed diet. There is a sweet spot, like the peak of the tax/revenue curve, that is the exact amount of buffet consumption that maximizes satisfaction.

We humans can feel and interpret sensory input from our stomachs that tells us whether we're hungry or full, and this is something like a physical equivalent of taking a gradient of a curve. If we're too hungry, we take some step with a predecided size, like one bite, toward reaching the sweet spot of satisfaction. If we're too full, we stop eating; we can't "un-eat" something we have already eaten. If our step size is small enough, we can be confident that we will not overstep the sweet spot by much. The process we go through when we are deciding how much to eat at a buffet is an iterative process involving repeated direction checks and small steps in adjustable directions—in other words, it's essentially the same as the gradient ascent algorithm we studied in this chapter.

Just as with the example of catching balls, we see in this buffet example that algorithms like gradient ascent are natural to human life and decision-making. They are natural to us even if we have never taken a math class or written a line of code. The tools in this chapter are merely meant to formalize and make precise the intuitions you already have.

When Not to Use an Algorithm

Often, learning an algorithm fills us with a feeling of power. We feel that if we are ever in a situation that requires maximization or minimization, we should immediately apply gradient ascent or descent and implicitly trust whatever results we find. However, sometimes more important than knowing an algorithm is knowing when not to use it, when it's inappropriate or insufficient for the task at hand, or when there is something better that we should try instead.

When should we use gradient ascent (and descent), and when should we not? Gradient ascent works well if we start with the right ingredients:

- A mathematical function to maximize
- Knowledge of where we currently are
- An unequivocal goal to maximize the function
- Ability to alter where we are

There are many situations in which one or more of these ingredients is missing. In the case of setting taxation rates, we used a hypothetical function relating tax rates to revenue. However, there's no consensus among economists about what that relationship is and what functional form it takes. So we can perform gradient ascent and descent all we like, but until we can all agree on what function we need to maximize, we cannot rely on the results we find.

In other situations, we may find that gradient ascent isn't very useful because we don't have the ability to take action to optimize our situation. For example, suppose that we derived an equation relating a person's height to their happiness. Maybe this function expresses how people who are too tall suffer because they cannot get comfortable on airplanes, and people who are too short suffer because they cannot excel at pickup basketball games, but some sweet spot in the middle of too tall and too short tends to maximize happiness. Even if we can express this function perfectly and apply gradient ascent to find the maximum, it will not be useful to us, because we do not have control over our height.

If we zoom out even further, we may have all the ingredients required for gradient ascent (or any other algorithm) and still wish to refrain for deeper philosophical reasons. For example, suppose you can precisely determine a tax-revenue function and you're elected prime minister with full control over the taxation rate in your country. Before you apply gradient ascent and climb to the revenue-maximizing peak, you may want to ask yourself if maximizing your tax revenue is the right goal to pursue in the first place. It could be that you are more concerned with freedom or economic dynamism or redistributive justice or even opinion polls than you are with state revenues. Even if you have decided that you want to maximize revenues, it's not clear that maximizing revenues in the short term (that is, this year) will lead to maximization of revenues in the long term.

Algorithms are powerful for practical purposes, enabling us to achieve goals like catching baseballs and finding revenue-maximizing taxation rates. But though algorithms can achieve goals effectively, they're not as suited to the more philosophical task of deciding which goals are worth pursuing in the first place. Algorithms can make us clever, but they cannot make us wise. It's important to remember that the great power of algorithms is useless or even harmful if it is used for the wrong ends.

Summary

This chapter introduced gradient ascent and gradient descent as simple and powerful algorithms used to find the maxima and minima of functions, respectively. We also talked about the serious potential problem of local extrema, and some philosophical considerations about when to use algorithms and when to gracefully refrain.

Hang on tight, because in the next chapter we discuss a variety of searching and sorting algorithms. Searching and sorting are fundamental and important in the world of algorithms. We'll also talk about "big O" notation and the standard ways to evaluate algorithm performance.

4

SORTING AND SEARCHING

There are a few workhorse algorithms we use in nearly every kind of program. Sometimes these algorithms are so fundamental that we take them for granted or don't even realize our code is relying on them.

Several methods for sorting and searching are among these fundamental algorithms. They're worth knowing because they're commonly used and beloved by algorithm enthusiasts (and the sadists who give coding interviews). The implementation of these algorithms can be short and simple, but every character matters, and since they are so commonly needed, computer scientists have striven to enable them to sort and search with mind-melting speed. So we'll also use this chapter to discuss algorithm speed and the special notation we use to compare algorithms' efficiencies.

We start by introducing insertion sort, a simple and intuitive sorting algorithm. We discuss the speed and efficiency of insertion sort and how to measure algorithm efficiency in general. Next, we look at merge sort, a faster algorithm that is the current state of the art for searching. We also explore sleep sort, a strange algorithm that isn't used much in practice but is interesting as a curiosity. Finally, we discuss binary search and show some interesting applications of searching, including inverting mathematical functions.

Insertion Sort

Imagine that you've been asked to sort all the files in a filing cabinet. Each file has a number assigned to it, and you need to rearrange the files so that the file with the lowest number is first in the cabinet, the file with the highest number is last, and the files' numbers proceed in order in between.

Whatever method you follow as you sort the filing cabinet, we can describe it as a "sorting algorithm." But before you even think of opening Python to code an algorithm for this, take a moment to pause and consider how you would sort such a filing cabinet in real life. This may seem like a mundane task, but allow the adventurer within you to creatively consider a broad range of possibilities.

In this section, we present a very simple sorting algorithm called *insertion sort*. This method relies on looking at each item in a list one at a time and inserting it into a new list that ends up being correctly sorted. Our algorithm's code will have two sections: an insertion section, which performs the humble task of inserting a file into a list, and a sorting section, which performs insertion repeatedly until we have completed our sorting task.

Putting the Insertion in Insertion Sort

First, consider the task of insertion itself. Imagine that you have a filing cabinet whose files are already perfectly sorted. If someone hands you one new file and asks you to insert it into the right (sorted) position in the filing cabinet, how do you accomplish that? The task may seem so simple that it doesn't warrant an explanation, or even the possibility of one (*just do it!* you might think). But in the world of algorithms, every task, however humble, must be explained completely.

The following method describes a reasonable algorithm for inserting one file into a sorted filing cabinet. We'll call the file we need to insert the "file to insert." We'll say that we can compare two files and call one file "higher than" the other one. This could mean that one file's assigned number is higher than the other's assigned number, or it could mean that it's higher in an alphabetical or other ordering.

1. Select the highest file in the filing cabinet. (We'll start at the back of the cabinet and work our way to the front.)
2. Compare the file you have selected with the file to insert.
3. If the file you have selected is lower than the file to insert, place the file to insert one position behind that file.
4. If the file you have selected is higher than the file to insert, select the next highest file in the filing cabinet.

5. Repeat steps 2 to 4 until you have inserted your file or compared it with every existing file. If you have not yet inserted your file after comparing it with every existing file, insert it at the beginning of the filing cabinet.

That method should more or less match the intuition you have for how to insert a record into a sorted list. If you prefer, you could also start at the beginning of the list, instead of the end, and follow an analogous process with the same results. Notice that we haven't just inserted a record; we've inserted a record *in the correct position*, so after insertion, we'll still have a sorted list. We can write a script in Python that executes this insertion algorithm. First, we can define our sorted filing cabinet. In this case, our filing cabinet will be a Python list, and our files will simply be numbers.

```
cabinet = [1,2,3,3,4,6,8,12]
```

Then, we can define the "file" (in this case, just a number) that we want to insert into our cabinet.

```
to_insert = 5
```

We proceed one at a time through every number in the list (every file in the cabinet). We'll define a variable called check_location. As advertised, it will store the location in the cabinet that we want to check. We start at the back of the cabinet:

```
check_location = len(cabinet) - 1
```

We'll also define a variable called insert_location. The goal of our algorithm is to determine the proper value of insert_location, and then it's a simple matter of inserting the file at the insert_location. We'll start out by assuming the insert_location is 0:

```
insert_location = 0
```

Then we can use a simple if statement to check whether the file to insert is higher than the file at the check_location. As soon as we encounter a number that's lower than the number to insert, we use its location to decide where to insert our new number. We add 1 because our insertion takes place just behind the lower number we found:

```
if to_insert > cabinet[check_location]:
    insert_location = check_location + 1
```

After we know the right insert_location, we can use a built-in Python method for list manipulation called insert to put the file into the cabinet:

```
cabinet.insert(insert_location,to_insert)
```

Running this code will not work to insert our file properly yet, however. We need to put these steps together in one coherent insertion function. This function combines all of the previous code and also adds a while loop. The while loop is used to iterate over the files in the cabinet, starting with the last file and proceeding until either we find the right insert_location or we have examined every file. The final code for our cabinet insertion is in Listing 4-1.

```
def insert_cabinet(cabinet,to_insert):
  check_location = len(cabinet) - 1
  insert_location = 0
  while(check_location >= 0):
    if to_insert > cabinet[check_location]:
        insert_location = check_location + 1
        check_location = - 1
    check_location = check_location - 1
  cabinet.insert(insert_location,to_insert)
  return(cabinet)

cabinet = [1,2,3,3,4,6,8,12]
newcabinet = insert_cabinet(cabinet,5)
print(newcabinet)
```

Listing 4-1: Inserting a numbered file into our cabinet

When you run the code in Listing 4-1, it will print out newcabinet, which you can see includes our new "file," 5, inserted into our cabinet at the correct location (between 4 and 6).

It's worthwhile to think for a moment about one edge case of insertion: inserting into an empty list. Our insertion algorithm mentioned "proceeding sequentially through every file in the filing cabinet." If there are no files in the filing cabinet, then there is nothing to proceed through sequentially. In this case, we need to heed only the last sentence, which tells us to insert our new file at the beginning of the cabinet. Of course, this is easier done than said, because the beginning of an empty cabinet is also the end and the middle of the cabinet. So all we need to do in this case is insert the file into the cabinet without regard to position. We can do this by using the insert() function in Python and inserting at location 0.

Sorting via Insertion

Now that we've rigorously defined insertion and know how to perform it, we're almost at the point where we can perform an insertion sort. Insertion sort is simple: it takes each element of an unsorted list one at a time and uses our insertion algorithm to insert it correctly into a new, sorted list. In filing cabinet terms, we start with an unsorted filing cabinet, which we'll call "old cabinet," and an empty cabinet, which we'll call "new cabinet." We remove the first element of our old unsorted cabinet and add it to our new empty cabinet, using the insertion algorithm. We do the same with the second element of the old cabinet, then the third, and so on until we have inserted every element of the old cabinet into the new cabinet. Then, we forget about the old cabinet and use only our new, sorted cabinet. Since we've been inserting using our insertion algorithm, and it always returns a sorted list, we know that our new cabinet will be sorted at the end of the process.

In Python, we start with an unsorted cabinet and an empty `newcabinet`:

```
cabinet = [8,4,6,1,2,5,3,7]
newcabinet = []
```

We implement insertion sort by repeatedly calling our `insert_cabinet()` function from Listing 4-1. In order to call it, we'll need to have a file in our "hand," which we accomplish by popping it out of the unsorted cabinet:

```
to_insert = cabinet.pop(0)
newcabinet = insert_cabinet(newcabinet, to_insert)
```

In this snippet, we used a method called `pop()`. This method removes a list element at a specified index. In this case, we removed the element of `cabinet` at index 0. After we use `pop()`, `cabinet` no longer contains that element, and we store it in the variable `to_insert` so that we can put it into the `newcabinet`.

We'll put all of this together in Listing 4-2, where we define an `insertion_sort()` function that loops through every element of our unsorted cabinet, inserting the elements one by one into `newcabinet`. Finally, at the end, we print out the result, a sorted cabinet called `sortedcabinet`.

```
cabinet = [8,4,6,1,2,5,3,7]
def insertion_sort(cabinet):
  newcabinet = []
  while len(cabinet) > 0:
    to_insert = cabinet.pop(0)
    newcabinet = insert_cabinet(newcabinet, to_insert)
  return(newcabinet)

sortedcabinet = insertion_sort(cabinet)
print(sortedcabinet)
```

Listing 4-2: An implementation of insertion sort

Now that we can do insertion sort, we can sort any list we encounter. We may be tempted to think that this means we have all the sorting knowledge we'll ever need. However, sorting is so fundamental and important that we want to be able to do it in the best possible way. Before we discuss alternatives to insertion sort, let's look at what it means for one algorithm to be better than another and, on an even more basic level, what it means for an algorithm to be good.

Measuring Algorithm Efficiency

Is insertion sort a good algorithm? This question is hard to answer unless we're sure about what we mean by "good." Insertion sort works—it sorts lists—so it's good in the sense that it accomplishes its purpose. Another point in its favor is that it's easy to understand and explain with reference to physical tasks that many people are familiar with. Yet another feather in its cap is that it doesn't take too many lines of code to express. So far, insertion sort seems like a good algorithm.

However, insertion sort has one crucial failing: it takes a long time to perform. The code in Listing 4-2 almost certainly ran in less than one second on your computer, so the "long time" that insertion sort takes is not the long time that it takes for a tiny seed to become a mighty redwood or even the long time that it takes to wait in line at the DMV. It's more like a long time in comparison to how long it takes a gnat to flap its wings once.

To fret about a gnat's wing flap as a "long time" may seem a little extreme. But there are several good reasons to push algorithms as close as possible to zero-second running times.

Why Aim for Efficiency?

The first reason to relentlessly pursue algorithm efficiency is that it can increase our raw capabilities. If your inefficient algorithm takes one minute to sort an eight-item list, that may not seem like a problem. But consider that such an inefficient algorithm might take an hour to sort a thousand-item list, and a week to sort a million-item list. It may take a year or a century to sort a billion-item list, or it may not be able to sort it at all. If we make the algorithm better able to sort an eight-item list (something that seems trivial since it saves us only a minute), it may make the difference between being able to sort a billion-item list in an hour rather than a century, which can open up many possibilities. Advanced machine-learning methods like k-means clustering and k-NN supervised learning rely on ordering long lists, and improving the performance of a fundamental algorithm like sorting can enable us to perform these methods on big datasets that would otherwise be beyond our grasp.

Even sorting short lists is important to do quickly if it's something that we have to do many times. The world's search engines, for example, collectively receive a trillion searches every few months and have to order each set of results from most to least relevant before delivering them to users. If they can cut the time required for one simple sort from one second to half a second, they cut their required processing time from a trillion seconds to half a trillion seconds. This saves time for users (saving a thousand seconds for half a billion people really adds up!) and reduces data processing costs, and by consuming less energy, efficient algorithms are even environmentally friendly.

The final reason to create faster algorithms is the same reason that people try to do better in any pursuit. Even though there is no obvious need for it, people try to run the 100-meter dash faster, play chess better, and cook a tastier pizza than anyone ever has before. They do these things for the same reason George Mallory said he wanted to climb Mount Everest: "because it's there." It's human nature to push the boundaries of the possible and strive to be better, faster, stronger, and more intelligent than anyone else. Algorithm researchers are trying to do better because, among other reasons, they wish to do something remarkable, whether or not it is practically useful.

Measuring Time Precisely

Since the time required for an algorithm to run is so important, we should be more precise than saying that insertion sort takes a "long time" or "less than a second." How long, exactly, does it take? For a literal answer, we can use the timeit module in Python. With timeit, we can create a timer that we start just before running our sorting code and end just afterward. When we check the difference between the starting time and the ending time, we find how long it took to run our code.

```
from timeit import default_timer as timer

start = timer()
cabinet = [8,4,6,1,2,5,3,7]
sortedcabinet = insertion_sort(cabinet)
end = timer()
print(end - start)
```

When I ran this code on my consumer-grade laptop, it ran in about 0.0017 seconds. This is a reasonable way to express how good insertion sort is—it can fully sort a list with eight items in 0.0017 seconds. If we want to compare insertion sort with any other sorting algorithm, we can compare the results of this timeit timing to see which is faster, and say the faster one is better.

However, using these timings to compare algorithm performance has some problems. For example, when I ran the timing code a second time on my laptop, I found that it ran in 0.0008 seconds. A third time, I found that it ran on another computer in 0.03 seconds. The precise timing you get depends on the speed and architecture of your hardware, the current load on your operating system (OS), the version of Python you're running, the OS's internal task schedulers, the efficiency of your code, and probably other chaotic vagaries of randomness and electron motion and the phases of the moon. Since we can get very different results in each timing attempt, it's hard to rely on timings to communicate about algorithms' comparative efficiency. One programmer may brag that they can sort a list in Y seconds, while another programmer laughs and says that their algorithm gets better performance in Z seconds. We might find out they are running exactly the same code, but on different hardware at different times, so their comparison is not of algorithm efficiency but rather of hardware speed and luck.

Counting Steps

Instead of using timings in seconds, a more reliable measure of algorithm performance is the number of steps required to execute the algorithm. The number of steps an algorithm takes is a feature of the algorithm itself and isn't dependent on the hardware architecture or even necessarily on the programming language. Listing 4-3 is our insertion sort code from Listings 4-1 and 4-2 with several lines added where we have specified stepcounter+=1. We increase our step counter every time we pick up a new file to insert from the old cabinet, every time we compare that file to another file in the new cabinet, and every time we insert the file into the new cabinet.

```
def insert_cabinet(cabinet,to_insert):
  check_location = len(cabinet) - 1
  insert_location = 0
  global stepcounter
  while(check_location >= 0):
    stepcounter += 1
    if to_insert > cabinet[check_location]:
        insert_location = check_location + 1
        check_location = - 1
    check_location = check_location - 1
  stepcounter += 1
  cabinet.insert(insert_location,to_insert)
  return(cabinet)

def insertion_sort(cabinet):
  newcabinet = []
  global stepcounter
  while len(cabinet) > 0:
    stepcounter += 1
    to_insert = cabinet.pop(0)
    newcabinet = insert_cabinet(newcabinet,to_insert)
  return(newcabinet)

cabinet = [8,4,6,1,2,5,3,7]
stepcounter = 0
sortedcabinet = insertion_sort(cabinet)
print(stepcounter)
```

Listing 4-3: Our insertion sort code with a step counter

In this case, we can run this code and see that it performs 36 steps in order to accomplish the insertion sort for a list of length 8. Let's try to perform insertion sort for lists of other lengths and see how many steps we take.

To do so, let's write a function that can check the number of steps required for insertion sort for unsorted lists of different lengths. Instead of manually writing out each unsorted list, we can use a simple list comprehension in Python to generate a random list of any specified length. We can import Python's random module to make the random creation of lists easier. Here's how we can create a random unsorted cabinet of length 10:

```
import random
size_of_cabinet = 10
cabinet = [int(1000 * random.random()) for i in range(size_of_cabinet)]
```

Our function will simply generate a list of some given length, run our insertion sort code, and return the final value it finds for stepcounter.

```
def check_steps(size_of_cabinet):
  cabinet = [int(1000 * random.random()) for i in range(size_of_cabinet)]
  global stepcounter
  stepcounter = 0
  sortedcabinet = insertion_sort(cabinet)
  return(stepcounter)
```

Let's create a list of all numbers between 1 and 100 and check the number of steps required to sort lists of each length.

```
random.seed(5040)
xs = list(range(1,100))
ys = [check_steps(x) for x in xs]
print(ys)
```

In this code, we start by calling the random.seed() function. This is not necessary but will ensure that you see the same results as those printed here if you run the same code. You can see that we define sets of values for *x*, stored in xs, and a set of values for *y*, stored in ys. The *x* values are simply the numbers between 1 and 100, and the *y* values are the number of steps required to sort randomly generated lists of each size corresponding to each *x*. If you look at the output, you can see how many steps insertion sort took to sort randomly generated lists of lengths 1, 2, 3 . . . , all the way to 99. We can plot the relationship between list length and sorting steps as follows. We'll import matplotlib.pyplot in order to accomplish the plotting.

```
import matplotlib.pyplot as plt
plt.plot(xs,ys)
plt.title('Steps Required for Insertion Sort for Random Cabinets')
plt.xlabel('Number of Files in Random Cabinet')
plt.ylabel('Steps Required to Sort Cabinet by Insertion Sort')
plt.show()
```

Figure 4-1 shows the output. You can see that the output curve is a little jagged—sometimes a longer list will be sorted in fewer steps than will a shorter list. The reason for this is that we generated every list randomly. Occasionally our random list generation code will create a list that's easy for insertion sort to deal with quickly (because it's already partially sorted), and occasionally it will create a list that is harder to deal with quickly, strictly through random chance. For this same reason, you may find that the output on your screen doesn't look exactly like the output printed here if you don't use the same random seed, but the general shape should be the same.

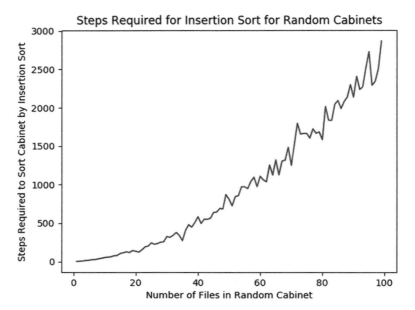

Figure 4-1: Insertion sort steps

Comparing to Well-Known Functions

Looking beyond the superficial jaggedness of Figure 4-1, we can examine the general shape of the curve and try to reason about its growth rate. The number of steps required appears to grow quite slowly between $x = 1$ and about $x = 10$. After that, it seems to slowly get steeper (and more jagged). Between about $x = 90$ and $x = 100$, the growth rate appears very steep indeed.

Saying that the plot gets gradually steeper as the list length increases is still not as precise as we want to be. Sometimes we talk colloquially about this kind of accelerating growth as "exponential." Are we dealing with exponential growth here? Strictly speaking, there is a function called the *exponential function* defined by e^x, where e is Euler's number, or about 2.71828. So does the number of steps required for insertion sort follow this exponential function that we could say fits the narrowest possible definition of exponential growth? We can get a clue about the answer by plotting our step curve together with an exponential growth curve, as follows. We will also import the numpy module in order to take the maximum and minimum of our step values.

```
import math
import numpy as np
random.seed(5040)
xs = list(range(1,100))
ys = [check_steps(x) for x in xs]
ys_exp = [math.exp(x) for x in xs]
plt.plot(xs,ys)
axes = plt.gca()
axes.set_ylim([np.min(ys),np.max(ys) + 140])
```

```
plt.plot(xs,ys_exp)
plt.title('Comparing Insertion Sort to the Exponential Function')
plt.xlabel('Number of Files in Random Cabinet')
plt.ylabel('Steps Required to Sort Cabinet')
plt.show()
```

Just like before, we define xs to be all the numbers between 1 and 100, and ys to be the number of steps required to sort randomly generated lists of each size corresponding to each x. We also define a variable called ys_exp, which is e^x for each of the values stored in xs. We then plot both ys and ys_exp on the same plot. The result enables us to see how the growth of the number of steps required to sort a list relates to true exponential growth.

Running this code creates the plot shown in Figure 4-2.

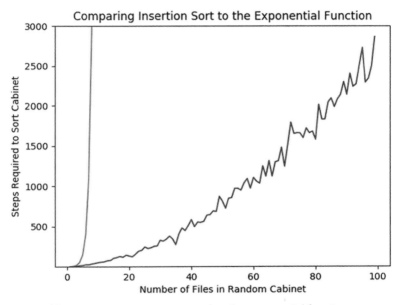

Figure 4-2: Insertion sort steps compared to the exponential function

We can see the true exponential growth curve shooting up toward infinity on the left side of the plot. Though the insertion sort step curve grows at an accelerating rate, its acceleration does not seem to get close to matching true exponential growth. If you plot other curves whose growth rate could also be called exponential, 2^x or 10^x, you'll see that all of these types of curves also grow much faster than our insertion sort step counter curve does. So if the insertion sort step curve doesn't match exponential growth, what kind of growth might it match? Let's try to plot a few more functions on the same plot. Here, we'll plot $y = x$, $y = x^{1.5}$, $y = x^2$, and $y = x^3$ along with the insertion sort step curve.

```
random.seed(5040)
xs = list(range(1,100))
ys = [check_steps(x) for x in xs]
xs_exp = [math.exp(x) for x in xs]
```

```
xs_squared = [x**2 for x in xs]
xs_threehalves = [x**1.5 for x in xs]
xs_cubed = [x**3 for x in xs]
plt.plot(xs,ys)
axes = plt.gca()
axes.set_ylim([np.min(ys),np.max(ys) + 140])
plt.plot(xs,xs_exp)
plt.plot(xs,xs)
plt.plot(xs,xs_squared)
plt.plot(xs,xs_cubed)
plt.plot(xs,xs_threehalves)
plt.title('Comparing Insertion Sort to Other Growth Rates')
plt.xlabel('Number of Files in Random Cabinet')
plt.ylabel('Steps Required to Sort Cabinet')
plt.show()
```

This results in Figure 4-3.

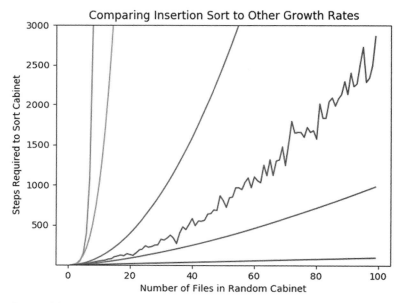

Figure 4-3: Insertion sort steps compared to other growth rates

There are five growth rates plotted in Figure 4-3, in addition to the jagged curve counting the steps required for insertion sort. You can see that the exponential curve grows the fastest, and next to it the cubic curve scarcely even makes an appearance on the plot because it also grows so fast. The $y = x$ curve grows extremely slowly compared to the other curves; you can see it at the very bottom of the plot.

The curves that are the closest to the insertion sort curve are $y = x^2$ and $y = x^{1.5}$. It isn't obvious which curve is most comparable to the insertion sort curve, so we cannot speak with certainty about the exact growth rate of insertion sort. But after plotting, we're able to make a statement like "if we are sorting a list with n elements, insertion sort will take somewhere between $n^{1.5}$ and n^2 steps." This is a more precise and robust statement than "as long as a gnat's wing flap" or ".002-ish seconds on my unique laptop this morning."

Adding Even More Theoretical Precision

To get even more precise, we should try to reason carefully about the steps required for insertion sort. Let's imagine, once again, that we have a new unsorted list with n elements. In Table 4-2, we proceed through each step of insertion sort individually and count the steps.

Table 4-2: Counting the Steps in Insertion Sort

Description of actions	Number of steps required for pulling the file from the old cabinet	Maximum number of steps required for comparing to other files	Number of steps required for inserting the file into the new cabinet
Take the first file from the old cabinet and insert it into the (empty) new cabinet.	1	0. (There are no files to compare to.)	1
Take the second file from the old cabinet and insert it into the new cabinet (that now contains one file).	1	1. (There's one file to compare to and we have to compare it.)	1
Take the third file from the old cabinet and insert it into the new cabinet (that now contains two files).	1	2 or fewer. (There are two files and we have to compare between 1 of them and all of them.)	1
Take the fourth file from the old cabinet and insert it into the new cabinet (that now contains three files).	1	3 or fewer. (There are three files and we have to compare between 1 of them and all of them.)	1
. . .	. . .	. . .	. . .
Take the nth file from the old cabinet and insert it into the new cabinet (that contains $n-1$ files).	1	$n-1$ or fewer. (There are $n-1$ files and we have to compare between one of them and all of them.)	1

If we add up all the steps described in this table, we get the following maximum total steps:

- Steps required for pulling files: n (1 step for pulling each of n files)
- Steps required for comparison: up to $1 + 2 + \ldots + (n-1)$
- Steps required for inserting files: n (1 step for inserting each of n files)

If we add these up, we get an expression like the following:

$$\text{maximum\_total\_steps} = n + (1 + 2 + \ldots + n)$$

We can simplify this expression using a handy identity:

$$1 + 2 + \ldots + n = \frac{n \times (n + 1)}{2}$$

If we use this identity and then add everything together and simplify, we find that the total number of steps required is

$$\text{maximum\_total\_steps} = \frac{n^2}{2} + \frac{3n}{2}$$

We finally have a very precise expression for the maximum total steps that could be required to perform insertion sort. But believe it or not, this expression may even be too precise, for several reasons. One is that it's the maximum number of steps required, but the minimum and the average could be much lower, and almost every conceivable list that we might want to sort would require fewer steps. Remember the jaggedness in the curve we plotted in Figure 4-1—there's always variation in how long it takes to perform an algorithm, depending on our choice of input.

Another reason that our expression for the maximum steps could be called too precise is that knowing the number of steps for an algorithm is most important for large values of n, but as n gets very large, a small part of the expression starts to dominate the rest in importance because of the sharply diverging growth rates of different functions.

Consider the expression $n^2 + n$. It is a sum of two terms: an n^2 term, and an n term. When $n = 10$, $n^2 + n$ is 110, which is 10% higher than n^2. When $n = 100$, $n^2 + n$ is 10,100, which is only 1% higher than n^2. As n grows, the n^2 term in the expression becomes more important than the n term because quadratic functions grow so much faster than linear ones. So if we have one algorithm that takes $n^2 + n$ steps to perform and another algorithm that takes n^2 steps to perform, as n grows very large, the difference between them will matter less and less. Both of them run in more or less n^2 steps.

Using Big O Notation

To say that an algorithm runs in more or less n^2 steps is a reasonable balance between the precision we want and the conciseness we want (and the randomness we have). The way we express this type of "more or less" relationship formally is by using *big O* notation (the O is short for *order*). We might say that a particular algorithm is "big O of n^2," or $O(n^2)$, if, in the worst case, it runs in more or less n^2 steps for large n. The technical definition states that the function $f(x)$ is big-O of the function $g(x)$ if there's some constant number M such that the absolute value of $f(x)$ is always less than M times $g(x)$ for all sufficiently large values of x.

In the case of insertion sort, when we look at our expression for the maximum number of steps required to perform the algorithm, we find that it's a sum of two terms: one is a multiple of n^2, and the other is a multiple of n. As we just discussed, the term that is a multiple of n will matter less and less as n grows, and the n^2 term will come to be the only one that we are concerned with. So the worst case of insertion sort is that it is a $O(n^2)$ ("big O of n^2") algorithm.

The quest for algorithm efficiency consists of seeking algorithms whose runtimes are big O of smaller and smaller functions. If we could find a way to alter insertion sort so that it is $O(n^{1.5})$ instead of $O(n^2)$, that would be a major breakthrough that would make a huge difference in runtimes for large values of n. We can use big O notation to talk not only about time but also about space. Some algorithms can gain speed by storing big datasets in memory. They might be big O of a small function for runtime but big O of a larger function for memory requirements. Depending on the circumstances, it may be wise to gain speed by eating up memory, or to free up memory by sacrificing speed. In this chapter, we'll focus on gaining speed and designing algorithms to have runtimes that are big O of the smallest possible functions, without regard to memory requirements.

After learning insertion sort and seeing that its runtime performance is $O(n^2)$, it's natural to wonder what level of improvement we can reasonably hope for. Could we find some holy grail algorithm that could sort any possible list in fewer than 10 steps? No. Every sorting algorithm will require at least n steps, because it will be necessary to consider each element of the list in turn, for each of the n elements. So any sorting algorithm will be at least $O(n)$. We cannot do better than $O(n)$, but can we do better than insertion sort's $O(n^2)$? We can. Next, we'll consider an algorithm that's known to be $O(n\log(n))$, a significant improvement over insertion sort.

Merge Sort

Merge sort is an algorithm that's much quicker than insertion sort. Just like insertion sort, merge sort contains two parts: a part that merges two lists and a part that repeatedly uses merging to accomplish the actual sorting. Let's consider the merging itself before we consider the sorting.

Suppose we have two filing cabinets that are both sorted individually but have never been compared to each other. We want to combine their contents into one final filing cabinet that is also completely sorted. We will call this task a *merge* of the two sorted filing cabinets. How should we approach this problem?

Once again, it's worthwhile to consider how we would do this with real filing cabinets before we open Python and start writing code. In this case, we can imagine having three filing cabinets in front of us: the two full, sorted filing cabinets whose files we want to merge, and a third, empty filing cabinet that we will insert files into and that will eventually contain all of the files from the original two cabinets. We can call our two original cabinets the "left" and "right" cabinets, imagining that they are placed on our left and right.

Merging

To merge, we can take the first file in both of the original cabinets simultaneously: the first left file with our left hand and the first right file with our right hand. Whichever file is lower is inserted into the new cabinet as its first file. To find the second file for the new cabinet, once again take the first file in the left and right cabinets, compare them, and insert whichever is lower into the last position in the new cabinet. When either the left cabinet or the right cabinet is empty, take the remaining files in the nonempty cabinet and place them all together at the end of the new cabinet. After this, your new cabinet will contain all the files from the left and right cabinets, sorted in order. We have successfully merged our original two cabinets.

In Python, we'll use the variables left and right to refer to our original sorted cabinets, and we'll define a newcabinet list, which will start empty and eventually contain all elements of both left and right, in order.

```
newcabinet = []
```

We'll define example cabinets that we'll call left and right:

```
left = [1,3,4,4,5,7,8,9]
right = [2,4,6,7,8,8,10,12,13,14]
```

To compare the respective first elements of our left and right cabinets, we'll use the following if statements (which won't be ready to run until we fill in the --*snip*-- sections):

```
if left[0] > right[0]:
    --snip--
elif left[0] <= right[0]:
    --snip--
```

Remember that if the first element of the left cabinet is lower than the first element of the right cabinet, we want to pop that element out of the left cabinet and insert it into the newcabinet, and vice versa. We can accomplish that by using Python's built-in pop() function, inserting it into our if statements as follows:

```
if left[0] > right[0]:
    to_insert = right.pop(0)
    newcabinet.append(to_insert)
elif left[0] <= right[0]:
    to_insert = left.pop(0)
    newcabinet.append(to_insert)
```

This process—checking the first elements of the left and right cabinets and popping the appropriate one into the new cabinet—needs to continue as long as both of the cabinets still have at least one file. That's why we will nest these if statements inside a while loop that checks the minimum length of left and right. As long as both left and right contain at least one file, it will continue its process:

```
while(min(len(left),len(right)) > 0):
    if left[0] > right[0]:
        to_insert = right.pop(0)
        newcabinet.append(to_insert)
    elif left[0] <= right[0]:
        to_insert = left.pop(0)
        newcabinet.append(to_insert)
```

Our while loop will stop executing as soon as either left or right runs out of files to insert. At that point, if left is empty, we'll insert all the files in right at the end of the new cabinet in their current order, and vice versa. We can accomplish that final insertion as follows:

```
if(len(left) > 0):
    for i in left:
        newcabinet.append(i)

if(len(right) > 0):
    for i in right:
        newcabinet.append(i)
```

Finally, we combine all of those snippets into our final merging algorithm in Python as shown in Listing 4-4.

```
def merging(left,right):
    newcabinet = []
    while(min(len(left),len(right)) > 0):
        if left[0] > right[0]:
            to_insert = right.pop(0)
            newcabinet.append(to_insert)
        elif left[0] <= right[0]:
            to_insert = left.pop(0)
            newcabinet.append(to_insert)
    if(len(left) > 0):
        for i in left:
            newcabinet.append(i)
    if(len(right)>0):
        for i in right:
            newcabinet.append(i)
    return(newcabinet)

left = [1,3,4,4,5,7,8,9]
right = [2,4,6,7,8,8,10,12,13,14]

newcab=merging(left,right)
```

Listing 4-4: An algorithm to merge two sorted lists

The code in Listing 4-4 creates `newcab`, a single list that contains all elements of `left` and `right`, merged and in order. You can run `print(newcab)` to see that our merging function worked.

From Merging to Sorting

Once we know how to merge, merge sort is within our grasp. Let's start by creating a simple merge sort function that works only on lists that have two or fewer elements. A one-element list is already sorted, so if we pass that as the input to our merge sort function, we should just return it unaltered. If we pass a two-element list to our merge sort function, we can split that list into two one-element lists (that are therefore already sorted) and call our merging function on those one-element lists to get a final, sorted two-element list. The following Python function accomplishes what we need:

```
import math

def mergesort_two_elements(cabinet):
    newcabinet = []
    if(len(cabinet) == 1):
        newcabinet = cabinet
    else:
        left = cabinet[:math.floor(len(cabinet)/2)]
        right = cabinet[math.floor(len(cabinet)/2):]
        newcabinet = merging(left,right)
    return(newcabinet)
```

This code relies on Python's list indexing syntax to split whatever cabinet we want to sort into a left cabinet and a right cabinet. You can see in the lines that define `left` and `right` that we're using `:math.floor(len(cabinet)/2)` and `math.floor(len(cabinet)/2):` to refer to the entire first half or the entire second half of the original cabinet, respectively. You can call this function with any one- or two-element cabinet—for example, `mergesort_two_elements([3,1])`—and see that it successfully returns a sorted cabinet.

Next, let's write a function that can sort a list that has four elements. If we split a four-element list into two sublists, each sublist will have two elements. We could follow our merging algorithm to combine these lists. However, recall that our merging algorithm is designed to combine two already sorted lists. These two lists may not be sorted, so using our merging algorithm will not successfully sort them. However, each of our sublists has only two elements, and we just wrote a function that can perform merge sort on lists with two elements. So we can split our four-element list into two sublists, call our merge sort function that works on two-element lists on each of those sublists, and then merge the two sorted lists together to get a sorted result with four elements. This Python function accomplishes that:

```
def mergesort_four_elements(cabinet):
    newcabinet = []
    if(len(cabinet) == 1):
        newcabinet = cabinet
```

```
    else:
        left = mergesort_two_elements(cabinet[:math.floor(len(cabinet)/2)])
        right = mergesort_two_elements(cabinet[math.floor(len(cabinet)/2):])
        newcabinet = merging(left,right)
    return(newcabinet)

cabinet = [2,6,4,1]
newcabinet = mergesort_four_elements(cabinet)
```

We could continue writing these functions to work on successively larger lists. But the breakthrough comes when we realize that we can collapse that whole process by using recursion. Consider the function in Listing 4-5, and compare it to the preceding mergesort_four_elements() function.

```
def mergesort(cabinet):
    newcabinet = []
    if(len(cabinet) == 1):
        newcabinet = cabinet
    else:
❶       left = mergesort(cabinet[:math.floor(len(cabinet)/2)])
❷       right = mergesort(cabinet[math.floor(len(cabinet)/2):])
        newcabinet = merging(left,right)
    return(newcabinet)
```

Listing 4-5: Implementing merge sort with recursion

You can see that this function is nearly identical to our mergesort_four_elements() to function. The crucial difference is that to create the sorted left and right cabinets, it doesn't call another function that works on smaller lists. Rather, it calls itself on the smaller list ❶❷. Merge sort is a *divide and conquer* algorithm. We start with a large, unsorted list. Then we split that list repeatedly into smaller and smaller chunks (the dividing) until we end up with sorted (conquered) one-item lists, and then we simply merge them back together successively until we have built back up to one big sorted list. We can call this merge sort function on a list of any size and check that it works:

```
cabinet = [4,1,3,2,6,3,18,2,9,7,3,1,2.5,-9]
newcabinet = mergesort(cabinet)
print(newcabinet)
```

When we put all of our merge sort code together, we get Listing 4-6.

```
def merging(left,right):
    newcabinet = []
    while(min(len(left),len(right)) > 0):
        if left[0] > right[0]:
            to_insert = right.pop(0)
            newcabinet.append(to_insert)
        elif left[0] <= right[0]:
            to_insert = left.pop(0)
            newcabinet.append(to_insert)
    if(len(left) > 0):
        for i in left:
            newcabinet.append(i)
```

```
        if(len(right) > 0):
            for i in right:
                newcabinet.append(i)
        return(newcabinet)

import math

def mergesort(cabinet):
    newcabinet = []
    if(len(cabinet) == 1):
        newcabinet=cabinet
    else:
        left = mergesort(cabinet[:math.floor(len(cabinet)/2)])
        right = mergesort(cabinet[math.floor(len(cabinet)/2):])
        newcabinet = merging(left,right)
    return(newcabinet)

cabinet = [4,1,3,2,6,3,18,2,9,7,3,1,2.5,-9]
newcabinet=mergesort(cabinet)
```

Listing 4-6: Our complete merge sort code

You could add a step counter to your merge sort code to check how many steps it takes to run and how it compares to insertion sort. The merge sort process consists of successively splitting the initial cabinet into sublists and then merging those sublists back together, preserving the sorting order. Every time we split a list, we're cutting it in half. The number of times a list of length n can be split in half before each sublist has only one element is about $\log(n)$ (where the log is to base 2), and the number of comparisons we have to make at each merge is at most n. So n or fewer comparisons for each of $\log(n)$ comparisons means that merge sort is O($n \times \log(n)$), which may not seem impressive but actually makes it the state of the art for sorting. In fact, when we call Python's built-in sorting function sorted as follows:

```
print(sorted(cabinet))
```

Python is using a hybrid version of merge sort and insertion sort behind the scenes to accomplish this sorting task. By learning merge sort and insertion sort, you've gotten up to speed with the quickest sorting algorithm computer scientists have been able to create, something that is used millions of times every day in every imaginable kind of application.

Sleep Sort

The enormous negative influence that the internet has had on humanity is occasionally counterbalanced by a small, shining treasure that it provides. Occasionally, the bowels of the internet even produce a scientific discovery that creeps into the world outside the purview of scientific journals or the "establishment." In 2011, an anonymous poster on the online image board 4chan proposed and provided code for a sorting algorithm that had never been published before and has since come to be called *sleep sort*.

Sleep sort wasn't designed to resemble any real-world situation, like inserting files into a filing cabinet. If we're seeking an analogy, we might consider the task of allocating lifeboat spots on the *Titanic* as it began to sink. We might want to allow children and younger people the first chance to get on the lifeboats, and then allow older people to try to get one of the remaining spots. If we make an announcement like "younger people get on the boats before older people," we'd face chaos as everyone would have to compare their ages—they would face a difficult sorting problem amidst the chaos of the sinking ship.

A sleep-sort approach to the *Titanic* lifeboats would be the following. We would announce, "Everyone please stand still and count to your age: 1, 2, 3, ... As soon as you have counted up to your current age, step forward to get on a lifeboat." We can imagine that 8-year-olds would finish their counting about one second before the 9-year-olds, and so would have a one-second head start and be able to get a spot on the boats before those who were 9. The 8- and 9-year-olds would similarly be able to get on the boats before the 10-year-olds, and so on. Without doing any comparisons at all, we'd rely on individuals' ability to pause for a length of time proportional to the metric we want to sort on and then insert themselves, and the sorting would happen effortlessly after that—with no direct inter-person comparisons.

This *Titanic* lifeboat process shows the idea of sleep sort: allow each element to insert itself directly, but only after a pause in proportion to the metric it's being sorted on. From a programming perspective, these pauses are called *sleeps* and can be implemented in most languages.

In Python, we can implement sleep sort as follows. We will import the threading module, which will enable us to create different computer processes for each element of our list to sleep and then insert itself. We'll also import the time.sleep module, which will enable us to put our different "threads" to sleep for the appropriate length of time.

```
import threading
from time import sleep

def sleep_sort(i):
    sleep(i)
    global sortedlist
    sortedlist.append(i)
    return(i)

items = [2, 4, 5, 2, 1, 7]
sortedlist = []
ignore_result = [threading.Thread(target = sleep_sort, args = (i,)).start() \
for i in items]
```

The sorted list will be stored in the sortedlist variable, and you can ignore the list we create called ignore_result. You can see that one advantage of sleep sort is that it can be written concisely in Python. It's also fun to print the sortedlist variable before the sorting is done (in this case, within about 7 seconds) because depending on exactly when you execute the print command, you'll see a different list. However, sleep sort also has some major disadvantages. One of these is that because it's not possible to sleep for a negative length of time, sleep sort cannot sort lists with negative numbers. Another disadvantage is that sleep sort's execution is highly dependent on outliers—if you append 1,000 to the list, you'll have to wait at least 1,000 seconds for the algorithm to finish executing. Yet another disadvantage is that numbers that are close to each other may be inserted in the wrong order if the threads are not executed perfectly concurrently. Finally, since sleep sort uses threading, it will not be able to execute (well) on hardware or software that does not enable threading (well).

If we had to express sleep sort's runtime in big O notation, we might say that it is $O(max(list))$. Unlike the runtime of every other well-known sorting algorithm, its runtime depends not on the size of the list but on the size of the elements of the list. This makes sleep sort hard to rely on, because we can only be confident about its performance with certain lists—even a short list may take far too long to sort if any of its elements are too large.

There may never be a practical use for sleep sort, even on a sinking ship. I include it here for a few reasons. First, because it is so different from all other extant sorting algorithms, it reminds us that even the most stale and static fields of research have room for creativity and innovation, and it provides a refreshingly new perspective on what may seem like a narrow field. Second, because it was designed and published anonymously and probably by someone outside the mainstream of research and practice, it reminds us that great thoughts and geniuses are found not only in fancy universities, established journals, and top firms, but also among the uncredentialed and unrecognized. Third, it represents a fascinating new generation of algorithms that are "native to computers," meaning that they are not a translation of something that can be done with a cabinet and two hands like many old algorithms, but are fundamentally based on capabilities that are unique to computers (in this case, sleeping and threading). Fourth, the computer-native ideas it relies on (sleeping and threading) are very useful and worth putting in any algorithmicist's toolbox for use in designing other algorithms. And fifth, I have an idiosyncratic affection for it, maybe just because it is a strange, creative misfit or maybe because I like its method of self-organizing order and the fact that I can use it if I'm ever in charge of saving a sinking ship.

From Sorting to Searching

Searching, like sorting, is fundamental to a variety of tasks in computer science (and in the rest of life). We may want to search for a name in a phone book, or (since we're living after the year 2000) we may need to access a database and find a relevant record.

Searching is often merely a corollary of sorting. In other words, once we have sorted a list, searching is very straightforward—the sorting is often the hard part.

Binary Search

Binary search is a quick and effective method for searching for an element in a sorted list. It works a little like a guessing game. Suppose that someone is thinking of a number from 1 to 100 and you are trying to guess it. You may guess 50 as your first guess. Your friend says that 50 is incorrect but allows you to guess again and gives you a hint: 50 is too high. Since 50 is too high, you guess 49. Again, you are incorrect, and your friend tells you that 49 is too high and gives you another chance to guess. You could guess 48, then 47, and so on until you get the right answer. But that could take a long time—if the correct number is 1, it will take you 50 guesses to get it, which seems like too many guesses considering there were only 100 total possibilities to begin with.

A better approach is to take larger jumps after you find out whether your guess is too high or too low. If 50 is too high, consider what we could learn from guessing 40 next instead of 49. If 40 is too low, we have eliminated 39 possibilities (1–39) and we'll definitely be able to guess in at most 9 more guesses (41–49). If 40 is too high, we've at least eliminated 9 possibilities (41–49) and we'll definitely be able to guess in at most 39 more guesses (1–39). So in the worst case, guessing 40 narrows down the possibilities from 49 (1–49) to 39 (1–39). By contrast, guessing 49 narrows down the possibilities from 49 (1–49) to 48 (1–48) in the worst case. Clearly, guessing 40 is a better searching strategy than guessing 49.

It turns out that the best searching strategy is to guess exactly the midpoint of the remaining possibilities. If you do that and then check whether your guess was too high or too low, you can always eliminate half of the remaining possibilities. If you eliminate half of the possibilities in each round of guessing, you can actually find the right value quite quickly ($O(\log(n))$ for those keeping score at home). For example, a list with 1,000 items will require only 10 guesses to find any element with a binary search strategy. If we're allowed to have only 20 guesses, we can correctly find the position of an element in a list with more than a million items. Incidentally, this is why we can write guessing-game apps that can correctly "read your mind" by asking only about 20 questions.

To implement this in Python, we will start by defining upper and lower bounds for what location a file can occupy in a filing cabinet. The lower bound will be 0, and the upper bound will be the length of the cabinet:

```
sorted_cabinet = [1,2,3,4,5]
upperbound = len(sorted_cabinet)
lowerbound = 0
```

To start, we will guess that the file is in the middle of the cabinet. We'll import Python's *math* library to use the floor() function, which can convert decimals to integers. Remember that guessing the halfway point gives us the maximum possible amount of information:

```
import math
guess = math.floor(len(sorted_cabinet)/2)
```

Next, we will check whether our guess is too low or too high. We'll take a different action depending on what we find. We use the `looking_for` variable for the value we are searching for:

```
if(sorted_cabinet[guess] > looking_for):
    --snip--
if(sorted_cabinet[guess] < looking_for):
    --snip--
```

If the file in the cabinet is too high, then we'll make our guess the new upper bound, since there is no use looking any higher in the cabinet. Then our new guess will be lower—to be precise, it will be halfway between the current guess and the lower bound:

```
looking_for = 3
if(sorted_cabinet[guess] > looking_for):
    upperbound = guess
    guess = math.floor((guess + lowerbound)/2)
```

We follow an analogous process if the file in the cabinet is too low:

```
if(sorted_cabinet[guess] < looking_for):
    lowerbound = guess
    guess = math.floor((guess + upperbound)/2)
```

Finally, we can put all of these pieces together into a `binarysearch()` function. The function contains a *while* loop that will run for as long as it takes until we find the part of the cabinet we've been looking for (Listing 4-7).

```
import math
sortedcabinet = [1,2,3,4,5,6,7,8,9,10]

def binarysearch(sorted_cabinet,looking_for):
    guess = math.floor(len(sorted_cabinet)/2)
    upperbound = len(sorted_cabinet)
    lowerbound = 0
    while(abs(sorted_cabinet[guess] - looking_for) > 0.0001):
        if(sorted_cabinet[guess] > looking_for):
            upperbound = guess
            guess = math.floor((guess + lowerbound)/2)
        if(sorted_cabinet[guess] < looking_for):
            lowerbound = guess
            guess = math.floor((guess + upperbound)/2)
    return(guess)

print(binarysearch(sortedcabinet,8))
```

Listing 4-7: An implementation of binary search

The final output of this code tells us that the number 8 is at position 7 in our sorted_cabinet. This is correct (remember that the index of Python lists starts at 0). This strategy of guessing in a way that eliminates half of the remaining possibilities is useful in many domains. For example, it's the basis for the most efficient strategy on average in the formerly popular board game *Guess Who*. It's also the best way (in theory) to look words up in a large, unfamiliar dictionary.

Applications of Binary Search

Besides guessing games and word lookups, binary search is used in a few other domains. For example, we can use the idea of binary search when debugging code. Suppose that we have written some code that doesn't work, but we aren't sure which part is faulty. We can use a binary search strategy to find the problem. We split the code in half and run both halves separately. Whichever half doesn't run properly is the half where the problem lies. Again, we split the problematic part in half, and test each half to further narrow down the possibilities until we find the offending line of code. A similar idea is implemented in the popular code version-control software Git as git bisect (although git bisect iterates through temporally separated versions of the code rather than through lines in one version).

Another application of binary search is inverting a mathematical function. For example, imagine that we have to write a function that can calculate the arcsin, or inverse sine, of a given number. In only a few lines, we can write a function that will call our binarysearch() function to get the right answer. To start, we need to define a domain; these are the values that we will search through to find a particular arcsin value. The sine function is periodic and takes on all of its possible values between $-pi/2$ and $pi/2$, so numbers in between those extremes will constitute our domain. Next, we calculate sine values for each value in the domain. We call binarysearch() to find the position of the number whose sine is the number we're looking for, and return the domain value with the corresponding index, like so:

```
def inverse_sin(number):
    domain = [x * math.pi/10000 - math.pi/2 for x in list(range(0,10000))]
    the_range = [math.sin(x) for x in domain]
    result = domain[binarysearch(the_range,number)]
    return(result)
```

You can run inverse_sin(0.9) and see that this function returns the correct answer: about 1.12.

This is not the only way to invert a function. Some functions can be inverted through algebraic manipulation. However, algebraic function inversion can be difficult or even impossible for many functions. The binary search method presented here, by contrast, can work for any function, and with its $O(\log(n))$ runtime, it's also lightning fast.

Summary

Sorting and searching may feel mundane to you, as if you've taken a break from an adventure around the world to attend a seminar on folding laundry. Maybe so, but remember that if you can fold clothes efficiently, you can pack more gear for your trek up Kilimanjaro. Sorting and searching algorithms can be enablers, helping you build newer and greater things on their shoulders. Besides that, it's worth studying sorting and searching algorithms closely because they are fundamental and common, and the ideas you see in them can be useful for the rest of your intellectual life. In this chapter, we discussed some fundamental and interesting sorting algorithms, plus binary search. We also discussed how to compare algorithms and use big O notation.

In the next chapter, we'll turn to a few applications of pure math. We'll see how we can use algorithms to explore the mathematical world, and how the mathematical world can help us understand our own.

5

PURE MATH

The quantitative precision of algorithms makes them naturally suited to applications in mathematics. In this chapter, we explore algorithms that are useful in pure mathematics and look at how mathematical ideas can improve any of our algorithms. We'll start by discussing continued fractions, an austere topic that will take us to the dizzying heights of the infinite and give us the power to find order in chaos. We'll continue by discussing square roots, a more prosaic but arguably more useful topic. Finally, we'll discuss randomness, including the mathematics of randomness and some important algorithms that generate random numbers.

Continued Fractions

In 1597, the great Johannes Kepler wrote about what he considered geometry's "two great treasures": the Pythagorean theorem and a number that has since come to be called the *golden ratio*. Often denoted by the Greek letter *phi*, the golden ratio is equal to about 1.618, and Kepler was only one of dozens of great thinkers who have been entranced by it. Like pi and a few other famous constants, such as the exponential base *e*, phi has a tendency to show up in unexpected places. People have found phi in many places in nature, and have painstakingly documented where it occurs in fine art, as in the annotated version of the Rokeby Venus shown in Figure 5-1.

In Figure 5-1, a phi enthusiast has added overlays that indicate that the ratios of some of these lengths, like b/a and d/c, seem to be equal to phi. Many great paintings have a composition that's amenable to this kind of phi-hunting.

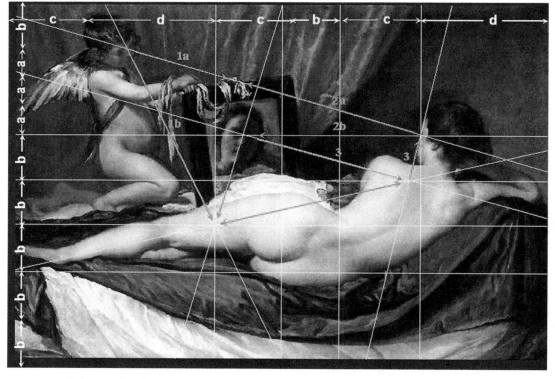

Figure 5-1: Phi/Venus (from https://commons.wikimedia.org/wiki/File:DV_The_Toilet_of_Venus_Gr.jpg)

Compressing and Communicating Phi

Phi's exact value is surprisingly hard to express. I could say that it's equal to 1.61803399 . . . . The ellipsis here is a way of cheating; it means that more numbers follow (an infinite number of numbers, in fact), but I haven't told you what those numbers are, so you still don't know the exact value of phi.

For some numbers with infinite decimal expansions, a fraction can represent them exactly. For example, the number 0.11111 . . . is equal to 1/9—here, the fraction provides an easy way to express the exact value of an infinitely continued decimal. Even if you didn't know the fractional representation, you could see the pattern of repeating 1s in 0.1111 . . . and thereby understand its exact value. Unfortunately, the golden ratio is what's called an *irrational number*, meaning that there are no two integers x and y that enable us to say that phi is equal to x/y. Moreover, no one has yet been able to discern any pattern in its digits.

We have an infinite decimal expansion with no clear pattern and no fractional representation. It may seem impossible to ever clearly express phi's exact value. But if we learn more about phi, we can find a way to express it both exactly and concisely. One of the things we know about phi is that it's the solution to this equation:

$$phi^2 - phi - 1 = 0$$

One way we might imagine expressing the exact value of phi would be to write "the solution to the equation written above this paragraph." This has the benefit of being concise and technically exact, but it means that we have to solve the equation somehow. That description also doesn't tell us the 200th or 500th digit in phi's expansion.

If we divide our equation by phi, we get the following:

$$phi - 1 - \frac{1}{phi} = 0$$

And if we rearrange that equation, we get this:

$$phi = 1 + \frac{1}{phi}$$

Now imagine if we attempted a strange substitution of this equation into itself:

$$phi = 1 + \frac{1}{phi} = 1 + \frac{1}{1 + \dfrac{1}{phi}}$$

Here, we rewrote the phi on the righthand side as 1 + 1/phi. We could do that same substitution again; why not?

$$phi = 1 + \cfrac{1}{phi} = 1 + \cfrac{1}{1 + \cfrac{1}{phi}} = 1 + \cfrac{1}{1 + \cfrac{1}{1 + \cfrac{1}{phi}}}$$

We can perform this substitution as many times as we like, with no end. As we continue, phi gets pushed more and more levels "in" to the corner of a growing fraction. Listing 5-1 shows an expression for phi with phi seven levels in.

$$phi = 1 + \cfrac{1}{1 + \cfrac{1}{1 + \cfrac{1}{1 + \cfrac{1}{1 + \cfrac{1}{1 + \cfrac{1}{1 + \cfrac{1}{phi}}}}}}}$$

Listing 5-1: A continued fraction with seven levels expressing the value of phi

If we imagine continuing this process, we can push phi infinity levels in. Then what we have left is shown in Listing 5-2.

$$phi = 1 + \cfrac{1}{1 + \cfrac{1}{1 + \cfrac{1}{1 + \cfrac{1}{1 + \cfrac{1}{1 + \cfrac{1}{1 + \ldots}}}}}}$$

Listing 5-2: An infinite continued fraction expressing the value of phi

In theory, after the infinity of 1s and plus signs and fraction bars represented by the ellipsis, we should insert a phi into Listing 5-2, just like it appears in the bottom right of Listing 5-1. But we will never get through all of those 1s (because there are an infinite number of them), so we are justified in forgetting entirely about the phi that's supposed to be nested in the righthand side.

More about Continued Fractions

The expressions just shown are called continued fractions. A *continued fraction* consists of sums and reciprocals nested in multiple layers. Continued fractions can be finite, like the one in Listing 5-1 that terminated after seven layers, or infinite, continuing forever without end like the one in

Listing 5-2. Continued fractions are especially useful for our purposes because they enable us to express the exact value of phi without needing to chop down an infinite forest to manufacture enough paper. In fact, mathematicians sometimes use an even more concise notation method that enables us to express a continued fraction in one simple line. Instead of writing all the fraction bars in a continued fraction, we can use square brackets ([ ]) to denote that we're working with a continued fraction, and use a semicolon to separate the digit that's "alone" from the digits that are together in a fraction. With this method, we can write the continued fraction for phi as the following:

$$phi = [1; 1,1,1,1 \ldots]$$

In this case, the ellipses are no longer losing information, since the continued fraction for phi has a clear pattern: it's all 1s, so we know its exact 100th or 1,000th element. This is one of those times when mathematics seems to deliver something miraculous to us: a way to concisely write down a number that we had thought was infinite, without pattern, and ineffable. But phi isn't the only possible continued fraction. We could write another continued fraction as follows:

$$mysterynumber = [2; 1,2,1,1,4,1,1,6,1,1,8, \ldots]$$

In this case, after the first few digits, we find a simple pattern: pairs of 1s alternate with increasing even numbers. The next values will be 1, 1, 10, 1, 1, 12, and so on. We can write the beginning of this continued fraction in a more conventional style as

$$mysterynumber = 2 + \cfrac{1}{1 + \cfrac{1}{2 + \cfrac{1}{1 + \cfrac{1}{1 + \cfrac{1}{4 + \cfrac{1}{1 + \cfrac{1}{\ldots}}}}}}}$$

In fact, this mystery number is none other than our old friend e, the base of the natural logarithm! The constant e, just like phi and other irrational numbers, has an infinite decimal expansion with no apparent pattern and cannot be represented by a finite fraction, and it seems like it's impossible to express its exact numeric value concisely. But by using the new concept of continued fractions and a new concise notation, we can write these apparently intractable numbers in one line. There are also several remarkable ways to use continued fractions to represent pi. This is a victory for data compression. It's also a victory in the perennial battle between order and chaos: where we thought there was nothing but encroaching chaos dominating the numbers we love, we find that there was always a deep order beneath the surface.

Our continued fraction for phi came from a special equation that works only for phi. But in fact, it is possible to generate a continued fraction representation of any number.

An Algorithm for Generating Continued Fractions

To find a continued fraction expansion for any number, we'll use an algorithm.

It's easiest to find continued fraction expansions for numbers that are integer fractions already. For example, consider the task of finding a continued fraction representation of 105/33. Our goal is to express this number in a form that looks like the following:

$$\frac{105}{33} = a + \cfrac{1}{b + \cfrac{1}{c + \cfrac{1}{d + \cfrac{1}{e + \cfrac{1}{f + \cfrac{1}{g + \cfrac{1}{\cdots}}}}}}}$$

where the ellipses could be referring to a finite rather than an infinite continuation. Our algorithm will generate a first, then b, then c, and proceed through terms of the alphabet sequentially until it reaches the final term or until we require it to stop.

If we interpret our example 105/33 as a division problem instead of a fraction, we find that 105/33 is 3, remainder 6. We can rewrite 105/33 as 3 + 6/33:

$$3 + \frac{6}{33} = a + \cfrac{1}{b + \cfrac{1}{c + \cfrac{1}{d + \cfrac{1}{e + \cfrac{1}{f + \cfrac{1}{g + \cfrac{1}{\cdots}}}}}}}$$

The left and the right sides of this equation both consist of an integer (3 and a) and a fraction (6/33 and the rest of the right side). We conclude that the integer parts are equal, so $a = 3$. After this, we have to find a suitable b, c, and so on such that the whole fractional part of the expression will evaluate to 6/33.

To find the right b, c, and the rest, look at what we have to solve after concluding that $a = 3$:

$$\frac{6}{33} = \cfrac{1}{b + \cfrac{1}{c + \cfrac{1}{d + \cfrac{1}{e + \cfrac{1}{f + \cfrac{1}{g + \cfrac{1}{\cdots}}}}}}}$$

If we take the reciprocal of both sides of this equation, we get the following equation:

$$\frac{33}{6} = b + \cfrac{1}{c + \cfrac{1}{d + \cfrac{1}{e + \cfrac{1}{f + \cfrac{1}{g + \cfrac{1}{h + \cfrac{1}{\cdots}}}}}}}$$

Our task is now to find b and c. We can do a division again; 33 divided by 6 is 5, with remainder 3, so we can rewrite 33/6 as 5 + 3/6:

$$5 + \frac{3}{6} = b + \cfrac{1}{c + \cfrac{1}{d + \cfrac{1}{e + \cfrac{1}{f + \cfrac{1}{g + \cfrac{1}{h + \cfrac{1}{\cdots}}}}}}}$$

We can see that both sides of the equation have an integer (5 and b) and a fraction (3/6 and the rest of the right side). We can conclude that the integer parts are equal, so $b = 5$. We have gotten another letter of the alphabet, and now we need to simplify 3/6 to progress further. If you can't tell immediately that 3/6 is equal to 1/2, you could follow the same process we did for 6/33: say that 3/6 expressed as a reciprocal is 1/(6/3), and we find that 6/3 is 2 remainder 0. The algorithm we're following is meant to complete when we have a remainder of 0, so we will realize that we've finished the process, and we can write our full continued fraction as in Listing 5-3.

$$\frac{105}{33} = 3 + \cfrac{1}{5 + \cfrac{1}{2}}$$

Listing 5-3: A continued fraction for 105/33

If this process of repeatedly dividing two integers to get a quotient and a remainder felt familiar to you, it should have. In fact, it's the same process we followed in Euclid's algorithm in Chapter 2! We follow the same steps but record different answers: for Euclid's algorithm, we recorded the final nonzero remainder as the final answer, and in the continued fraction generation algorithm, we recorded every quotient (every letter of the alphabet) along the way. As happens so often in math, we have found an unexpected connection—in this case, between the generation of a continued fraction and the discovery of a greatest common divisor.

We can implement this continued fraction generation algorithm in Python as follows.

We'll assume that we're starting with a fraction of the form x/y. First, we decide which of x and y is bigger and which is smaller:

```
x = 105
y = 33
big = max(x,y)
small = min(x,y)
```

Next, we'll take the quotient of the bigger divided by the smaller of the two, just as we did with 105/33. When we found that the result was 3, remainder 6, we concluded that 3 was the first term (a) in the continued fraction. We can take this quotient and store the result as follows:

```
import math
output = []
quotient = math.floor(big/small)
output.append(quotient)
```

In this case, we are ready to obtain a full alphabet of results (a, b, c, and so on), so we create an empty list called output and append our first result to it.

Finally, we have to repeat the process, just as we did for 33/6. Remember that 33 was previously the small variable, but now it's the big one, and the remainder of our division process is the new small variable. Since the remainder is always smaller than the divisor, big and small will always be correctly labeled. We accomplish this switcheroo in Python as follows:

```
new_small = big % small
big = small
small = new_small
```

At this point, we have completed one round of the algorithm, and we need to repeat it for our next set of numbers (33 and 6). In order to accomplish the process concisely, we can put it all in a loop, as in Listing 5-4.

```
import math
def continued_fraction(x,y,length_tolerance):
    output = []
    big = max(x,y)
    small = min(x,y)
```

```
    while small > 0 and len(output) < length_tolerance:
        quotient = math.floor(big/small)
        output.append(quotient)
        new_small = big % small
        big = small
        small = new_small
    return(output)
```

Listing 5-4: An algorithm for expressing fractions as continued fractions

Here, we took *x* and *y* as inputs, and we defined a `length_tolerance` variable. Remember that some continued fractions are infinite in length, and others are extremely long. By including a `length_tolerance` variable in the function, we can stop our process early if the output is getting unwieldy, and thereby avoid getting caught in an infinite loop.

Remember that when we performed Euclid's algorithm, we used a recursive solution. In this case, we used a `while` loop instead. Recursion is well suited to Euclid's algorithm because it required only one final output number at the very end. Here, however, we want to collect a sequence of numbers in a list. A loop is better suited to that kind of sequential collection.

We can run our new `continued_fraction` generation function as follows:

```
print(continued_fraction(105,33,10))
```

We'll get the following simple output:

```
[3,5,2]
```

We can see that the numbers here are the same as the key integers on the right side of Listing 5-3.

We may want to check that a particular continued fraction correctly expresses a number we're interested in. In order to do this, we should define a `get_number()` function that converts a continued fraction to a decimal number, as in Listing 5-5.

```
def get_number(continued_fraction):
    index = -1
    number = continued_fraction[index]

    while abs(index) < len(continued_fraction):
        next = continued_fraction[index - 1]
        number = 1/number + next
        index -= 1
    return(number)
```

Listing 5-5: Converting a continued fraction to a decimal representation of a number

We don't need to worry about the details of this function since we're just using it to check our continued fractions. We can check that the function works by running `get_number([3,5,2])` and seeing that we get 3.181818 . . . as the output, which is another way to write 105/33 (the number we started with).

From Decimals to Continued Fractions

What if, instead of starting with some x/y as an input to our continued fraction algorithm, we start with a decimal number, like 1.4142135623730951? We'll need to make a few adjustments, but we can more or less follow the same process we followed for fractions. Remember that our goal is to find a, b, c, and the rest of the alphabet in the following type of expression:

$$1.4142135623730951 = a + \cfrac{1}{b + \cfrac{1}{c + \cfrac{1}{d + \cfrac{1}{e + \cfrac{1}{f + \cfrac{1}{g + \cfrac{1}{\cdots}}}}}}}$$

Finding a is as simple as it gets—it's just the part of the decimal number to the left of the decimal point. We can define this first_term (a in our equation) and the leftover as follows:

```
x = 1.4142135623730951
output = []
first_term = int(x)
leftover = x - int(x)
output.append(first_term)
```

Just like before, we're storing our successive answers in a list called output.

After solving for a, we have a leftover, and we need to find a continued fraction representation for it:

$$0.4142135623730951 = \cfrac{1}{b + \cfrac{1}{c + \cfrac{1}{d + \cfrac{1}{e + \cfrac{1}{f + \cfrac{1}{g + \cfrac{1}{\cdots}}}}}}}$$

Again, we can take a reciprocal of this:

$$\frac{1}{0.4142135623730951} = 2.4142135623730945 = b + \cfrac{1}{c + \cfrac{1}{d + \cfrac{1}{e + \cfrac{1}{f + \cfrac{1}{g + \cfrac{1}{\cdots}}}}}}$$

Our next term, *b*, will be the integer part to the left of the decimal point in this new term—in this case, 2. And then we will repeat the process: taking a reciprocal of a decimal part, finding the integer part to the left of the decimal, and so on.

In Python, we accomplish each round of this as follows:

```
next_term = math.floor(1/leftover)
leftover = 1/leftover - next_term
output.append(next_term)
```

We can put the whole process together into one function as in Listing 5-6.

```
def continued_fraction_decimal(x,error_tolerance,length_tolerance):
    output = []
    first_term = int(x)
    leftover = x - int(x)
    output.append(first_term)
    error = leftover
    while error > error_tolerance and len(output) <length_tolerance:
        next_term = math.floor(1/leftover)
        leftover = 1/leftover - next_term
        output.append(next_term)
        error = abs(get_number(output) - x)
    return(output)
```

Listing 5-6: Finding continued fractions from decimal numbers

In this case, we include a length_tolerance term just like before. We also add an error_tolerance term, which allows us to exit the algorithm if we get an approximation that's "close enough" to the exact answer. To find out whether we are close enough, we take the difference between x, the number we are trying to approximate, and the decimal value of the continued fraction terms we have calculated so far. To get that decimal value, we can use the same get_number() function we wrote in Listing 5-5.

We can try our new function easily as follows:

```
print(continued_fraction_decimal(1.4142135623730951,0.00001,100))
```

We get the following output:

```
[1, 2, 2, 2, 2, 2, 2, 2]
```

We can write this continued fraction as follows (using an approximate equal sign because our continued fraction is an approximation to within a tiny error and we don't have the time to calculate every element of an infinite sequence of terms):

$$1.4142135623730951 \approx 1 + \cfrac{1}{2 + \cfrac{1}{2 + \cfrac{1}{2 + \cfrac{1}{2 + \cfrac{1}{2 + \cfrac{1}{2 + \cfrac{1}{2}}}}}}}$$

Notice that there are 2s all along the diagonal in the fraction on the right. We've found the first seven terms of another infinite continued fraction whose infinite expansion consists of all 2s. We could write its continued fraction expansion as [1,2,2,2,2, . . .]. This is the continued fraction expansion of $\sqrt{2}$, another irrational number that can't be represented as an integer fraction, has no pattern in its decimal digit, and yet has a convenient and easily memorable representation as a continued fraction.

From Fractions to Radicals

If you're interested in continued fractions, I recommend that you read about Srinivasa Ramanujan, who during his short life traveled mentally to the edges of infinity and brought some gems back for us to treasure. In addition to continued fractions, Ramanujan was interested in *continued square roots* (also known as *nested radicals*)—for example, the following three infinitely nested radicals:

$$x = \sqrt{2 + \sqrt{2 + \sqrt{2 + \ldots}}}$$

and

$$y = \sqrt{1 + 2 \times \sqrt{1 + 3 \times \sqrt{1 + 4 \times \sqrt{1 + \ldots}}}}$$

and

$$z = \sqrt{1 + \sqrt{1 + \sqrt{1 + \ldots}}}$$

It turns out that $x = 2$ (an old anonymous result), $y = 3$ (as proved by Ramanujan), and z is none other than phi, the golden ratio! I encourage you to try to think of a method for generating nested radical representations in Python. Square roots are obviously interesting if we take them to infinite lengths, but it turns out that they're interesting even if we just consider them alone.

Square Roots

We take handheld calculators for granted, but when we think about what they can do, they're actually quite impressive. For example, you may remember learning in geometry class that the sine is defined in terms of triangle lengths: the length of the angle's opposite side divided by the length of the hypotenuse. But if that is the definition of a sine, how can a calculator have a sin button that performs this calculation instantaneously? Does the calculator draw a right triangle in its innards, get out a ruler and measure the lengths of the sides, and then divide them? We might ask a similar question for square roots: the square root is the inverse of a square, and there's no straightforward, closed-form arithmetic formula for it that a calculator could use. I imagine that you can already guess the answer: there is an algorithm for quick calculations of square roots.

The Babylonian Algorithm

Suppose that we need to find the square root of a number x. As with any math problem, we can try a guess-and-check strategy. Let's say that our best guess for the square root of x is some number y. We can calculate y^2, and if it's equal to x, we're done (having achieved a rare completion of the one-step "lucky guess algorithm").

If our guess y is not exactly the square root of x, then we'll want to guess again, and we'll want our next guess to take us closer to the true value of the square root of x. The Babylonian algorithm provides a way to systematically improve our guesses until we converge on the right answer. It's a simple algorithm and requires only division and averaging:

1. Make a guess, y, for the value of the square root of x.
2. Calculate $z = x/y$.
3. Find the average of z and y. This average is your new value of y, or your new guess for the value of the square root of x.
4. Repeat steps 2 and 3 until $y^2 - x$ is sufficiently small.

We described the Babylonian algorithm in four steps. A pure mathematician, by contrast, might express the entire thing in one equation:

$$y_{n+1} = \frac{y_n + \dfrac{x}{y_n}}{2}$$

In this case, the mathematician would be relying on the common mathematical practice of describing infinite sequences by continued subscripts, as in: $(y_1, y_2, \ldots y_n, \ldots)$. If you know the nth term of this infinite sequence, you can get the $n + 1$th term from the equation above. This sequence will converge to $\sqrt{x}$, or in other words $y_\infty = \sqrt{x}$. Whether you prefer the clarity of the four-step description, the elegant concision of an equation, or the practicality of the code we will write is a matter of taste, but it helps to be familiar with all the possible ways to describe an algorithm.

You can understand why the Babylonian algorithm works if you consider these two simple cases:

- **If $y < \sqrt{x}$**, then $y^2 < x$. So $\dfrac{x}{y^2} > 1$ so $x \times \dfrac{x}{y^2} > x$.

  But notice that $x \times \dfrac{x}{y^2} = \dfrac{x^2}{y^2} = (\dfrac{x}{y})^2 = z^2$. So $z^2 > x$. **This means that $z > \sqrt{x}$**.

- **If $y > \sqrt{x}$**, then $y^2 > x$. So $\dfrac{x}{y^2} < 1$, so $x \times \dfrac{x}{y^2} < x$.

  But notice that $x \times \dfrac{x}{y^2} = \dfrac{x^2}{y^2} = (\dfrac{x}{y})^2 = z^2$. So $z^2 < x$. **This means that $z < \sqrt{x}$**.

We can write these cases more succinctly by removing some text:

- If $y < \sqrt{x}$, then $z > \sqrt{x}$.
- If $y > \sqrt{x}$, then $z < \sqrt{x}$.

If y is an underestimate for the correct value of $\sqrt{x}$, then z is an overestimate. If y is an overestimate for the correct value of $\sqrt{x}$, then z is an underestimate. Step 3 of the Babylonian algorithm asks us to average an overestimate and an underestimate of the truth. The average of the underestimate and the overestimate will be higher than the underestimate and lower than the overestimate, so it will be closer to the truth than whichever of y or z was a worse guess. Eventually, after many rounds of gradual improvement of our guesses, we arrive at the true value of $\sqrt{x}$.

Square Roots in Python

The Babylonian algorithm is not hard to implement in Python. We can define a function that takes x, y, and an error_tolerance variable as its arguments. We create a while loop that runs repeatedly until our error is sufficiently small. At each iteration of the while loop, we calculate z, we update the value of y to be the average of y and z (just like steps 2 and 3 in the algorithm describe), and we update our error, which is $y^2 - x$. Listing 5-7 shows this function.

```
def square_root(x,y,error_tolerance):
    our_error = error_tolerance * 2
    while(our_error > error_tolerance):
        z = x/y
        y = (y + z)/2
        our_error = y**2 - x
    return y
```

Listing 5-7: A function to calculate square roots using the Babylonian algorithm

You may notice that the Babylonian algorithm shares some traits with gradient ascent and the outfielder algorithm. All consist of taking small, iterative steps until getting close enough to a final goal. This is a common structure for algorithms.

We can check our square root function as follows:

```
print(square_root(5,1,.000000000000001))
```

We can see that the number 2.23606797749979 is printed in the console. You can check whether this is the same number we get from the `math.sqrt()` method that's standard in Python:

```
print(math.sqrt(5))
```

We get exactly the same output: 2.23606797749979. We've successfully written our own function that calculates square roots. If you're ever stranded on a desert island with no ability to download Python modules like the `math` module, you can rest assured that you can write functions like `math.sqrt()` on your own, and you can thank the Babylonians for their help in giving us the algorithm for it.

Random Number Generators

So far we've taken chaos and found order within it. Mathematics is good at that, but in this section, we'll consider a quite opposite goal: finding chaos in order. In other words, we're going to look at how to algorithmically create randomness.

There's a constant need for random numbers. Video games depend on randomly selected numbers to keep gamers surprised by game characters' positions and movements. Several of the most powerful machine learning methods (including random forests and neural networks) rely heavily on random selections to function properly. The same goes for powerful statistical methods, like bootstrapping, that use randomness to make a static dataset better resemble the chaotic world. Corporations and research scientists perform A/B tests that rely on randomly assigning subjects to conditions so that the conditions' effects can be properly compared. The list goes on; there's a huge, constant demand for randomness in most technological fields.

The Possibility of Randomness

The only problem with the huge demand for random numbers is that we're not quite certain that they actually exist. Some people believe that the universe is deterministic: that like colliding billiard balls, if something moves, its movement was caused by some other completely traceable movement, which was in turn caused by some other movement, and so on. If the universe behaved like billiard balls on a table, then by knowing the current state of every particle in the universe, we would be able to determine the complete past and future of the universe with certainty. If so, then any event—winning the lottery, running into a long-lost friend on the other side of the world, being hit by a meteor—is not actually random, as we might be tempted to think of it, but merely the fully predetermined consequence of the way the universe was set up around a dozen billion years ago. This would mean that there is no randomness, that we are stuck in a player piano's melody and things appear random only because we don't know enough about them.

The mathematical rules of physics as we understand them are consistent with a deterministic universe, but they are also consistent with a nondeterministic universe in which randomness really does exist and, as some have put it, God "plays dice." They are also consistent with a "many worlds" scenario in which every possible version of an event occurs, but in different universes that are inaccessible from each other. All these interpretations of the laws of physics are further complicated if we try to find a place for free will in the cosmos. The interpretation of mathematical physics that we accept depends not on our mathematical understanding but rather on our philosophical inclinations—any position is acceptable mathematically.

Whether or not the universe itself contains randomness, your laptop doesn't—or at least it isn't supposed to. Computers are meant to be our perfectly obedient servants and do only what we explicitly command them to do, exactly when and how we command them to do it. To ask a computer to run a video game, perform machine learning via a random forest, or administer a randomized experiment is to ask a supposedly deterministic machine to generate something nondeterministic: a random number. This is an impossible request.

Since a computer cannot deliver true randomness, we've designed algorithms that can deliver the next-best thing: *pseudorandomness*. Pseudorandom number generation algorithms are important for all the reasons that random numbers are important. Since true randomness is impossible on a computer (and may be impossible in the universe at large), pseudorandom number generation algorithms must be designed with great care so that their outputs resemble true randomness as closely as possible. The way we judge whether a pseudorandom number generation algorithm truly resembles randomness depends on mathematical definitions and theory that we'll explore soon.

Let's start by looking at a simple pseudorandom number generation algorithm and examine how much its outputs appear to resemble randomness.

Linear Congruential Generators

One of the simplest examples of a *pseudorandom number generator (PRNG)* is the *linear congruential generator (LCG)*. To implement this algorithm, you'll have to choose three numbers, which we'll call n_1, n_2, and n_3. The LCG starts with some natural number (like 1) and then simply applies the following equation to get the next number:

$$next = (previous \times n_1 + n_2) \; mod \; n_3$$

This is the whole algorithm, which you could say takes only one step. In Python, we'll write % instead of *mod*, and we can write a full LCG function as in Listing 5-8.

```
def next_random(previous,n1,n2,n3):
    the_next = (previous * n1 + n2) % n3
    return(the_next)
```

Listing 5-8: A linear congruential generator

Note that the `next_random()` function is deterministic, meaning that if we put the same input in, we'll always get the same output. Once again, our PRNG has to be this way because computers are always deterministic. LCGs do not generate truly random numbers, but rather numbers that look random, or are *pseudorandom*.

In order to judge this algorithm for its ability to generate pseudorandom numbers, it might help to look at many of its outputs together. Instead of getting one random number at a time, we could compile an entire list with a function that repeatedly calls the `next_random()` function we just created, as follows:

```
def list_random(n1,n2,n3):
    output = [1]
    while len(output) <=n3:
        output.append(next_random(output[len(output) - 1],n1,n2,n3))
    return(output)
```

Consider the list we get by running `list_random(29,23,32)`:

```
[1, 20, 27, 6, 5, 8, 31, 26, 9, 28, 3, 14, 13, 16, 7, 2, 17, 4, 11, 22, 21,
24, 15, 10, 25, 12, 19, 30, 29, 0, 23, 18, 1]
```

It's not easy to detect a simple pattern in this list, which is exactly what we wanted. One thing we can notice is that it contains only numbers between 0 and 32. We may also notice that this list's last element is 1, the same as its first element. If we wanted more random numbers, we could extend this list by calling the `next_random()` function on its last element, 1. However, remember that the `next_random()` function is deterministic. If we extend our list, all we would get is repetition of the beginning of the list, since the next "random" number after 1 will always be 20, the next random number after 20 will always be 27, and so on. If we continued, we would eventually get to the number 1 again and repeat the whole list forever. The number of unique values that we obtain before they repeat is called the *period* of our PRNG. In this case, the period of our LCG is 32.

Judging a PRNG

The fact that this random number generation method will eventually start to repeat is a potential weakness because it allows people to predict what's coming next, which is exactly what we don't want to happen in situations where we're seeking randomness. Suppose that we used our LCG to govern an online roulette application for a roulette wheel with 32 slots. A savvy gambler who observed the roulette wheel long enough might notice that the winning numbers were following a regular pattern that repeated every 32 spins, and they may win all our money by placing bets on the number they now know with certainty will win in each round.

The idea of a savvy gambler trying to win at roulette is useful for evaluating any PRNG. If we are governing a roulette wheel with true randomness, no gambler will ever be able to win reliably. But any slight weakness, or deviation from true randomness, in the PRNG governing our roulette wheel could be exploited by a sufficiently savvy gambler. Even if we are creating a PRNG for a purpose that has nothing to do with roulette, we can ask ourselves, "If I use this PRNG to govern a roulette application, would I lose all my money?" This intuitive "roulette test" is a reasonable criterion for judging how good any PRNG is. Our LCG might pass the roulette test if we never do more than 32 spins, but after that, a gambler could notice the repeating pattern of outputs and start to place bets with perfect accuracy. The short period of our LCG has caused it to fail the roulette test.

Because of this, it helps to ensure that a PRNG has a long period. But in a case like a roulette wheel with only 32 slots, no deterministic algorithm can have a period longer than 32. That's why we often judge a PRNG by whether it has a *full period* rather than a long period. Consider the PRNG that we get by generating list_random(1,2,24):

```
[1, 3, 5, 7, 9, 11, 13, 15, 17, 19, 21, 23, 1, 3, 5, 7, 9, 11, 13, 15, 17, 19,
21, 23, 1]
```

In this case, the period is 12, which may be long enough for very simple purposes, but it is not a full period because it does not encompass every possible value in its range. Once again, a savvy gambler might notice that even numbers are never chosen by the roulette wheel (not to mention the simple pattern the chosen odd numbers follow) and thereby increase their winnings at our expense.

Related to the idea of a long, full period is the idea of *uniform distribution*, by which we mean that each number within the PRNG's range has an equal likelihood of being output. If we run list_random(1,18,36), we get:

```
[1, 19, 1, 19, 1, 19, 1, 19, 1, 19, 1, 19, 1, 19, 1, 19, 1, 19, 1, 19, 1, 19,
1, 19, 1, 19, 1, 19, 1, 19, 1, 19, 1, 19, 1, 19, 1]
```

Here, 1 and 19 each have a 50 percent likelihood of being output by the PRNG, while each other number has a likelihood of 0 percent. A roulette player would have a very easy time with this non-uniform PRNG. By contrast, in the case of list_random(29,23,32), we find that every number has about a 3.1 percent likelihood of being output.

We can see that these mathematical criteria for judging PRNGs have some relation to each other: the lack of a long or full period can be the cause of a lack of uniform distribution. From a more practical perspective, these mathematical properties are important only because they cause our roulette app to lose money. To state it more generally, the only important test of a PRNG is whether a pattern can be detected in it.

Unfortunately, the ability to detect a pattern is hard to pin down concisely in mathematical or scientific language. So we look for long, full period and uniform distribution as markers that give us a hint about pattern detection.

But of course, they're not the only clues that enable us to detect a pattern. Consider the LCG denoted by list_random(1,1,37). This outputs the following list:

```
[1, 2, 3, 4, 5, 6, 7, 8, 9, 10, 11, 12, 13, 14, 15, 16, 17, 18, 19, 20, 21,
22, 23, 24, 25, 26, 27, 28, 29, 30, 31, 32, 33, 34, 35, 36, 0, 1]
```

This has a long period (37), a full period (37), and a uniform distribution (each number has likelihood 1/37 of being output). However, we can still detect a pattern in it (the number goes up by 1 every round until it gets to 36, and then it repeats from 0). It passes the mathematical tests we devised, but it definitely fails the roulette test.

The Diehard Tests for Randomness

There is no single silver-bullet test that indicates whether there's an exploitable pattern in a PRNG. Researchers have devised many creative tests to evaluate the extent to which a collection of random numbers is resistant to pattern detection (or in other words can pass the roulette test). One collection of such tests is called the *Diehard* tests. There are 12 Diehard tests, each of which evaluates a collection of random numbers in a different way. Collections of numbers that pass every Diehard test are deemed to have a very strong resemblance to true randomness. One of the Diehard tests, called the *overlapping sums test,* takes the entire list of random numbers and finds sums of sections of consecutive numbers from the list. The collection of all these sums should follow the mathematical pattern colloquially called a *bell curve*. We can implement a function that generates a list of overlapping sums in Python as follows:

```
def overlapping_sums(the_list,sum_length):
    length_of_list = len(the_list)
    the_list.extend(the_list)
    output = []
    for n in range(0,length_of_list):
        output.append(sum(the_list[n:(n + sum_length)]))
    return(output)
```

We can run this test on a new random list like so:

```
import matplotlib.pyplot as plt
overlap = overlapping_sums(list_random(211111,111112,300007),12)
plt.hist(overlap, 20, facecolor = 'blue', alpha = 0.5)
plt.title('Results of the Overlapping Sums Test')
plt.xlabel('Sum of Elements of Overlapping Consecutive Sections of List')
plt.ylabel('Frequency of Sum')
plt.show()
```

We created a new random list by running list_random(211111,111112,300007). This new random list is long enough to make the overlapping sums test perform well. The output of this code is a histogram that records the frequency of the observed sums. If the list resembles a truly random collection, we expect some of the sums to be high and some to be low, but we expect most of them to be near the middle of the possible range of values. This is exactly what we see in the plot output (Figure 5-2).

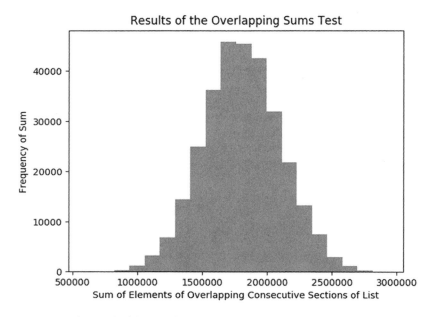

Figure 5-2: The result of the overlapping sums test for an LCG

If you squint, you can see that this plot resembles a bell. Remember that the Diehard overlapping sums test says that our list passes if it closely resembles a bell curve, which is a specific mathematically important curve (Figure 5-3).

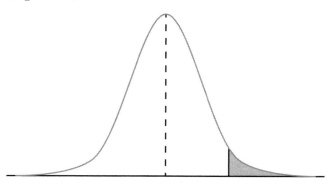

Figure 5-3: A bell curve, or Gaussian normal curve (source: Wikimedia Commons)

The bell curve, like the golden ratio, appears in many sometimes surprising places in math and the universe. In this case, we interpret the close resemblance between our overlapping sums test results and the bell curve as evidence that our PRNG resembles true randomness.

Knowledge of the deep mathematics of randomness can help you as you design random number generators. However, you can do almost as well just by sticking with a commonsense idea of how to win at roulette.

Linear Feedback Shift Registers

LCGs are easy to implement but are not sophisticated enough for many applications of PRNGs; a savvy roulette player could crack an LCG in no time at all. Let's look at a more advanced and reliable type of algorithm called *linear feedback shift registers (LFSRs)*, which can serve as a jumping-off point for the advanced study of PRNG algorithms.

LFSRs were designed with computer architecture in mind. At the lowest level, data in computers is stored as a series of 0s and 1s called *bits*. We can illustrate a potential string of 10 bits as shown in Figure 5-4.

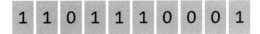

Figure 5-4: A string of 10 bits

After starting with these bits, we can proceed through a simple LFSR algorithm. We start by calculating a simple sum of a subset of the bits—for example, the sum of the 4th bit, 6th bit, 8th bit, and 10th bit (we could also choose other subsets). In this case, that sum is 3. Our computer architecture can only store 0s and 1s, so we take our sum mod 2, and end up with 1 as our final sum. Then we remove our rightmost bit and shift every remaining bit one position to the right (Figure 5-5).

Figure 5-5: Bits after removal and shifting

Since we removed a bit and shifted everything, we have an empty space where we should insert a new bit. The bit we insert here is the sum we calculated before. After that insertion, we have the new state of our bits (Figure 5-6).

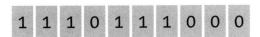

Figure 5-6: Bits after replacement with a sum of selected bits

We take the bit we removed from the right side as the output of the algorithm, the pseudorandom number that this algorithm is supposed to generate. And now that we have a new set of 10 ordered bits, we can run a new round of the algorithm and get a new pseudorandom bit just as before. We can repeat this process as long as we'd like.

In Python, we can implement a feedback shift register relatively simply. Instead of directly overwriting individual bits on the hard drive, we will just create a list of bits like the following:

```
bits = [1,1,1]
```

We can define the sum of the bits in the specified locations with one line. We store it in a variable called xor_result, because taking a sum mod 2 is also called the *exclusive OR* or *XOR operation*. If you have studied formal logic, you may have encountered XOR before—it has a logical definition and an equivalent mathematical definition; here we will use the mathematical definition. Since we are working with a short bit-string, we don't sum the 4th, 6th, 8th, and 10th bits (since those don't exist), but instead sum the 2nd and 3rd bits:

```
xor_result = (bits[1] + bits[2]) % 2
```

Then, we can take out the rightmost element of the bits easily with Python's handy pop() function, storing the result in a variable called output:

```
output = bits.pop()
```

We can then insert our sum with the insert() function, specifying position 0 since we want it to be on the left side of our list:

```
bits.insert(0,xor_result)
```

Now let's put it all together into one function that will return two outputs: a pseudorandom bit and a new state for the bits series (Listing 5-9).

```
def feedback_shift(bits):
    xor_result = (bits[1] + bits[2]) % 2
    output = bits.pop()
    bits.insert(0,xor_result)
    return(bits,output)
```

Listing 5-9: A function that implements an LFSR, completing our goal for this section

Just as we did with the LCG, we can create a function that will generate an entire list of our output bits:

```
def feedback_shift_list(bits_this):
    bits_output = [bits_this.copy()]
    random_output = []
    bits_next = bits_this.copy()
```

```
    while(len(bits_output) < 2**len(bits_this)):
        bits_next,next = feedback_shift(bits_next)
        bits_output.append(bits_next.copy())
        random_output.append(next)
    return(bits_output,random_output)
```

In this case, we run the while loop until we expect the series to repeat. Since there are $2^3 = 8$ possible states for our bits list, we can expect a period of at most 8. Actually, LFSRs typically cannot output a full set of zeros, so in practice we expect a period of at most $2^3 - 1 = 7$. We can run the following code to find all possible outputs and check the period:

```
bitslist = feedback_shift_list([1,1,1])[0]
```

Sure enough, the output that we stored in bitslist is

```
[[1, 1, 1], [0, 1, 1], [0, 0, 1], [1, 0, 0], [0, 1, 0], [1, 0, 1], [1, 1, 0],
[1, 1, 1]]
```

We can see that our LFSR outputs all seven possible bit-strings that are not all 0s. We have a full-period LFSR, and also one that shows a uniform distribution of outputs. If we use more input bits, the maximum possible period grows exponentially: with 10 bits, the maximum possible period is $2^{10} - 1 = 1023$, and with only 20 bits, it is $2^{20} - 1 = 1,048,575$.

We can check the list of pseudorandom bits that our simple LFSR generates with the following:

```
pseudorandom_bits = feedback_shift_list([1,1,1])[1]
```

The output that we stored in pseudorandom_bits looks reasonably random given how simple our LFSR and its input are:

```
[1, 1, 1, 0, 0, 1, 0]
```

LFSRs are used to generate pseudorandom numbers in a variety of applications, including white noise. We present them here to give you a taste of advanced PRNGs. The most widely used PRNG in practice today is the *Mersenne Twister*, which is a modified, generalized feedback shift register—essentially a much more convoluted version of the LFSR presented here. If you continue to progress in your study of PRNGs, you will find a great deal of convolution and advanced mathematics, but all of it will build on the ideas presented here: deterministic, mathematical formulas that can resemble randomness as evaluated by stringent mathematical tests.

Summary

Mathematics and algorithms will always have a close relationship. The more deeply you dive into one field, the more ready you will be to take on advanced ideas in the other. Math may seem arcane and impractical, but it is a long game: theoretical advances in math sometimes lead to practical technologies only many centuries later. In this chapter we discussed continued fractions and an algorithm for generating continued fraction representations of any number. We also discussed square roots, and examined an algorithm that handheld calculators use to calculate them. Finally, we discussed randomness, including two algorithms for generating pseudorandom numbers, and mathematical principles that we can use to evaluate lists that claim to be random.

In the next chapter, we will discuss optimization, including a powerful method you can use to travel the world or forge a sword.

6

ADVANCED OPTIMIZATION

You already know optimization. In Chapter 3, we covered gradient ascent/descent, which lets us "climb hills" to find a maximum or minimum. Any optimization problem can be thought of as a version of hill climbing: we strive to find the best possible outcome out of a huge range of possibilities. The gradient ascent tool is simple and elegant, but it has an Achilles' heel: it can lead us to find a peak that is only locally optimal, not globally optimal. In the hill-climbing analogy, it might take us to the top of a foothill, when going downhill for just a little while would enable us to start scaling the huge mountain that we actually want to climb. Dealing with this issue is the most difficult and crucial aspect of advanced optimization.

In this chapter, we discuss a more advanced optimization algorithm using a case study. We'll consider the traveling salesman problem, as well as several of its possible solutions and their shortcomings. Finally, we'll introduce simulated annealing, an advanced optimization algorithm that overcomes these shortcomings and can perform global, rather than just local, optimization.

Life of a Salesman

The *traveling salesman problem (TSP)* is an extremely famous problem in computer science and combinatorics. Imagine that a traveling salesman wishes to visit a collection of many cities to peddle his wares. For any number of reasons—lost income opportunities, the cost of gas for his car, his head aching after a long journey (Figure 6-1)—it's costly to travel between cities.

Figure 6-1: A traveling salesman in Naples

The TSP asks us to determine the order of travel between cities that will minimize travel costs. Like all the best problems in science, it's easy to state and extremely difficult to solve.

Setting Up the Problem

Let's fire up Python and start exploring. First, we'll randomly generate a map for our salesman to traverse. We start by selecting some number N that will represent the number of cities we want on the map. Let's say $N = 40$. Then we'll select 40 sets of coordinates: one x value and one y value for each city. We'll use the numpy module to do the random selection:

```
import numpy as np
random_seed = 1729
np.random.seed(random_seed)
N = 40
x = np.random.rand(N)
y = np.random.rand(N)
```

In this snippet, we used the numpy module's random.seed() method. This method takes any number you pass to it and uses that number as a "seed" for its pseudorandom number generation algorithm (see Chapter 5 for more about pseudorandom number generation). This means that if you use the same seed we used in the preceding snippet, you'll generate the same random numbers we generate here, so it will be easier to follow the code and you'll get plots and results that are identical to these.

Next, we'll zip the x values and y values together to create cities, a list containing the coordinate pair for each of our 40 randomly generated city locations.

```
points = zip(x,y)
cities = list(points)
```

If you run print(cities) in the Python console, you can see a list containing the randomly generated points. Each of these points represents a city. We won't bother to give any city a name. Instead, we can refer to the first city as cities[0], the second as cities[1], and so on.

We already have everything we need to propose a solution to the TSP. Our first proposed solution will be to simply visit all the cities in the order in which they appear in the cities list. We can define an itinerary variable that will store this order in a list:

```
itinerary = list(range(0,N))
```

This is just another way of writing the following:

```
itinerary = [0,1,2,3,4,5,6,7,8,9,10,11,12,13,14,15,16,17,18,19,20,21,22,23,24,25,26,27,28,29, \
30,31,32,33,34,35,36,37,38,39]
```

The order of the numbers in our itinerary is the order in which we're proposing to visit our cities: first city 0, then city 1, and so on.

Next, we'll need to judge this itinerary and decide whether it represents a good or at least acceptable solution to the TSP. Remember that the point of the TSP is to minimize the cost the salesman faces as he travels between cities. So what is the cost of travel? We can specify whatever cost function we want: maybe certain roads have more traffic than others, maybe there are rivers that are hard to cross, or maybe it's harder to travel north than east or vice versa. But let's start simply: let's say it costs one dollar to travel a distance of 1, no matter which direction and no matter which cities we're traveling between. We won't specify any distance units in this chapter because our algorithms work the same whether we're traveling miles or kilometers or light-years. In this case, minimizing the cost is the same as minimizing the distance traveled.

To determine the distance required by a particular itinerary, we need to define two new functions. First, we need a function that will generate a collection of lines that connect all of our points. After that, we need to sum up the distances represented by those lines. We can start by defining an empty list that we'll use to store information about our lines:

```
lines = []
```

Next, we can iterate over every city in our itinerary, at each step adding a new line to our lines collection that connects the current city and the city after it.

```
for j in range(0,len(itinerary) - 1):
    lines.append([cities[itinerary[j]],cities[itinerary[j + 1]]])
```

If you run print(lines), you can see how we're storing information about lines in Python. Each line is stored as a list that contains the coordinates of two cities. For example, you can see the first line by running print(lines[0]), which will show you the following output:

```
[(0.21215859519373315, 0.1421890509660515), (0.25901824052776146,
0.4415438502354807)]
```

We can put these elements together in one function called genlines (short for "generate lines"), which takes cities and itinerary as arguments and returns a collection of lines connecting each city in our list of cities, in the order specified in the itinerary:

```
def genlines(cities,itinerary):
    lines = []
    for j in range(0,len(itinerary) - 1):
        lines.append([cities[itinerary[j]],cities[itinerary[j + 1]]])
    return(lines)
```

Now that we have a way to generate a collection of lines between each two cities in any itinerary, we can create a function that measures the total distances along those lines. It will start by defining our total distance as 0, and then for every element in our lines list, it will add the length of that line to the distance variable. We'll use the Pythagorean theorem to get these line lengths.

Using the Pythagorean theorem to calculate distances on Earth is not quite correct; the surface of the Earth is curved, so more sophisticated geometry is required to get true distances between points on Earth. We're ignoring this small complexity and assuming that our salesman can burrow through the curved crust of the Earth to take direct routes, or else that he lives in some Flatland-esque geometrical utopia in which distances are easy to calculate using ancient Greek methods. Especially for short distances, the Pythagorean theorem provides a very good approximation to the true distance.

```
import math
def howfar(lines):
    distance = 0
    for j in range(0,len(lines)):
        distance += math.sqrt(abs(lines[j][1][0] - lines[j][0][0])**2 + \
        abs(lines[j][1][1] - lines[j][0][1])**2)
    return(distance)
```

This function takes a list of lines as its input and outputs the sum of the lengths of every line. Now that we have these functions, we can call them together with our itinerary to determine the total distance our salesman has to travel:

```
totaldistance = howfar(genlines(cities,itinerary))
print(totaldistance)
```

When I ran this code, I found that the totaldistance was about 16.81. You should get the same results if you use the same random seed. If you use a different seed or set of cities, your results will vary slightly.

To get a sense of what this result means, it will help to plot our itinerary. For that, we can create a plotitinerary() function:

```
import matplotlib.collections as mc
import matplotlib.pylab as pl
def plotitinerary(cities,itin,plottitle,thename):
    lc = mc.LineCollection(genlines(cities,itin), linewidths=2)
    fig, ax = pl.subplots()
    ax.add_collection(lc)
    ax.autoscale()
    ax.margins(0.1)
    pl.scatter(x, y)
    pl.title(plottitle)
    pl.xlabel('X Coordinate')
    pl.ylabel('Y Coordinate')
    pl.savefig(str(thename) + '.png')
    pl.close()
```

The `plotitinerary()` function takes `cities`, `itin`, `plottitle`, and `thename` as arguments, where `cities` is our list of cities, `itin` is the itinerary we want to plot, `plottitle` is the title that will appear at the top of our plot, and `thename` is the name that we will give to the png plot output. The function uses the `pylab` module for plotting and `matplotlib`'s `collections` module to create a collection of lines. Then it plots the points of the itinerary and the lines we've created connecting them.

If you plot the itinerary with `plotitinerary(cities,itinerary,'TSP - Random Itinerary','figure2')`, you'll generate the plot shown in Figure 6-2.

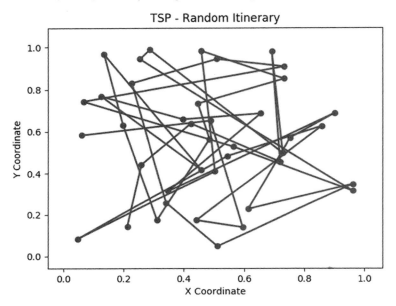

Figure 6-2: The itinerary resulting from visiting the cities in the random order in which they were generated

Maybe you can tell just by looking at Figure 6-2 that we haven't yet found the best solution to the TSP. The itinerary we've given our poor salesman has him whizzing all the way across the map to an extremely distant city several times, when it seems obvious that he could do much better by stopping at some other cities along the way. The goal of the rest of this chapter is to use algorithms to find an itinerary with the minimum traveling distance.

The first potential solution we'll discuss is the simplest and has the worst performance. After that, we'll discuss solutions that trade a little complexity for a lot of performance improvement.

Brains vs. Brawn

It might occur to you to make a list of every possible itinerary that can connect our cities and evaluate them one by one to see which is best. If we want to visit three cities, the following is an exhaustive list of every order in which they can be visited:

- 1, 2, 3
- 1, 3, 2
- 2, 3, 1
- 2, 1, 3
- 3, 1, 2
- 3, 2, 1

It shouldn't take long to evaluate which is best by measuring each of the lengths one by one and comparing what we find for each of them. This is called a *brute force* solution. It refers not to physical force, but to the effort of checking an exhaustive list by using the brawn of our CPUs rather than the brains of an algorithm designer, who could find a more elegant approach with a quicker runtime.

Sometimes a brute force solution is exactly the right approach. They tend to be easy to write code for, and they work reliably. Their major weakness is their runtime, which is never better and usually much worse than algorithmic solutions.

In the case of the TSP, the required runtime grows far too fast for a brute force solution to be practical for any number of cities higher than about 20. To see this, consider the following argument about how many possible itineraries there are to check if we are working with four cities and trying to find every possible order of visiting them:

1. When we choose the first city to visit, we have four choices, since there are four cities and we haven't visited any of them yet. So the total number of ways to choose the first city is 4.

2. When we choose the second city to visit, we have three choices, since there are four cities total and we've already visited one of them. So the total number of ways to choose the first two cities is $4 \times 3 = 12$.

3. When we choose the third city to visit, we have two choices, since there are four cities total and we've already visited two of them. So the total number of ways to choose the first three cities is $4 \times 3 \times 2 = 24$.

4. When we choose the fourth city to visit, we have one choice, since there are four cities total and we've already visited three of them. So the total number of ways to choose all four cities is $4 \times 3 \times 2 \times 1 = 24$.

You should've noticed the pattern here: when we have N cities to visit, the total number of possible itineraries is $N \times (N-1) \times (N-2) \times \ldots \times 3 \times 2 \times 1$, otherwise known as $N!$ ("N factorial"). The factorial function grows incredibly fast: while 3! is only 6 (which we can brute force without even using a computer), we find that 10! is over 3 million (easy enough to brute force on a modern computer), and 18! is over 6 quadrillion, 25! is over 15 septillion, and 35! and above starts to push the edge of what's possible to brute force on today's technology given the current expectation for the longevity of the universe.

This phenomenon is called *combinatorial explosion*. Combinatorial explosion doesn't have a rigorous mathematical definition, but it refers to cases like this, in which apparently small sets can, when considered in combinations and permutations, lead to a number of possible choices far beyond the size of the original set and beyond any size that we know how to work with using brute force.

The number of possible itineraries that connect the 90 zip codes in Rhode Island, for example, is much larger than the estimated number of atoms in the universe, even though Rhode Island is much smaller than the universe. Similarly, a chess board can host more possible chess games than the number of atoms in the universe despite the fact that a chess board is even smaller than Rhode Island. These paradoxical situations, in which the nearly infinite can spring forth from the assuredly bounded, make good algorithm design all the more important, since brute force can never investigate all possible solutions of the hardest problems. Combinatorial explosion means that we have to consider algorithmic solutions to the TSP because we don't have enough CPUs in the whole world to calculate a brute force solution.

The Nearest Neighbor Algorithm

Next we'll consider a simple, intuitive method called the *nearest neighbor* algorithm. We start with the first city on the list. Then we simply find the closest unvisited city to the first city and visit that city second. At every step, we simply look at where we are and choose the closest unvisited city as the next city on our itinerary. This minimizes the travel distance at each step, although it may not minimize the total travel distance. Note that rather than looking at every possible itinerary, as we would in a brute force search, we find only the nearest neighbor at each step. This gives us a runtime that's very fast even for very large N.

Implementing Nearest Neighbor Search

We'll start by writing a function that can find the nearest neighbor of any given city. Suppose that we have a point called point and a list of cities called cities. The distance between point and the jth element of cities is given by the following Pythagorean-style formula:

```
point = [0.5,0.5]
j = 10
distance = math.sqrt((point[0] - cities[j][0])**2 + (point[1] - cities[j][1])**2)
```

If we want to find which element of cities is closest to our point (the point's nearest neighbor), we need to iterate over every element of cities and check the distance between the point and every city, as in Listing 6-1.

```
def findnearest(cities,idx,nnitinerary):
    point = cities[idx]
    mindistance = float('inf')
    minidx = - 1
    for j in range(0,len(cities)):
        distance = math.sqrt((point[0] - cities[j][0])**2 + (point[1] - cities[j][1])**2)
        if distance < mindistance and distance > 0 and j not in nnitinerary:
            mindistance = distance
            minidx = j
    return(minidx)
```

Listing 6-1: The findnearest() function, which finds the nearest city to a given city

After we have this findnearest() function, we're ready to implement the nearest neighbor algorithm. Our goal is to create an itinerary called nnitinerary. We'll start by saying that the first city in cities is where our salesman starts:

```
nnitinerary = [0]
```

If our itinerary needs to have N cities, our goal is to iterate over all the numbers between 0 and $N-1$, find for each of those numbers the nearest neighbor to the most recent city we visited, and append that city to our itinerary. We'll accomplish that with the function in Listing 6-2, donn() (short for "do nearest neighbor"). It starts with the first city in cities, and at every step adds the closest city to the most recently added city until every city has been added to the itinerary.

```
def donn(cities,N):
    nnitinerary = [0]
    for j in range(0,N - 1):
        next = findnearest(cities,nnitinerary[len(nnitinerary) - 1],nnitinerary)
        nnitinerary.append(next)
    return(nnitinerary)
```

Listing 6-2: A function that successively finds the nearest neighbor to each city and returns a complete itinerary

We already have everything we need to check the performance of the nearest neighbor algorithm. First, we can plot the nearest neighbor itinerary:

```
plotitinerary(cities,donn(cities,N),'TSP - Nearest Neighbor','figure3')
```

Figure 6-3 shows the result we get.

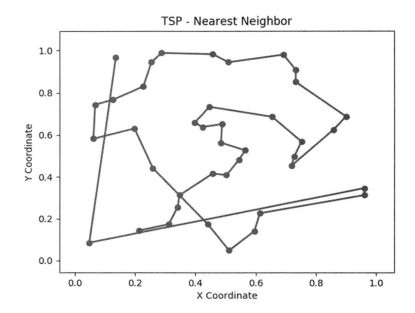

Figure 6-3: The itinerary generated by the nearest neighbor algorithm

We can also check how far the salesman had to travel using this new itinerary:

```
print(howfar(genlines(cities,donn(cities,N))))
```

In this case, we find that whereas the salesman travels a distance of 16.81 following the random path, our algorithm has pushed down the distance to 6.29. Remember that we're not using units, so we could interpret this as 6.29 miles (or kilometers or parsecs). The important thing is that it's less than the 16.81 miles or kilometers or parsecs we found from the random itinerary. This is a significant improvement, all from a very simple, intuitive algorithm. In Figure 6-3, the performance improvement is evident; there are fewer journeys to opposite ends of the map and more short trips between cities that are close to each other.

Checking for Further Improvements

If you look closely at Figure 6-2 or Figure 6-3, you might be able to imagine some specific improvements that could be made. You could even attempt those improvements yourself and check whether they worked by using our howfar() function. For example, maybe you look at our initial random itinerary:

```
initial_itinerary = [0,1,2,3,4,5,6,7,8,9,10,11,12,13,14,15,16,17,18,19,20,21,22,23,24,25,26, \
27,28,29,30,31,32,33,34,35,36,37,38,39]
```

and you think you could improve the itinerary by switching the order of the salesman's visits to city 6 and city 30. You can switch them by defining this new itinerary with the numbers in question switched (shown in bold):

```
new_itinerary = [0,1,2,3,4,5,30,7,8,9,10,11,12,13,14,15,16,17,18,19,20,21,22,23,24,25,26,27, \
28,29,6,31,32,33,34,35,36,37,38,39]
```

We can then do a simple comparison to check whether the switch we performed has decreased the total distance:

```
print(howfar(genlines(cities,initial_itinerary)))
print(howfar(genlines(cities,new_itinerary)))
```

If the new_itinerary is better than the initial_itinerary, we might want to throw out the initial_itinerary and keep the new one. In this case, we find that the new itinerary has a total distance of about 16.79, a very slight improvement on our initial itinerary. After finding one small improvement, we can run the same process again: pick two cities, exchange their locations in the itinerary, and check whether the distance has decreased. We can continue this process indefinitely, and at each step expect a reasonable chance that we can find a way to decrease the traveling distance. After repeating this process many times, we can (we hope) obtain an itinerary with a very low total distance.

It's simple enough to write a function that can perform this switch-and-check process automatically (Listing 6-3):

```
def perturb(cities,itinerary):
    neighborids1 = math.floor(np.random.rand() * (len(itinerary)))
    neighborids2 = math.floor(np.random.rand() * (len(itinerary)))

    itinerary2 = itinerary.copy()

    itinerary2[neighborids1] = itinerary[neighborids2]
    itinerary2[neighborids2] = itinerary[neighborids1]

    distance1 = howfar(genlines(cities,itinerary))
    distance2 = howfar(genlines(cities,itinerary2))

    itinerarytoreturn = itinerary.copy()

    if(distance1 > distance2):
        itinerarytoreturn = itinerary2.copy()

    return(itinerarytoreturn.copy())
```

Listing 6-3: A function that makes a small change to an itinerary, compares it to the original itinerary, and returns whichever itinerary is shorter

The perturb() function takes any list of cities and any itinerary as its arguments. Then, it defines two variables: neighborids1 and neihborids2, which are randomly selected integers between 0 and the length of the itinerary. Next, it creates a new itinerary called itinerary2, which is the same as the original itinerary except that the cities at neighborids1 and neighborids2 have switched places. Then it calculates distance1, the total distance of the original itinerary, and distance2, the total distance of itinerary2. If distance2 is smaller than distance1, it returns the new itinerary (with the switch). Otherwise, it returns the original itinerary. So we send an itinerary to this function, and it always returns an itinerary either as good as or better than the one we sent it. We call this function perturb() because it perturbs the given itinerary in an attempt to improve it.

Now that we have a perturb() function, let's call it repeatedly on a random itinerary. In fact, let's call it not just one time but 2 million times in an attempt to get the lowest traveling distance possible:

```
itinerary = [0,1,2,3,4,5,6,7,8,9,10,11,12,13,14,15,16,17,18,19,20,21,22,23,24,25,26,27,28,29, \
30,31,32,33,34,35,36,37,38,39]

np.random.seed(random_seed)
itinerary_ps = itinerary.copy()
for n in range(0,len(itinerary) * 50000):
    itinerary_ps = perturb(cities,itinerary_ps)

print(howfar(genlines(cities,itinerary_ps)))
```

We have just implemented something that might be called a *perturb search* algorithm. It's searching through many thousands of possible itineraries in the hopes of finding a good one, just like a brute force search. However, it's better because while a brute force search would consider every possible itinerary indiscriminately, this is a *guided search* that is considering a set of itineraries that are monotonically decreasing in total traveling distance, so it should arrive at a good solution faster than brute force. We only need to make a few small additions to this perturb search algorithm in order to implement simulated annealing, the capstone algorithm of this chapter.

Before we jump into the code for simulated annealing, we'll go over what kind of improvement it offers over the algorithms we've discussed so far. We also want to introduce a temperature function that allows us to implement the features of simulated annealing in Python.

Algorithms for the Avaricious

The nearest neighbor and perturb search algorithms that we've considered so far belong to a class of algorithms called *greedy* algorithms. Greedy algorithms proceed in steps, and they make choices that are locally optimal at each step but may not be globally optimal once all the steps are considered. In the case of our nearest neighbor algorithm, at each step, we look for the closest city to where we are at that step, without any regard to the rest of the cities. Visiting the closest city is locally optimal because it minimizes the distance we travel at the step we're on. However, since it doesn't take into account all cities at once, it may not be globally optimal—it may lead us to take strange paths around the map that eventually make the total trip extremely long and expensive for the salesman even though each individual step looked good at the time.

The "greediness" refers to the shortsightedness of this locally optimizing decision process. We can understand these greedy approaches to optimization problems with reference to the problem of trying to find the highest point in a complex, hilly terrain, where "high" points are analogous to better, optimal solutions (short distances in the TSP), and "low" points are analogous to worse, suboptimal solutions (long distances in the TSP). A greedy approach to finding the highest point in a hilly terrain would be to always go up, but that might take us to the top of a little foothill instead of the top of the highest mountain. Sometimes it's better to go down to the bottom of the foothill in order to start the more important ascent of the bigger mountain. Because greedy algorithms search only for local improvements, they will never allow us to go down and can get us stuck on local extrema. This is exactly the problem discussed in Chapter 3.

With that understanding, we're finally ready to introduce the idea that will enable us to resolve the local optimization problem caused by greedy algorithms. The idea is to give up the naive commitment to always climbing. In the case of the TSP, we may sometimes have to perturb to worse itineraries so that later we can get the best possible itineraries, just as we go down a foothill in order to ultimately go up a mountain. In other words, in order to do better eventually, we have to do worse initially.

Introducing the Temperature Function

To do worse with the intention of eventually doing better is a delicate undertaking. If we're overzealous in our willingness to do worse, we might go downward at every step and get to a low point instead of a high one. We need to find a way to do worse only a little, only occasionally, and only in the context of learning how to eventually do better.

Imagine again that we're in a complex, hilly terrain. We start in the late afternoon and know that we have two hours to find the highest point in the whole terrain. Suppose we don't have a watch to keep track of our time, but we know that the air gradually cools down in the evening, so we decide to use the temperature as a way to gauge approximately how much time we have left to find the highest point.

At the beginning of our two hours, when it's relatively hot outside, it is natural for us to be open to creative exploration. Since we have a long time remaining, it's not a big risk to travel downward a little in order to understand the terrain better and see some new places. But as it gets cooler and we near the end of our two hours, we'll be less open to broad exploration. We'll be more narrowly focused on improvements and less willing to travel downward.

Take a moment to think about this strategy and why it's the best way to get to the highest point. We already talked about why we want to go down occasionally: so that we can avoid a "local optimum," or the top of a foothill next to a huge mountain. But when should we go down? Consider the last 10 seconds of our two-hour time period. No matter where we are, we should go as directly upward as we can at that time. It's no use to go down to explore new foothills and find new mountains during our last 10 seconds, since even if we found a promising mountain, we wouldn't have time to climb it, and if we make a mistake and slip downward during our last 10 seconds, we won't have time to correct it. Thus, the last 10 seconds is when we should go directly up and not consider going down at all.

By contrast, consider the first 10 seconds of our two-hour time period. During that time, there's no need to rush directly upward. At the beginning, we can learn the most from going a little downward to explore. If we make a mistake in the first 10 seconds, there's plenty of time to correct it later. We'll have plenty of time to take advantage of anything we learn or any mountains we find. During the first 10 seconds, it pays to be the most open about going down and the least zealous about going directly up.

You can understand the remainder of the two hours by thinking of the same ideas. If we consider the time 10 minutes before the end, we'll have a more moderate version of the mindset we had 10 seconds before the end. Since the end is near, we'll be motivated to go directly upward. However, 10 minutes is longer than 10 seconds, so we have some small amount of openness to a little bit of downward exploration just in case we discover something promising. By the same token, the time 10 minutes after the beginning will lead us to a more moderate version of the mindset we had 10 seconds after the beginning. The full two-hour time period will have a gradient of intention: a willingness to sometimes go down at first, followed by a gradually strengthening zeal to go only up.

In order to model this scenario in Python, we can define a function. We'll start with a hot temperature and a willingness to explore and go downward, and we'll end with a cool temperature and an unwillingness to go downward. Our temperature function is relatively simple. It takes t as an argument, where t stands for time:

```python
temperature = lambda t: 1/(t + 1)
```

You can see a simple plot of the temperature function by running the following code in the Python console. This code starts by importing `matplotlib` functionality and then defines ts, a variable containing a range of t values between 1 and 100. Finally, it plots the temperature associated with each t value. Again, we're not worried about units or exact magnitude here because this is a hypothetical situation meant to show the general shape of a cooling function. So we use 1 to represent our maximum temperature, 0 to represent our minimum temperature, 0 to represent our minimum time, and 99 to represent our maximum time, without specifying units.

```python
import matplotlib.pyplot as plt
ts = list(range(0,100))
plt.plot(ts, [temperature(t) for t in ts])
plt.title('The Temperature Function')
plt.xlabel('Time')
plt.ylabel('Temperature')
plt.show()
```

The plot looks like Figure 6-4.

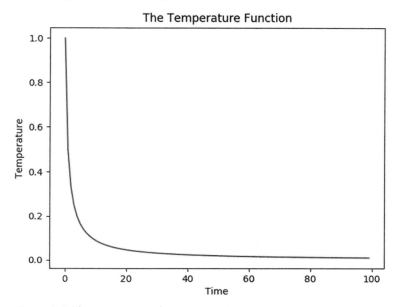

Figure 6-4: The temperature decreases as time goes on

This plot shows the temperature we'll experience during our hypothetical optimization. The temperature is used as a schedule that will govern our optimization: our willingness to go down is proportional to the temperature at any given time.

We now have all the ingredients we need to fully implement simulated annealing. Go ahead—dive right in before you overthink it.

Simulated Annealing

Let's bring all of our ideas together: the temperature function, the search problem in hilly terrain, the perturb search algorithm, and the TSP. In the context of the TSP, the complex, hilly terrain that we're in consists of every possible solution to the TSP. We can imagine that a better solution corresponds to a higher point in the terrain, and a worse solution corresponds to a lower point in the terrain. When we apply the perturb() function, we're moving to a different point in the terrain, hoping that point is as high as possible.

We'll use the temperature function to guide our exploration of this terrain. When we start, our high temperature will dictate more openness to choosing a worse itinerary. Closer to the end of the process, we'll be less open to choosing worse itineraries and more focused on "greedy" optimization.

The algorithm we'll implement, *simulated annealing*, is a modified form of the perturb search algorithm. The essential difference is that in simulated annealing, we're sometimes willing to accept itinerary changes that *increase* the distance traveled, because this enables us to avoid the problem of local optimization. Our willingness to accept worse itineraries depends on the current temperature.

Let's modify our perturb() function with this latest change. We'll add a new argument: time, which we'll have to pass to perturb(). The time argument measures how far we are through the simulated annealing process; we start with time 1 the first time we call perturb(), and then time will be 2, 3, and so on as many times as we call the perturb() function. We'll add a line that specifies the temperature function and a line that selects a random number. If the random number is lower than the temperature, then we'll be willing to accept a worse itinerary. If the random number is higher than the temperature, then we won't be willing to accept a worse itinerary. That way, we'll have occasional, but not constant, times when we accept worse itineraries, and our likelihood of accepting a worse itinerary will decrease over time as our temperature cools. We'll call this new function perturb_sa1(), where sa is short for simulated annealing. Listing 6-4 shows our new perturb_sa1() function with these changes.

```
def perturb_sa1(cities,itinerary,time):
    neighborids1 = math.floor(np.random.rand() * (len(itinerary)))
    neighborids2 = math.floor(np.random.rand() * (len(itinerary)))

    itinerary2 = itinerary.copy()

    itinerary2[neighborids1] = itinerary[neighborids2]
    itinerary2[neighborids2] = itinerary[neighborids1]

    distance1 = howfar(genlines(cities,itinerary))
    distance2 = howfar(genlines(cities,itinerary2))

    itinerarytoreturn = itinerary.copy()

    randomdraw = np.random.rand()
    temperature = 1/((time/1000) + 1)

    if((distance2 > distance1 and (randomdraw) < (temperature)) or (distance1 > distance2)):
        itinerarytoreturn=itinerary2.copy()

    return(itinerarytoreturn.copy())
```

Listing 6-4: An updated version of our perturb() function that takes into account the temperature and a random draw

Just by adding those two short lines, a new argument, and a new if condition (all shown in bold in Listing 6-4), we already have a very simple simulated annealing function. We also changed the temperature function a little; because we'll be calling this function with very high time values, we use time/1000 instead of time as part of the denominator argument in our temperature function. We can compare the performance of simulated annealing with the perturb search algorithm and the nearest neighbor algorithm as follows:

```
itinerary = [0,1,2,3,4,5,6,7,8,9,10,11,12,13,14,15,16,17,18,19,20,21,22,23,24,25,26,27,28,29, \
30,31,32,33,34,35,36,37,38,39]
np.random.seed(random_seed)

itinerary_sa = itinerary.copy()
for n in range(0,len(itinerary) * 50000):
    itinerary_sa = perturb_sa1(cities,itinerary_sa,n)

print(howfar(genlines(cities,itinerary))) #random itinerary
print(howfar(genlines(cities,itinerary_ps))) #perturb search
print(howfar(genlines(cities,itinerary_sa))) #simulated annealing
print(howfar(genlines(cities,donn(cities,N)))) #nearest neighbor
```

Congratulations! You can perform simulated annealing. You can see that a random itinerary has distance 16.81, while a nearest neighbor itinerary has distance 6.29, just like we observed before. The perturb search itinerary has distance 7.38, and the simulated annealing itinerary has distance 5.92. In this case, we've found that perturb search performs better than a random itinerary, that nearest neighbor performs better than perturb search and a random itinerary, and simulated annealing performs better than all the others. When you try other random seeds, you may see different results, including cases where simulated annealing does not perform as well as nearest neighbor. This is because simulated annealing is a sensitive process, and several aspects of it need to be tuned precisely in order for it to work well and reliably. After we do that tuning, it will consistently give us significantly better performance than simpler, greedy optimization algorithms. The rest of the chapter is concerned with the finer details of simulated annealing, including how to tune it to get the best possible performance.

METAPHOR-BASED METAHEURISTICS

The peculiarities of simulated annealing are easier to understand if you know its origin. Annealing is a process from metallurgy, in which metals are heated up and then gradually cooled. When the metal is hot, many of the bonds between particles in the metal are broken. As the metal cools, new bonds are formed between particles that lead to the metal having different, more desirable properties. Simulated annealing is like annealing in the sense that when our temperature is hot, we "break" things by accepting worse solutions, in the hope that then, as the temperature cools, we can fix them in a way that makes them better than they were before.

(continued)

The metaphor is a little contrived, and isn't one that non-metallurgists find intuitive. Simulated annealing is something called a *metaphor-based metaheuristic*. There are many other metaphor-based metaheuristics that take an existing process found in nature or human society and find a way to adapt it to solve an optimization problem. They have names like ant colony optimization, cuckoo search, cuttlefish optimization, cat swarm optimization, shuffled frog leaping, emperor penguins colony, harmony search (based on the improvisation of jazz musicians), and the rain water algorithm. Some of these analogies are contrived and not very useful, but sometimes they can provide or inspire a real insight into a serious problem. In either case, they're nearly always interesting to learn and fun to code.

Tuning Our Algorithm

As mentioned, simulated annealing is a sensitive process. The code we've introduced shows how to do it in a basic way, but we'll want to make changes to the details in order to do better. This process of changing small details or parameters of an algorithm in order to get better performance without changing its main approach is often called *tuning*, and it can make big differences in difficult cases like this one.

Our perturb() function makes a small change in the itinerary: it switches the place of two cities. But this isn't the only possible way to perturb an itinerary. It's hard to know in advance which perturbing methods will perform best, but we can always try a few.

Another natural way to perturb an itinerary is to reverse some portion of it: take a subset of cities, and visit them in the opposite order. In Python, we can implement this reversal in one line. If we choose two cities in the itinerary, with indices small and big, the following snippet shows how to reverse the order of all the cities between them:

```
small = 10
big = 20
itinerary = [0,1,2,3,4,5,6,7,8,9,10,11,12,13,14,15,16,17,18,19,20,21,22,23,24,25,26,27,28,29, \
30,31,32,33,34,35,36,37,38,39]
itinerary[small:big] = itinerary[small:big][::-1]
print(itinerary)
```

When you run this snippet, you can see that the output shows an itinerary with cities 10 through 19 in reverse order:

```
[0, 1, 2, 3, 4, 5, 6, 7, 8, 9, 19, 18, 17, 16, 15, 14, 13, 12, 11, 10, 20, 21, 
22, 23, 24, 25, 26, 27, 28, 29, 30, 31, 32, 33, 34, 35, 36, 37, 38, 39]
```

Another way to perturb an itinerary is to lift a section from where it is and place it in another part of the itinerary. For example, we might take the following itinerary:

```
itinerary = [0,1,2,3,4,5,6,7,8,9]
```

and move the whole section [1,2,3,4] to later in the itinerary by converting it to the following new itinerary:

```
itinerary = [0,5,6,7,8,1,2,3,4,9]
```

We can do this type of lifting and moving with the following Python snippet, which will move a chosen section to a random location:

```
small = 1
big = 5
itinerary = [0,1,2,3,4,5,6,7,8,9]
tempitin = itinerary[small:big]
del(itinerary[small:big])
np.random.seed(random_seed + 1)
neighborids3 = math.floor(np.random.rand() * (len(itinerary)))
for j in range(0,len(tempitin)):
    itinerary.insert(neighborids3 + j,tempitin[j])
```

We can update our perturb() function so that it randomly alternates between these different perturbing methods. We'll do this by making another random selection of a number between 0 and 1. If this new random number lies in a certain range (say, 0–0.45), we'll perturb by reversing a subset of cities, but if it lies in another range (say, 0.45–0.55), we'll perturb by switching the places of two cities. If it lies in a final range (say, 0.55–1), we'll perturb by lifting and moving a subset of cities. In this way, our perturb() function can randomly alternate between each type of perturbing. We can put this random selection and these types of perturbing into our new function, now called perturb_sa2(), as shown in Listing 6-5.

```
def perturb_sa2(cities,itinerary,time):
    neighborids1 = math.floor(np.random.rand() * (len(itinerary)))
    neighborids2 = math.floor(np.random.rand() * (len(itinerary)))

    itinerary2 = itinerary.copy()

    randomdraw2 = np.random.rand()
    small = min(neighborids1,neighborids2)
    big = max(neighborids1,neighborids2)
    if(randomdraw2 >= 0.55):
        itinerary2[small:big] = itinerary2[small:big][:: - 1]
    elif(randomdraw2 < 0.45):
        tempitin = itinerary[small:big]
        del(itinerary2[small:big])
```

```
        neighborids3 = math.floor(np.random.rand() * (len(itinerary)))
        for j in range(0,len(tempitin)):
            itinerary2.insert(neighborids3 + j,tempitin[j])
    else:
        itinerary2[neighborids1] = itinerary[neighborids2]
        itinerary2[neighborids2] = itinerary[neighborids1]

    distance1 = howfar(genlines(cities,itinerary))
    distance2 = howfar(genlines(cities,itinerary2))

    itinerarytoreturn = itinerary.copy()

    randomdraw = np.random.rand()
    temperature = 1/((time/1000) + 1)

    if((distance2 > distance1 and (randomdraw) < (temperature)) or (distance1 > distance2)):
        itinerarytoreturn = itinerary2.copy()

    return(itinerarytoreturn.copy())
```

Listing 6-5: Now, we use several different methods to perturb our itinerary.

Our perturb() function is now more complex and more flexible; it can make several different types of changes to itineraries based on random draws. Flexibility is not necessarily a goal worth pursuing for its own sake, and complexity is definitely not. In order to judge whether the complexity and flexibility are worth adding in this case (and in every case), we should check whether they improve performance. This is the nature of tuning: as with tuning a musical instrument, you don't know beforehand exactly how tight a string needs to be—you have to tighten or loosen a little, listen to how it sounds, and adjust. When you test the changes here (shown in bold in Listing 6-5), you'll be able to see that they do improve performance compared to the code we were running before.

Avoiding Major Setbacks

The whole point of simulated annealing is that we need to do worse in order to do better. However, we want to avoid making changes that leave us *too much* worse off. The way we set up the perturb() function, it will accept a worse itinerary any time our random selection is less than the temperature. It does this using the following conditional (which is not meant to be run alone):

```
if((distance2 > distance1 and randomdraw < temperature) or (distance1 > distance2)):
```

We may want to change that condition so that our willingness to accept a worse itinerary depends not only on the temperature but also on how much worse our hypothetical change makes the itinerary. If it makes it just a little worse, we'll be more willing to accept it than if it makes it much worse.

To account for this, we'll incorporate into our conditional a measurement of how much worse our new itinerary is. The following conditional (which is also not meant to be run alone) is an effective way to accomplish this:

```
scale = 3.5
if((distance2 > distance1 and (randomdraw) < (math.exp(scale*(distance1-distance2)) *
temperature)) or (distance1 > distance2)):
```

When we put this conditional in our code, we have the function in Listing 6-6, where we show only the very end of the perturb() function.

```
--snip--
# beginning of perturb function goes here

    scale = 3.5
    if((distance2 > distance1 and (randomdraw) < (math.exp(scale * (distance1 - distance2)) *
temperature)) or (distance1 > distance2)):
        itinerarytoreturn = itinerary2.copy()

    return(itinerarytoreturn.copy())
```

Allowing Resets

During the simulated annealing process, we may unwittingly accept a change to our itinerary that's unequivocally bad. In that case, it may be useful to keep track of the best itinerary we've encountered so far and allow our algorithm to reset to that best itinerary under certain conditions. Listing 6-6 provides the code to do this, highlighted in bold in a new, full perturbing function for simulated annealing.

```
def perturb_sa3(cities,itinerary,time,maxitin):
    neighborids1 = math.floor(np.random.rand() * (len(itinerary)))
    neighborids2 = math.floor(np.random.rand() * (len(itinerary)))
    global mindistance
    global minitinerary
    global minidx
    itinerary2 = itinerary.copy()
    randomdraw = np.random.rand()

    randomdraw2 = np.random.rand()
    small = min(neighborids1,neighborids2)
    big = max(neighborids1,neighborids2)
    if(randomdraw2>=0.55):
        itinerary2[small:big] = itinerary2[small:big][::- 1 ]
    elif(randomdraw2 < 0.45):
        tempitin = itinerary[small:big]
        del(itinerary2[small:big])
        neighborids3 = math.floor(np.random.rand() * (len(itinerary)))
        for j in range(0,len(tempitin)):
            itinerary2.insert(neighborids3 + j,tempitin[j])
```

```
    else:
        itinerary2[neighborids1] = itinerary[neighborids2]
        itinerary2[neighborids2] = itinerary[neighborids1]

    temperature=1/(time/(maxitin/10)+1)

    distance1 = howfar(genlines(cities,itinerary))
    distance2 = howfar(genlines(cities,itinerary2))

    itinerarytoreturn = itinerary.copy()

    scale = 3.5
    if((distance2 > distance1 and (randomdraw) < (math.exp(scale*(distance1 - distance2)) * \
temperature)) or (distance1 > distance2)):
        itinerarytoreturn = itinerary2.copy()

    reset = True
    resetthresh = 0.04
    if(reset and (time - minidx) > (maxitin * resetthresh)):
        itinerarytoreturn = minitinerary
        minidx = time

    if(howfar(genlines(cities,itinerarytoreturn)) < mindistance):
        mindistance = howfar(genlines(cities,itinerary2))
        minitinerary = itinerarytoreturn
        minidx = time

    if(abs(time - maxitin) <= 1):
        itinerarytoreturn = minitinerary.copy()

    return(itinerarytoreturn.copy())
```

Listing 6-6: This function performs the full simulated annealing process and returns an optimized itinerary.

Here, we define global variables for the minimum distance achieved so far, the itinerary that achieved it, and the time at which it was achieved. If the time progresses very far without finding anything better than the itinerary that achieved our minimum distance, we can conclude that the changes we made after that point were mistakes, and we allow resetting to that best itinerary. We'll reset only if we've attempted many perturbations without finding an improvement on our previous best, and a variable called resetthresh will determine how long we should wait before resetting. Finally, we add a new argument called maxitin, which tells the function how many total times we intend to call this function, so that we know where exactly in the process we are. We use maxitin in our temperature function as well so that the temperature curve can adjust flexibly to however many perturbations we intend to perform. When our time is up, we return the itinerary that gave us the best results so far.

Testing Our Performance

Now that we have made these edits and improvements, we can create a function called siman() (short for simulated annealing), which will create our global variables, and then call our newest perturb() function repeatedly, eventually arriving at an itinerary with a very low traveling distance (Listing 6-7).

```
def siman(itinerary,cities):
    newitinerary = itinerary.copy()
    global mindistance
    global minitinerary
    global minidx
    mindistance = howfar(genlines(cities,itinerary))
    minitinerary = itinerary
    minidx = 0

    maxitin = len(itinerary) * 50000
    for t in range(0,maxitin):
        newitinerary = perturb_sa3(cities,newitinerary,t,maxitin)

    return(newitinerary.copy())
```

Listing 6-7: This function performs the full simulated annealing process and returns an optimized itinerary.

Next, we call our siman() function and compare its results to the results of our nearest neighbor algorithm:

```
np.random.seed(random_seed)
itinerary = list(range(N))
nnitin = donn(cities,N)
nnresult = howfar(genlines(cities,nnitin))
simanitinerary = siman(itinerary,cities)
simanresult = howfar(genlines(cities,simanitinerary))
print(nnresult)
print(simanresult)
print(simanresult/nnresult)
```

When we run this code, we find that our final simulated annealing function yields an itinerary with distance 5.32. Compared to the nearest-neighbor itinerary distance of 6.29, this is an improvement of more than 15 percent. This may seem underwhelming to you: we spent more than a dozen pages grappling with difficult concepts only to shave about 15 percent from our total distance. This is a reasonable complaint, and it may be that you never need to have better performance than the performance offered by the nearest neighbor algorithm. But imagine offering the CEO of a global logistics company like UPS or DHL a way to decrease travel costs by 15 percent, and seeing the pupils of their eyes turn to dollar signs as they think of the billions of dollars this would represent. Logistics remains a major driver of high costs and environmental pollution in every business in the world, and doing well at solving the TSP will always make a big practical difference. Besides this, the TSP is extremely important academically, as a benchmark for comparing optimization methods and as a gateway to investigating advanced theoretical ideas.

You can plot the itinerary we got as the final result of simulated annealing by running `plotitinerary(cities,simanitinerary,'Traveling Salesman Itinerary - Simulated Annealing','figure5')`. You'll see the plot in Figure 6-5.

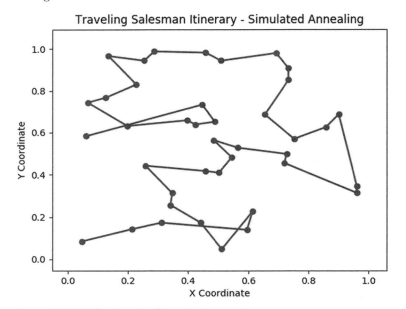

Figure 6-5: The final result of simulated annealing

On one hand, it's just a plot of randomly generated points with lines connecting them. On the other, it's the result of an optimization process that we performed over hundreds of thousands of iterations, relentlessly pursuing perfection among nearly infinite possibilities, and in that way it is beautiful.

Summary

In this chapter, we discussed the traveling salesman problem as a case study in advanced optimization. We discussed a few approaches to the problem, including brute force search, nearest neighbor search, and finally simulated annealing, a powerful solution that enables doing worse in order to do better. I hope that by working through the difficult case of the TSP, you have gained skills that you can apply to other optimization problems. There will always be a practical need for advanced optimization in business and in science.

In the next chapter, we turn our attention to geometry, examining powerful algorithms that enable geometric manipulations and constructions. Let the adventure continue!

7

GEOMETRY

We humans have a deep, intuitive grasp of geometry. Every time we maneuver a couch through a hallway, draw a picture in *Pictionary,* or judge how far away another car on the highway is, we're engaging in some kind of geometric reasoning, often depending on algorithms that we've unconsciously mastered. By now, you won't be surprised to learn that advanced geometry is a natural fit for algorithmic reasoning.

In this chapter, we'll use a geometric algorithm to solve the postmaster problem. We'll begin with a description of the problem and see how we can solve it using Voronoi diagrams. The rest of the chapter explains how to algorithmically generate this solution.

The Postmaster Problem

Imagine that you are Benjamin Franklin, and you have been appointed the first postmaster general of a new nation. The existing independent post offices had been built haphazardly as the nation grew, and your job is to turn these chaotic parts into a well-functioning whole. Suppose that in one town, four post offices are placed among the homes, as in Figure 7-1.

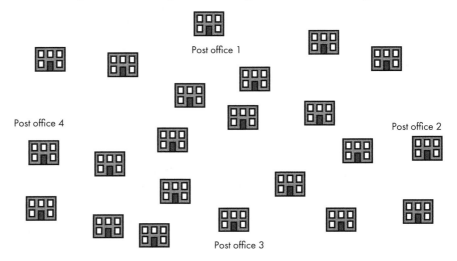

Figure 7-1: A town and its post offices

Since there has never been a postmaster in your new nation, there has been no oversight to optimize the post offices' deliveries. It could be that post office 4 is assigned to deliver to a home that's closer to post offices 2 and 3, and at the same time post office 2 is assigned to deliver to a home that's closer to post office 4, as in Figure 7-2.

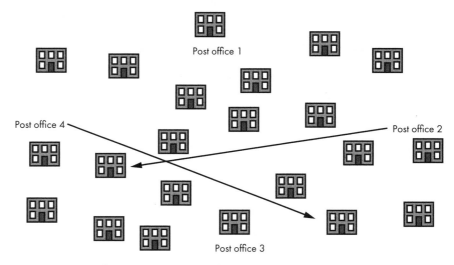

Figure 7-2: Post offices 2 and 4 have inefficient assignments.

You can rearrange the delivery assignments so that each home receives deliveries from the ideal post office. The ideal post office for a delivery assignment could be the one with the most free staff, the one that possesses suitable equipment for traversing an area, or the one with the institutional knowledge to find all the addresses in an area. But probably, the ideal post office for a delivery assignment is simply the closest one. You may notice that this is similar to the traveling salesman problem (TSP), at least in the sense that we are moving objects around a map and want to decrease the distance we have to travel. However, the TSP is the problem of one traveler optimizing the order of a set route, while here you have the problem of many travelers (letter carriers) optimizing the assignment of many routes. In fact, this problem and the TSP can be solved consecutively for maximum gain: after you make the assignments of which post office should deliver to which homes, the individual letter carriers can use the TSP to decide the order in which to visit those homes.

The simplest approach to this problem, which we might call the *postmaster problem*, is to consider each house in turn, calculating the distance between the house and each of the four post offices, and assigning the closest post office to deliver to the house in question.

This approach has a few weaknesses. First, it does not provide an easy way to make assignments when new houses are built; every newly built house has to go through the same laborious process of comparison with every existing post office. Second, doing calculations at the individual house level does not allow us to learn about a region as a whole. For example, maybe an entire neighborhood lies within the shadow of one post office but lies many miles away from all other post offices. It would be best to conclude in one step that the whole neighborhood should be served by the same close post office. Unfortunately, our method requires us to repeat the calculation for every house in the neighborhood, only to get the same result each time.

By calculating distances for each house individually, we're repeating work that we wouldn't have to do if we could somehow make generalizations about entire neighborhoods or regions. And that work will add up. In megacities of tens of millions of inhabitants, with many post offices and quick construction rates like we see today around the world, this approach would be unnecessarily slow and computing-resource-heavy.

A more elegant approach would be to consider the map as a whole and separate it into distinct regions, each of which represents one post office's assigned service area. By drawing just two straight lines, we can accomplish that with our hypothetical town (Figure 7-3).

The regions we have drawn indicate areas of closest proximity, meaning that for every single house, point, and pixel, the closest post office is the one that shares its region. Now that the entire map is subdivided, we can easily assign any new construction to its closest post office simply by checking which region it's in.

A diagram that subdivides a map into regions of closest proximity, as ours does, is called a *Voronoi diagram*. Voronoi diagrams have a long history going all the way back to René Descartes. They were used to analyze water pump placement in London to provide evidence for how cholera was spread, and they're still used in physics and materials science to represent crystal structures. This chapter will introduce an algorithm for generating a Voronoi diagram for any set of points, thereby solving the postmaster problem.

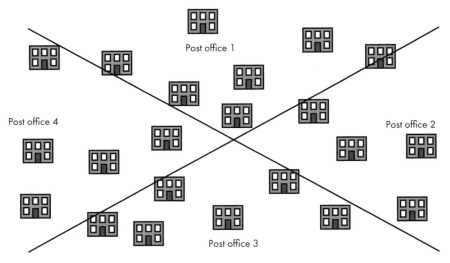

Figure 7-3: Voronoi diagram separating our town into optimal postal delivery regions

Triangles 101

Let's back up and start with the simplest elements of the algorithms we'll explore. We're working in geometry, in which the simplest element of analysis is the point. We'll represent points as lists with two elements: an x-coordinate and a y-coordinate, like the following example:

```
point = [0.2,0.8]
```

At the next level of complexity, we combine points to form triangles. We'll represent a triangle as a list of three points:

```
triangle = [[0.2,0.8],[0.5,0.2],[0.8,0.7]]
```

Let's also define a helper function that can convert a set of three disparate points into a triangle. All this little function does is collect three points into a list and return the list:

```
def points_to_triangle(point1,point2,point3):
    triangle = [list(point1),list(point2),list(point3)]
    return(triangle)
```

It will be helpful to be able to visualize the triangles we're working with. Let's create a simple function that will take any triangle and plot it. First, we'll use the genlines() function that we defined in Chapter 6. Remember that this function takes a collection of points and converts them into lines. Again, it's a very simple function, just appending points to a list called lines:

```
def genlines(listpoints,itinerary):
    lines = []
    for j in range(len(itinerary)-1):
        lines.append([listpoints[itinerary[j]],listpoints[itinerary[j+1]]])
    return(lines)
```

Next, we'll create our simple plotting function. It will take a triangle we pass to it, split it into its *x* and *y* values, call genlines() to create a collection of lines based on those values, plot the points and lines, and finally save the figure to a *.png* file. It uses the pylab module for plotting and code from the matplotlib module to create the line collection. Listing 7-1 shows this function.

```
import pylab as pl
from matplotlib import collections as mc
def plot_triangle_simple(triangle,thename):
    fig, ax = pl.subplots()

    xs = [triangle[0][0],triangle[1][0],triangle[2][0]]
    ys = [triangle[0][1],triangle[1][1],triangle[2][1]]

    itin=[0,1,2,0]

    thelines = genlines(triangle,itin)

    lc = mc.LineCollection(genlines(triangle,itin), linewidths=2)

    ax.add_collection(lc)

    ax.margins(0.1)
    pl.scatter(xs, ys)
    pl.savefig(str(thename) + '.png')
    pl.close()
```

Listing 7-1: A function for plotting triangles

Now, we can select three points, convert them to a triangle, and plot the triangle, all in one line:

```
plot_triangle_simple(points_to_triangle((0.2,0.8),(0.5,0.2),(0.8,0.7)),'tri')
```

Figure 7-4 shows the output.

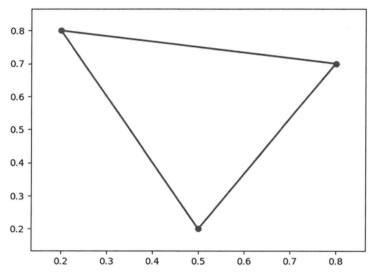

Figure 7-4: A humble triangle

It will also come in handy to have a function that allows us to calculate the distance between any two points using the Pythagorean theorem:

```
def get_distance(point1,point2):
    distance = math.sqrt((point1[0] - point2[0])**2 + (point1[1] - point2[1])**2)
    return(distance)
```

Finally, a reminder of the meaning of some common terms in geometry:

Bisect   To divide a line into two equal segments. Bisecting a line finds its midpoint.

Equilateral   Meaning "equal sides." We use this term to describe a shape in all which all sides have equal length.

Perpendicular   The way we describe two lines that form a 90-degree angle.

Vertex   The point at which two edges of a shape meet.

Advanced Graduate-Level Triangle Studies

The scientist and philosopher Gottfried Wilhelm Leibniz thought that our world was the best of all possible worlds because it was the "simplest in hypotheses and richest in phenomena." He thought that the laws of science could be boiled down to a few simple rules but that those rules led to the complex variety and beauty of the world we observe. This may not be true for the universe, but it is certainly true for triangles. Starting with something that is extremely simple in hypothesis (the idea of a shape with three sides), we enter a world that is extremely rich in phenomena.

Finding the Circumcenter

To begin to see the richness of the phenomena of the world of triangles, consider the following simple algorithm, which you can try with any triangle:

1. Find the midpoint of each side of the triangle.
2. Draw a line from each vertex of the triangle to the midpoint of the vertex's opposite side.

After you follow this algorithm, you will see something like Figure 7-5.

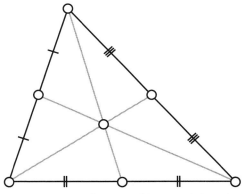

Figure 7-5: Triangle centroid (source Wikimedia Commons)

Remarkably, all the lines you drew meet in a single point that looks something like the "center" of the triangle. All three lines will meet at a single point no matter what triangle you start with. The point where they meet is commonly called the *centroid* of the triangle, and it's always on the inside in a place that looks like it could be called the triangle's center.

Some shapes, like circles, always have one point that can unambiguously be called the shape's center. But triangles aren't like this: the centroid is one center-ish point, but there are other points that could also be considered centers. Consider this new algorithm for any triangle:

1. Bisect each side of the triangle.
2. Draw a line perpendicular to each side through the side's midpoint.

In this case, the lines do not typically go through the vertices like they did when we drew a centroid. Compare Figure 7-5 with Figure 7-6.

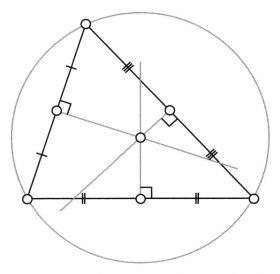

Figure 7-6: Triangle circumcenter (source: Wikimedia Commons)

Notice that the lines do all meet, again in a point that is not the centroid, but is often inside the triangle. This point has another interesting property: it's the center of the unique circle that goes through all three vertices of our triangle. Here is another of the rich phenomena related to triangles: every triangle has one unique circle that goes through all three of its points. This circle is called the *circumcircle* because it is the circle that circumscribes the triangle. The algorithm we just outlined finds the center of that circumcircle. For this reason, the point where all three of these lines meet is called the *circumcenter*.

Like the centroid, the circumcenter is a point that could be called the center of a triangle, but they are not the only candidates—an encyclopedia at *https://faculty.evansville.edu/ck6/encyclopedia/ETC.html* contains a list of 40,000 (so far) points that could be called triangle centers for one reason or another. As the encyclopedia itself says, the definition of a triangle center is one that "is satisfied by infinitely many objects, of which only finitely many will ever be published." Remarkably, starting with three simple points and three straight sides, we get a potentially infinite encyclopedia of unique centers—Leibniz would be so pleased.

We can write a function that finds the circumcenter and *circumradius* (the radius of the circumcircle) for any given triangle. This function relies on conversion to complex numbers. It takes a triangle as its input and returns a center and a radius as its output:

```
def triangle_to_circumcenter(triangle):
    x,y,z = complex(triangle[0][0],triangle[0][1]), complex(triangle[1][0],triangle[1][1]), \
    complex(triangle[2][0],triangle[2][1])
    w = z - x
    w /= y - x
    c = (x-y) * (w-abs(w)**2)/2j/w.imag - x
    radius = abs(c + x)
    return((0 - c.real,0 - c.imag),radius)
```

The specific details of how this function calculates the center and radius are complex. We won't dwell on it here, but I encourage you to walk through the code on your own, if you'd like.

Increasing Our Plotting Capabilities

Now that we can find a circumcenter and a circumradius for every triangle, let's improve our plot_triangle() function so it can plot everything. Listing 7-2 shows the new function.

```
def plot_triangle(triangles,centers,radii,thename):
    fig, ax = pl.subplots()
    ax.set_xlim([0,1])
    ax.set_ylim([0,1])
    for i in range(0,len(triangles)):
        triangle = triangles[i]
        center = centers[i]
        radius = radii[i]
        itin = [0,1,2,0]
        thelines = genlines(triangle,itin)
        xs = [triangle[0][0],triangle[1][0],triangle[2][0]]
        ys = [triangle[0][1],triangle[1][1],triangle[2][1]]

        lc = mc.LineCollection(genlines(triangle,itin), linewidths = 2)

        ax.add_collection(lc)
        ax.margins(0.1)
        pl.scatter(xs, ys)
        pl.scatter(center[0],center[1])

        circle = pl.Circle(center, radius, color = 'b', fill = False)

        ax.add_artist(circle)
    pl.savefig(str(thename) + '.png')
    pl.close()
```

Listing 7-2: Our improved plot_triangle() function, which plots the circumcenter and cicrumcircle

We start by adding two new arguments: a centers variable that's a list of the respective circumcenters of all triangles, and a radii variable that's a list of the radius of every triangle's circumcircle. Note that we take arguments that consist of lists, since this function is meant to draw multiple triangles instead of just one triangle. We'll use pylab's circle-drawing capabilities to draw the circles. Later, we'll be working with multiple triangles at the same time. It will be useful to have a plotting function that can plot multiple triangles instead of just one. We'll put a loop in our plotting function that will loop through every triangle and center and plot each of them successively.

We can call this function with a list of triangles that we define:

```
triangle1 = points_to_triangle((0.1,0.1),(0.3,0.6),(0.5,0.2))
center1,radius1 = triangle_to_circumcenter(triangle1)
```

```
triangle2 = points_to_triangle((0.8,0.1),(0.7,0.5),(0.8,0.9))
center2,radius2 = triangle_to_circumcenter(triangle2)
plot_triangle([triangle1,triangle2],[center1,center2],[radius1,radius2],'two')
```

Our output is shown in Figure 7-7.

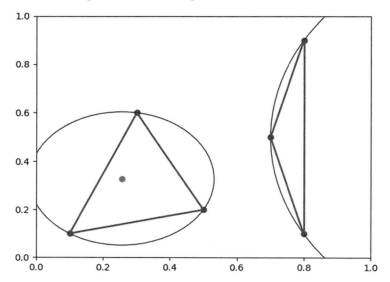

Figure 7-7: Two triangles with circumcenter and circumcircles

Notice that our first triangle is close to equilateral. Its circumcircle is small and its circumcenter lies within it. Our second triangle is a narrow, sliver triangle. Its circumcircle is large and its circumcenter is far outside the plot boundaries. Every triangle has a unique circumcircle, and different triangle shapes lead to different kinds of circumcircles. It could be worthwhile to explore different triangle shapes and the circumcircles they lead to on your own. Later, the differences between these triangles' circumcircles will be important.

Delaunay Triangulation

We're ready for the first major algorithm of this chapter. It takes a set of points as its input and returns a set of triangles as its output. In this context, turning a set of points into a set of triangles is called *triangulation*.

The points_to_triangle() function we defined near the beginning of the chapter is the simplest possible triangulation algorithm. However, it's quite limited because it works only if we give it exactly three input points. If we want to triangulate three points, there's only one possible way to do so: output a triangle consisting of exactly those three points. If we want to triangulate more than three points, there will inevitably be more than one way to triangulate. For example, consider the two distinct ways to triangulate the same seven points shown in Figure 7-8.

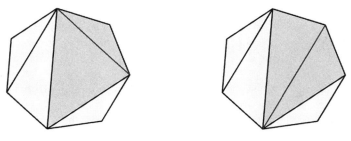

Figure 7-8: Two different ways to triangulate seven points (Wikimedia Commons)

In fact, there are 42 possible ways to triangulate this regular heptagon Figure 7-9).

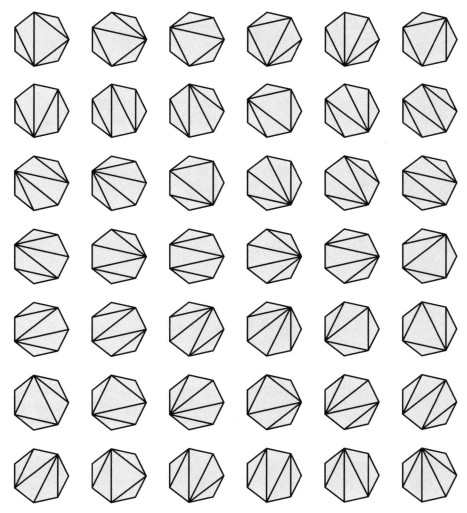

Figure 7-9: All 42 possible ways to triangulate seven points (source: Wikipedia)

If you have more than seven points and they are irregularly placed, the number of possible triangulations can rise to staggering magnitudes.

We can accomplish triangulation manually by getting pen and paper and connecting dots. Unsurprisingly, we can do it better and faster by using an algorithm.

There are a several different triangulation algorithms. Some are meant to have a quick runtime, others are meant to be simple, and still others are meant to yield triangulations that have specific desirable properties. What we'll cover here is called the *Bowyer-Watson algorithm*, and it's designed to take a set of points as its input and output a Delaunay triangulation.

A *Delaunay triangulation (DT)* aims to avoid narrow, sliver triangles. It tends to output triangles that are somewhere close to equilateral. Remember that equilateral triangles have relatively small circumcircles and sliver triangles have relatively large circumcircles. With that in mind, consider the technical definition of a DT: for a set of points, it is the set of triangles connecting all the points in which no point is inside the circumcircle of any of the triangles. The large circumcircles of sliver triangles would be very likely to encompass one or more of the other points in the set, so a rule stating that no point can be inside any circumcircle leads to relatively few sliver triangles. If this is unclear, don't fret—you'll see it visualized in the next section.

Incrementally Generating Delaunay Triangulations

Our eventual goal is to write a function that will take any set of points and output a full Delaunay triangulation. But let's start with something simple: we'll write a function that takes an existing DT of *n* points and also one point that we want to add to it, and outputs a DT of *n* + 1 points. This "Delaunay expanding" function will get us very close to being able to write a full DT function.

NOTE *The example and images in this section are courtesy of LeatherBee (*https://leatherbee .org/index.php/2018/10/06/terrain-generation-3-voronoi-diagrams/*).*

First, suppose that we already have the DT of nine points shown in Figure 7-10.

Now suppose we want to add a 10th point to our DT (Figure 7-11).

A DT has only one rule: no point can lie within a circumcircle of any of its triangles. So we check the circumcircle of every circle in our existing DT, to determine whether point 10 lies within any of them. We find that point 10 lies within the circumcircles of three triangles (Figure 7-12).

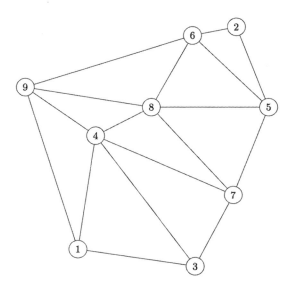

Figure 7-10: A DT with nine points

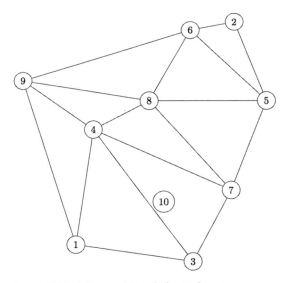

Figure 7-11: A 9-point DT with the 10th point we want to add

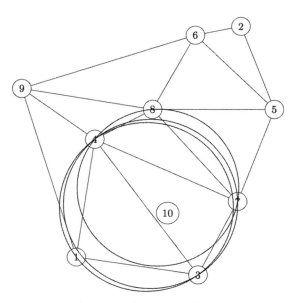

Figure 7-12: Three triangles in the DT have circumcircles containing point 10.

These triangles are no longer allowed to be in our DT, so we will remove them, yielding Figure 7-13.

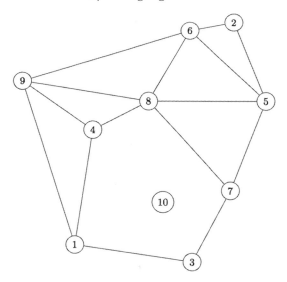

Figure 7-13: We have removed the invalid triangles.

We haven't finished yet. We need to fill in the hole that we've created and make sure that point 10 is properly connected to the other points. If we don't, then we won't have a collection of triangles, we'll just have points and lines. The way we connect point 10 can be described simply: add an edge connecting point 10 to every vertex of the largest empty polygon that point 10 lies within (Figure 7-14).

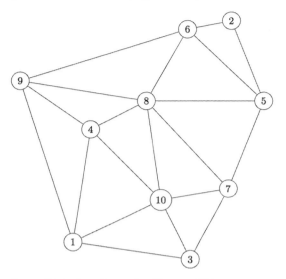

Figure 7-14: Completing the 10-point DT by reconnecting valid triangles

Voilà! We started with a 9-point DT, added a new point, and now have a 10-point DT. This process may seem straightforward. Unfortunately, as is often the case with geometric algorithms, what seems clear and intuitive to the human eye can be tricky to write code for. But let's not allow this to deter us, brave adventurers.

Implementing Delaunay Triangulations

Let's start by assuming that we already have a DT, which we'll call delaunay. It will be nothing more than a list of triangles. We can even start with one triangle alone:

```
delaunay = [points_to_triangle((0.2,0.8),(0.5,0.2),(0.8,0.7))]
```

Next, we'll define a point that we want to add to it, called point_to_add:

```
point_to_add = [0.5,0.5]
```

We first need to determine which, if any, triangles in the existing DT are now invalid because their circumcircle contains the point_to_add. We'll do the following:

1. Use a loop to iterate over every triangle in the existing DT.
2. For each triangle, find the circumcenter and radius of its circumcircle.

3. Find the distance between the `point_to_add` and this circumcenter.

4. If this distance is less than the circumradius, then the new point is inside the triangle's circumcircle. We can then conclude this triangle is invalid and needs to be removed from the DT.

We can accomplish these steps with the following code snippet:

```
import math
invalid_triangles = []
delaunay_index = 0
while delaunay_index < len(delaunay):
    circumcenter,radius = triangle_to_circumcenter(delaunay[delaunay_index])
    new_distance = get_distance(circumcenter,point_to_add)
    if(new_distance < radius):
        invalid_triangles.append(delaunay[delaunay_index])
    delaunay_index += 1
```

This snippet creates an empty list called `invalid_triangles`, loops through every triangle in our existing DT, and checks whether a particular triangle is invalid. It does this by checking whether the distance between the `point_to_add` and the circumcenter is less than the circumcircle's radius. If a triangle is invalid, we append it to the `invalid_triangles` list.

Now we have a list of invalid triangles. Since they are invalid, we want to remove them. Eventually, we'll also need to add new triangles to our DT. To do that, it will help to have a list of every point that is in one of the invalid triangles, as those points will be in our new, valid triangles.

Our next code snippet removes all invalid triangles from our DT, and we also get a collection of the points that make them up.

```
points_in_invalid = []

for i in range(len(invalid_triangles)):
    delaunay.remove(invalid_triangles[i])
    for j in range(0,len(invalid_triangles[i])):
        points_in_invalid.append(invalid_triangles[i][j])

❶ points_in_invalid = [list(x) for x in set(tuple(x) for x in points_in_invalid)]
```

We first create an empty list called `points_in_invalid`. Then, we loop through `invalid_triangles`, using Python's `remove()` method to take each invalid triangle out of the existing DT. We then loop through every point in the triangle to add it to the `points_in_invalid` list. Finally, since we may have added some duplicate points to the `points_in_invalid` list, we'll use a list comprehension ❶ to re-create `points_in_invalid` with only unique values.

The final step in our algorithm is the trickiest one. We have to add new triangles to replace the invalid ones. Each new triangle will have the `point_to_add` as one of its points, and and two points from the existing DT as its other points. However, we can't add every possible combination of `point_to_add` and two existing points.

In Figures 7-13 and 7-14, notice that the new triangles we needed to add were all triangles with point 10 as one of their points, and with edges selected from the empty polygon that contained point 10. This may seem simple enough after a visual check, but it's not straightforward to write code for it.

We need to find a simple geometric rule that can be easily explained in Python's hyper-literal style of interpretation. Think of the rules that could be used to generate the new triangles in Figure 7-14. As is common in mathematical situations, we could find multiple equivalent sets of rules. We could have rules related to points, since one definition of a triangle is a set of three points. We could have other rules related to lines, since another, equivalent definition of triangles is a set of three line segments. We could use any set of rules; we just want the one that will be the simplest to understand and implement in our code. One possible rule is that we should consider every possible combination of points in the invalid triangles with the point_to_add, but we should add one of those triangles only if the edge not containing the point_to_add occurs exactly once in the list of invalid triangles. This rule works because the edges that occur exactly once will be the edges of the outer polygon surrounding the new point (in Figure 7-13, the edges in question are the edges of the polygon connecting points 1, 4, 8, 7, and 3).

The following code implements this rule:

```
for i in range(len(points_in_invalid)):
    for j in range(i + 1,len(points_in_invalid)):
        #count the number of times both of these are in the bad triangles
        count_occurrences = 0
        for k in range(len(invalid_triangles)):
            count_occurrences += 1 * (points_in_invalid[i] in invalid_triangles[k]) * \
            (points_in_invalid[j] in invalid_triangles[k])
        if(count_occurrences == 1):
            delaunay.append(points_to_triangle(points_in_invalid[i], points_in_invalid[j], \
point_to_add))
```

Here we loop through every point in points_in_invalid. For each one, we loop through every following point in points_in_invalid. This double loop enables us to consider every combination of two points that was in an invalid triangle. For each combination, we loop through all the invalid triangles and count how many times those two points are together in an invalid triangle. If they are together in exactly one invalid triangle, then we conclude that they should be together in one of our new triangles, and we add a new triangle to our DT that consists of those two points together with our new point.

We have completed the steps that are required to add a new point to an existing DT. So we can take a DT that has n points, add a new point, and end up with a DT that has $n + 1$ points. Now, we need to learn to use this capability to take a set of n points and build a DT from scratch, from zero points all the way to n points. After we get the DT started, it's really quite simple: we just need to loop through the process that goes from n points to $n + 1$ points over and over until we have added all of our points.

There is just one more complication. For reasons that we'll discuss later, we want to add three more points to the collection of points whose DT we're generating. These points will lie far outside our chosen points, which we can ensure by finding the uppermost and leftmost points, adding a new point that is higher and farther left than either of those, and doing similarly for the lowermost and rightmost points and the lowermost and leftmost points. We'll se these points together as the first triangle of our DT. We'll start with a DT that connects three points: the three points in the new triangle just mentioned. Then, we'll follow the logic that we've already seen to turn a three-point DT into a four-point DT, then into a five-point DT, and so on until we've added all of our points.

In Listing 7-3, we can combine the code we wrote earlier to create a function called gen_delaunay(), which takes a set of points as its input and outputs a full DT.

```python
def gen_delaunay(points):
    delaunay = [points_to_triangle([-5,-5],[-5,10],[10,-5])]
    number_of_points = 0


    while number_of_points < len(points): ❶
        point_to_add = points[number_of_points]

        delaunay_index = 0

        invalid_triangles = [] ❷
        while delaunay_index < len(delaunay):
            circumcenter,radius = triangle_to_circumcenter(delaunay[delaunay_index])
            new_distance = get_distance(circumcenter,point_to_add)
            if(new_distance < radius):
                invalid_triangles.append(delaunay[delaunay_index])
            delaunay_index += 1

        points_in_invalid = [] ❸
        for i in range(0,len(invalid_triangles)):
            delaunay.remove(invalid_triangles[i])
            for j in range(0,len(invalid_triangles[i])):
                points_in_invalid.append(invalid_triangles[i][j])
        points_in_invalid = [list(x) for x in set(tuple(x) for x in points_in_invalid)]

        for i in range(0,len(points_in_invalid)): ❹
            for j in range(i + 1,len(points_in_invalid)):
                #count the number of times both of these are in the bad triangles
                count_occurrences = 0
                for k in range(0,len(invalid_triangles)):
                    count_occurrences += 1 * (points_in_invalid[i] in invalid_triangles[k]) * \
                    (points_in_invalid[j] in invalid_triangles[k])
                if(count_occurrences == 1):
                    delaunay.append(points_to_triangle(points_in_invalid[i], \
points_in_invalid[j], point_to_add))

        number_of_points += 1

    return(delaunay)
```

Listing 7-3: A function that takes a set of points and returns a Delaunay triangulation

The full DT generation function starts by adding the new outside triangle mentioned earlier. It then loops through every point in our collection of points ❶. For every point, it creates a list of invalid triangles: every triangle that's in the DT whose circumcircle includes the point we're currently looking at ❷. It removes those invalid triangles from the DT and creates a collection of points using each point that was in those invalid triangles ❸. Then, using those points, it adds new triangles that follow the rules of Delaunay triangulations ❹. It accomplishes this incrementally, using exactly the code that we have already introduced. Finally, it returns delaunay, a list containing the collection of triangles that constitutes our DT.

We can easily call this function to generate a DT for any collection of points. In the following code, we specify a number for N and generate N random points (x and y values). Then, we zip the x and y values, put them together into a list, pass them to our gen_delaunay() function, and get back a full, valid DT that we store in a variable called the_delaunay:

```
N=15
import numpy as np
np.random.seed(5201314)
xs = np.random.rand(N)
ys = np.random.rand(N)
points = zip(xs,ys)
listpoints = list(points)
the_delaunay = gen_delaunay(listpoints)
```

We'll use the_delaunay in the next section to generate a Voronoi diagram.

From Delaunay to Voronoi

Now that we've completed our DT generation algorithm, the Voronoi diagram generation algorithm is within our grasp. We can turn a set of points into a Voronoi diagram by following this algorithm:

1. Find the DT of a set of points.
2. Take the circumcenter of every triangle in the DT.
3. Draw lines connecting the circumcenters of all triangles in the DT that share an edge.

We already know how to do step 1 (we did it in the previous section), and we can accomplish step 2 withthe triangle_to_circumcenter() function. So the only thing we need is a code snippet that can accomplish step 3.

The code we write for step 3 will live in our plotting function. Remember that we pass a set of triangles and circumcenters to that function as its inputs. Our code will need to create a collection of lines connecting circumcenters. But it will not connect all of the circumcenters, only those from triangles that share an edge.

We're storing our triangles as collections of points, not edges. But it's still easy to check whether two of our triangles share an edge; we just check whether they share exactly two points. If they share only one point, then they have vertices that meet but no common edge. If they share three points, they are the same triangle and so will have the same circumcenter. Our code will loop through every triangle, and for each triangle, it will loop through every triangle again, and check the number of points that the two triangles share. If the number of common points is exactly two, then it will add a line between the circumcenters of the triangles in question. The lines between the circumcenters will be the boundaries of our Voronoi diagram. The following code snippet shows how we'll loop through triangles, but it's part of a larger plotting function, so don't run it yet:

```
--snip--
for j in range(len(triangles)):
    commonpoints = 0
    for k in range(len(triangles[i])):
        for n in range(len(triangles[j])):
            if triangles[i][k] == triangles[j][n]:
                commonpoints += 1
    if commonpoints == 2:
        lines.append([list(centers[i][0]),list(centers[j][0])])
```

This code will be added to our plotting function, since our final goal is a plotted Voronoi diagram.

While we're at it, we can make several other useful additions to our plotting function. The new plotting function is shown in Listing 7-4, with the changes in bold:

```
def plot_triangle_circum(triangles,centers,plotcircles,plotpoints, \
plottriangles,plotvoronoi,plotvpoints,thename):
    fig, ax = pl.subplots()
    ax.set_xlim([-0.1,1.1])
    ax.set_ylim([-0.1,1.1])

    lines=[]
    for i in range(0,len(triangles)):
        triangle = triangles[i]
        center = centers[i][0]
        radius = centers[i][1]
        itin = [0,1,2,0]
        thelines = genlines(triangle,itin)
        xs = [triangle[0][0],triangle[1][0],triangle[2][0]]
        ys = [triangle[0][1],triangle[1][1],triangle[2][1]]

        lc = mc.LineCollection(genlines(triangle,itin), linewidths=2)
        if(plottriangles):
            ax.add_collection(lc)
        if(plotpoints):
            pl.scatter(xs, ys)

    ax.margins(0.1)
```

```
❶ if(plotvpoints):
        pl.scatter(center[0],center[1])

    circle = pl.Circle(center, radius, color = 'b', fill = False)
    if(plotcircles):
        ax.add_artist(circle)

❷ if(plotvoronoi):
        for j in range(0,len(triangles)):
            commonpoints = 0
            for k in range(0,len(triangles[i])):
                for n in range(0,len(triangles[j])):
                    if triangles[i][k] == triangles[j][n]:
                        commonpoints += 1
            if commonpoints == 2:
                lines.append([list(centers[i][0]),list(centers[j][0])])

    lc = mc.LineCollection(lines, linewidths = 1)

    ax.add_collection(lc)

pl.savefig(str(thename) + '.png')
pl.close()
```

Listing 7-4: A function that plots triangles, circumcenters, circumcircles, Voronoi points, and Voronoi boundaries

First, we add new arguments that specify exactly what we want to plot. Remember that in this chapter we have worked with points, edges, triangles, circumcircles, circumcenters, DTs, and Voronoi boundaries. It could be overwhelming to the eye to plot all of these together, so we will add plotcircles to specify whether we want to plot our circumcircles, plotpoints to specify whether we want to plot our collection of points, plottriangles to specify whether we want to plot our DT, plotvoronoi to specify whether we want to plot our Voronoi diagram edges, and plotvpoints which to specify whether we want to plot our circumcenters (which are the vertices of the Voronoi diagram edges). The new additions are shown in bold. One addition plots the Voronoi vertices (circumcenters), if we have specified in our arguments that we want to plot them ❶. The longer addition plots the Voronoi edges ❷. We've also specified a few if statements that allow us to plot, or not plot, triangles, vertices, and circumcircles, as we prefer.

We're almost ready to call this plotting function and see our final Voronoi diagram. However, first we need to get the circumcenters of every triangle in our DT. Luckily, this is very easy. We can create an empty list called circumcenters and append the circumcenter of every triangle in our DT to that list, as follows:

```
circumcenters = []
for i in range(0,len(the_delaunay)):
    circumcenters.append(triangle_to_circumcenter(the_delaunay[i]))
```

Finally, we'll call our plotting function, specifying that we want it to draw the Voronoi boundaries:

```
plot_triangle_circum(the_delaunay,circumcenters,False,True,False,True,False,'final')
```

Figure 7-15 shows our output.

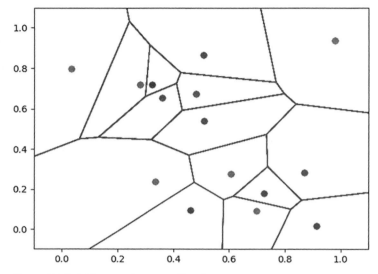

Figure 7-15: A Voronoi diagram. Phew!

We've transformed a set of points into a Voronoi diagram in mere seconds. You can see that the boundaries in this Voronoi diagram run right up to the edge of the plot. If we increased the size of the plot, the Voronoi edges would continue even farther. Remember that Voronoi edges connect the centers of circumcircles of triangles in our DT. But our DT could be connecting very few points that are close together in the center of our plot, so all the circumcenters could lie within a small area in the middle of our plot. If that happened, the edges of our Voronoi diagram wouldn't extend to the edges of the plot space. This is why we added the new outer triangle in the first line of our `gen_delaunay()` function; by having a triangle whose points are far outside our plot area, we can be confident that there will always be Voronoi edges that run to the edge of our map, so that (for example) we will know which post office to assign to deliver to new suburbs built on or outside the edge of the city.

Finally, you might enjoy playing with our plotting function. For example, if you set all of its input arguments to `True`, you can generate a messy but beautiful plot of all the elements we have discussed in this chapter:

```
plot_triangle_circum(the_delaunay,circumcenters,True,True,True,True,True,'everything')
```

Our output is shown in Figure 7-16.

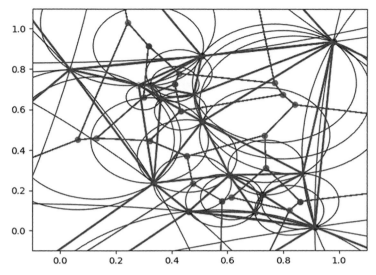

Figure 7-16: Magic eye

You can use this image to convince your roommates and family members that you are doing top-secret particle collision analysis work for CERN, or maybe you could use it to apply for an art fellowship as a spiritual successor to Piet Mondrian. As you look at this Voronoi diagram with its DT and circumcircles, you could imagine post offices, water pumps, crystal structures, or any other possible application of Voronoi diagrams. Or you could just imagine points, triangles, and lines and revel in the pure joys of geometry.

Summary

This chapter introduced methods for writing code to do geometric reasoning. We started by drawing simple points, lines, and triangles. We proceeded to discuss different ways to find the center of a triangle, and how this enables us to generate a Delaunay triangulation for any set of points. Finally, we went over simple steps for using a Delaunay triangulation to generate a Voronoi diagram, which can be used to solve the postmaster problem or to contribute to any of a variety of other applications. They are complex in some ways, but in the end they boil down to elementary manipulations of points, lines, and triangles.

In the next chapter, we discuss algorithms that can be used to work with languages. In particular, we'll talk about how an algorithm can correct text that's missing spaces and how to write a program that can predict what word should come next in a natural phrase.

8

LANGUAGE

In this chapter, we step into the messy world of human language. We'll start by discussing the differences between language and math that make language algorithms difficult. We'll continue by building a space insertion algorithm that can take any text in any language and insert spaces wherever they're missing. After that, we'll build a phrase completion algorithm that can imitate the style of a writer and find the most fitting next word in a phrase.

The algorithms in this chapter rely heavily on two tools that we haven't used before: list comprehensions and corpuses. *List comprehensions* enable us to quickly generate lists using the logic of loops and iterations. They're optimized to run very quickly in Python and they're easy to write concisely, but they can be hard to read and their syntax takes some getting used to. A *corpus* is a body of text that will "teach" our algorithm the language and style we want it to use.

Why Language Algorithms Are Hard

The application of algorithmic thinking to language goes back at least as far as Descartes, who noticed that although there are infinite numbers, anyone with a rudimentary understanding of arithmetic knows how to create or interpret a number they've never encountered before. For example, maybe you've never encountered the number 14,326—never counted that high, never read a financial report about that many dollars, never mashed exactly those keys on the keyboard. And yet I'm confident that you can easily grasp exactly how high it is, what numbers are higher or lower than it, and how to manipulate it in equations.

The algorithm that lets us easily understand hitherto unimagined numbers is simply a combination of the 10 digits (0–9), memorized in order, and the place system. We know that 14,326 is one higher than 14,325 because the digit 6 comes one after the digit 5 in order, they occupy the same place in their respective numbers, and the digits in all the other places are the same. Knowing the digits and the place system enables us to instantly have an idea of how 14,326 is similar to 14,325 and how both are larger than 12 and smaller than 1,000,000. We can also understand at a glance that 14,326 is similar to 4,326 in some respects but differs greatly in size.

Language is not the same. If you are learning English and you see the word *stage* for the first time, you cannot reliably reason about its meaning simply by noting its similarity to *stale* or *stake* or *state* or *stave* or *stade* or *sage*, even though those words differ from *stage* about as much as 14,326 does from 14,325. Nor can you reliably suppose that a bacterium is larger than an elk because of the number of syllables and characters in the words. Even supposedly reliable rules of language, like adding *s* to form plurals in English, can lead us badly astray when we infer that the word "princes" refers to less of something than the word "princess."

In order to use algorithms with language, we must either make language simpler, so that the short mathematical algorithms we have explored so far can reliably work with it, or make our algorithms smarter, so that they can deal with the messy complexity of human language as it has developed naturally. We'll do the latter.

Space Insertion

Imagine that you are the chief algorithm officer at a large old company that has a warehouse full of handwritten paper records. The chief record digitization officer has been conducting a long-term project of scanning those paper records to image files, and then using text recognition technology to convert the images to text that can be easily stored in the company's databases. However, some of the handwriting on the records is awful and the text recognition technology is imperfect, so the final digital text that is extracted from a paper record is sometimes incorrect. You've been given only the digitized text and you're asked to find a way to correct the mistakes without referring to the paper originals.

Suppose that you read the first digitized sentence into Python and find that it's a quote from G. K. Chesterton: "The one perfectly divine thing, the one glimpse of God's paradise given on earth, is to fight a losing battle— and not lose it." You take this imperfectly digitized text and store it in a variable called text:

```
text = "The oneperfectly divine thing, the oneglimpse of God's paradisegiven
on earth, is to fight a losingbattle - and notlose it."
```

You'll notice that this text is in English, and while the spelling of each word is correct, there are missing spaces throughout: oneperfectly should actually be one perfectly, paradisegiven should be paradise given, and so on. (Missing a space is uncommon for humans, but text recognition technology often makes this kind of mistake.) In order to do your job, you'll have to insert spaces at the appropriate spots in this text. For a fluent English speaker, this task may not seem difficult to do manually. However, imagine that you need to do it quickly for millions of scanned pages—you will obviously need to write an algorithm that can do it for you.

Defining a Word List and Finding Words

The first thing we will do is teach our algorithm some English words. This isn't very hard: we can define a list called word_list and populate it with words. Let's start with just a few words:

```
word_list = ['The','one','perfectly','divine']
```

In this chapter, we'll create and manipulate lists using list comprehensions, which you'll probably like after you get used to them. The following is a very simple list comprehension that creates a copy of our word_list:

```
word_list_copy = [word for word in word_list]
```

You can see that the syntax for word in word_list is very similar to the syntax for a for loop. But we don't need a colon or extra lines. In this case, the list comprehension is as simple as possible, just specifying that we want each word in word_list to be in our new list, word_list_copy. This may not be so useful, but we can concisely add logic to make it more useful. For example, if we want to find every word in our word list that contains the letter n, all it takes is the simple addition of an if statement:

```
has_n = [word for word in word_list if 'n' in word]
```

We can run print(has_n) to see that the result is what we expect:

```
['one', 'divine']
```

Later in the chapter, you'll see more complex list comprehensions, including some that have nested loops. However, all of them follow the same basic pattern: a for loop specifying iteration, with optional if statements describing the logic of what we want to select for our final list output.

We'll use Python's re module to access text manipulation tools. One of re's useful functions is finditer(), which can search our text to find the location of any word in our word_list. We use finditer() in a list comprehension like so:

```
import re
locs = list(set([(m.start(),m.end()) for word in word_list for m in re.finditer(word, text)]))
```

That line is a little dense, so take a moment to make sure you understand it. We're defining a variable called locs, short for "locations"; this variable will contain the locations in the text of every word in our word list. We'll use a list comprehension to get this list of locations.

The list comprehension takes place inside the square brackets ([]). We use for word in word_list to iterate over every word in our word_list. For each word, we call re.finditer(), which finds the selected word in our text and returns a list of every location where that word occurs. We iterate over these locations, and each individual location is stored in m. When we access m.start() and m.end(), we'll get the location in the text of the beginning and end of the word, respectively. Notice—and get used to—the order of the for loops, since some people find it the opposite of the order they expected.

The whole list comprehension is enveloped by list(set()). This is a convenient way to get a list that contains only unique values with no duplicates. Our list comprehension alone might have multiple identical elements, but converting it to a set automatically removes duplicates, and then converting it back to a list puts it in the format we want: a list of unique word locations. You can run print(locs) to see the result of the whole operation:

```
[(17, 23), (7, 16), (0, 3), (35, 38), (4, 7)]
```

In Python, ordered pairs like these are called *tuples*, and these tuples show the locations of each word from word_list in our text. For example, when we run text[17:23] (using the numbers from the third tuple in the preceding list), we find that it's divine. Here, d is the 17th character of our text, i is the 18th character of our text, and so on until e, the final letter of divine, is the 22nd character of our text, so the tuple is rounded off with 23. You can check that the other tuples also refer to the locations of words in our word_list.

Notice that text[4:7] is one, and text[7:16] is perfectly. The end of the word one runs into the beginning of the word perfectly without any intervening space. If we hadn't noticed that immediately by reading the text, we could have caught it by looking at the tuples (4, 7) and (7, 16) in our locs variable: since 7 is the second element of (4, 7) and also the first element of (7, 16), we know that one word ends in the same index where another word begins. In order to find places where we need to insert spaces, we'll look for cases like this: where the end of one valid word is at the same place as the beginning of another valid word.

Dealing with Compound Words

Unfortunately, two valid words appearing together without a space is not conclusive evidence that a space is missing. Consider the word *butterfly*. We know that *butter* is a valid word and *fly* is a valid word, but we can't necessarily conclude that *butterfly* was written in error, because *butterfly* is also a valid word. So we need to check not only for valid words that appear together without a space but also for valid words that, when mashed together without a space, do not together form another valid word. This means that in our text, we need to check whether `oneperfectly` is a word, whether `paradisegiven` is a word, and so on.

In order to check this, we need to find all the spaces in our text. We can look at all the substrings between two consecutive spaces and call those potential words. If a potential word is not in our word list, then we'll conclude that it's invalid. We can check each invalid word to see whether it's made up of a combination of two smaller words; if it is, we'll conclude that there's a missing space and add it back in, right between the two valid words that have combined to form the invalid word.

Checking Between Existing Spaces for Potential Words

We can use `re.finditer()` again to find all the spaces in our text, which we'll store in a variable called `spacestarts`. We'll also add two more elements to our `spacestarts` variable: one to represent the location of the beginning of the text and one to represent the location of the end. This ensures that we find every potential word, since words at the very beginning and end will be the only words that are not between spaces. We also add a line that sorts the `spacestarts` list:

```
spacestarts = [m.start() for m in re.finditer(' ', text)]
spacestarts.append(-1)
spacestarts.append(len(text))
spacestarts.sort()
```

The list `spacestarts` records the locations of the spaces in our text. We got these locations by using a list comprehension and the `re.finditer()` tool. In this case, `re.finditer()` finds the location of every space in the text and stores it in a list, which refers to each individual element as `m`. For each of those `m` elements, which are spaces, we get the location where the space begins by using the `start()` function. We are looking for potential words between those spaces. It will be useful to have another list that records the locations of characters that come just after a space; these will be the locations of the first character of each potential word. We'll call that list `spacestarts_affine`, since in technical terms, this new list is an affine transformation of the `spacestarts` list. *Affine* is often used to refer to linear transformations, such as adding 1 to each location, which we'll do here. We'll also sort this list:

```
spacestarts_affine = [ss+1 for ss in spacestarts]
spacestarts_affine.sort()
```

Next, we can get all the substrings that are between two spaces:

```
between_spaces = [(spacestarts[k] + 1,spacestarts[k + 1]) for k in range(0,len(spacestarts) - 1 )]
```

The variable we're creating here is called between_spaces, and it's a list of tuples of the form (*location of beginning of substring*, *location of end of substring*), like (17, 23). The way we get these tuples is through a list comprehension. This list comprehension iterates over k. In this case, k takes on the values of integers between 0 and one less than the length of the spacestarts list. For each k, we will generate one tuple. The first element of the tuple is spacestarts[k]+1, which is one position after the location of each space. The second element of the tuple is spacestarts[k+1], which is the location of the next space in the text. This way, our final output contains tuples that indicate the beginning and end of each substring between spaces.

Now, consider all of the potential words that are between spaces, and find the ones that are not valid (not in our word list):

```
between_spaces_notvalid = [loc for loc in between_spaces if \
text[loc[0]:loc[1]] not in word_list]
```

Looking at between_spaces_notvalid, we can see that it's a list of the locations of all invalid potential words in our text:

```
[(4, 16), (24, 30), (31, 34), (35, 45), (46, 48), (49, 54), (55, 68), (69,
71), (72, 78), (79, 81), (82, 84), (85, 90), (91, 92), (93, 105), (106, 107),
(108, 111), (112, 119), (120, 123)]
```

Our code thinks that all these locations refer to invalid words. However, if you look at some of the words referred to here, they look pretty valid. For example, text[103:106] outputs the valid word and. The reason our code thinks that and is an invalid word is that it isn't in our word list. Of course, we could add it to our word list manually and continue using that approach as we need our code to recognize words. But remember that we want this space insertion algorithm to work for millions of pages of scanned text, and they may contain many thousands of unique words. It would be helpful if we could import a word list that already contained a substantial body of valid English words. Such a collection of words is referred to as a *corpus*.

Using an Imported Corpus to Check for Valid Words

Luckily, there are existing Python modules that allow us to import a full corpus with just a few lines. First, we need to download the corpus:

```
import nltk
nltk.download('brown')
```

We've downloaded a corpus called brown from the module called nltk. Next, we'll import the corpus:

```
from nltk.corpus import brown
wordlist = set(brown.words())
word_list = list(wordlist)
```

We have imported the corpus and converted its collection of words into a Python list. Before we use this new word_list, however, we should do some cleanup to remove what it thinks are words but are actually punctuation marks:

```
word_list = [word.replace('*','') for word in word_list]
word_list = [word.replace('[','') for word in word_list]
word_list = [word.replace(']','') for word in word_list]
word_list = [word.replace('?','') for word in word_list]
word_list = [word.replace('.','') for word in word_list]
word_list = [word.replace('+','') for word in word_list]
word_list = [word.replace('/','') for word in word_list]
word_list = [word.replace(';','') for word in word_list]
word_list = [word.replace(':','') for word in word_list]
word_list = [word.replace(',','') for word in word_list]
word_list = [word.replace(')','') for word in word_list]
word_list = [word.replace('(','') for word in word_list]
word_list.remove('')
```

These lines use the remove() and replace() functions to replace punctuation with empty strings and then remove the empty strings. Now that we have a suitable word list, we'll be able to recognize invalid words more accurately. We can rerun our check for invalid words using our new word_list and get better results:

```
between_spaces_notvalid = [loc for loc in between_spaces if \
text[loc[0]:loc[1]] not in word_list]
```

When we print the list between_spaces_notvalid, we get a shorter and more accurate list:

```
[(4, 16), (24, 30), (35, 45), (55, 68), (72, 78), (93, 105), (112, 119), (120, 123)]
```

Now that we have found the invalid potential words in our text, we'll check in our word list for words that could be combined to form those invalid words. We can begin by looking for words that start just after a space. These words could be the first half of an invalid word:

```
partial_words = [loc for loc in locs if loc[0] in spacestarts_affine and \
loc[1] not in spacestarts]
```

Our list comprehension iterates over every element of our locs variable, which contains the location of every word in the text. It checks whether locs[0], the beginning of the word, is in spacestarts_affine, a list containing the characters that come just after a space. Then it checks whether loc[1] is not in spacestarts, which checks whether the word ends where a space begins. If a word starts after a space and doesn't end at the same place as a space, we put it in our partial_words variable, because this could be a word that needs to have a space inserted after it.

Next, let's look for words that end with a space. These could be the second half of an invalid word. To find them, we make some small changes to the previous logic:

```
partial_words_end = [loc for loc in locs if loc[0] not in spacestarts_affine \
and loc[1] in spacestarts]
```

Now we can start inserting spaces.

Finding First and Second Halves of Potential Words

Let's start by inserting a space into oneperfectly. We'll define a variable called loc that stores the location of oneperfectly in our text:

```
loc = between_spaces_notvalid[0]
```

We now need to check whether any of the words in partial_words could be the first half of oneperfectly. For a valid word to be the first half of oneperfectly, it would have to have the same beginning location in the text , but not the same ending location, as oneperfectly. We'll write a list comprehension that finds the ending location of every valid word that begins at the same location as oneperfectly:

```
endsofbeginnings = [loc2[1] for loc2 in partial_words if loc2[0] == loc[0] \
and (loc2[1] - loc[0]) > 1]
```

We've specified loc2[0] == loc[0], which says that our valid word must start at the same place as oneperfectly. We've also specified (loc2[1]-loc[0])>1, which ensures that the valid word we find is more than one character long. This is not strictly necessary, but it can help us avoid false positives. Think of words like *avoid, aside, along, irate,* and *iconic,* in which the first letter could be considered a word on its own but probably shouldn't be.

Our list endsofbeginnings should include the ending location of every valid word that begins at the same place as oneperfectly. Let's use a list comprehension to create a similar variable, called beginningsofends, that will find the beginning location of every valid word that ends at the same place as oneperfectly:

```
beginningsofends = [loc2[0] for loc2 in partial_words_end if loc2[1] == loc[1] and \
(loc2[1] - loc[0]) > 1]
```

We've specified loc2[1] == loc[1], which says that our valid word must end at the same place as oneperfectly. We've also specified (loc2[1]-loc[0])>1, which ensures that the valid word we find is more than one character long, just as we did before.

We're almost home; we just need to find whether any locations are contained in both endsofbeginnings and beginningsofends. If there are, that means that our invalid word is indeed a combination of two valid words without a space. We can use the `intersection()` function to find all elements that are shared by both lists:

```
pivot = list(set(endsofbeginnings).intersection(beginningsofends))
```

We use the `list(set())` syntax again; just like before, it's to make sure that our list contains only unique values, with no duplicates. We call the result `pivot`. It's possible that `pivot` will contain more than one element. This would mean that there are more than two possible combinations of valid words that could compose our invalid word. If this happens, we'll have to decide which combination is the one the original writer intended. This cannot be done with certainty. For example, consider the invalid word *choosespain*. It's possible that this invalid word is from a travel brochure for Iberia ("Choose Spain!"), but it's also possible that it's from a description of a masochist ("chooses pain"). Because of the huge quantity of words in our language and the numerous ways they can be combined, sometimes we can't be certain which is right. A more sophisticated approach would take into account context—whether other words around *choosespain* tend to be about olives and bullfighting or about whips and superfluous dentist appointments. Such an approach would be difficult to do well and impossible to do perfectly, illustrating again the difficulty of language algorithms in general. In our case, we'll take the smallest element of `pivot`, not because this is certainly the correct one, but just because we have to take one:

```
import numpy as np
pivot = np.min(pivot)
```

Finally, we can write one line that replaces our invalid word with the two valid component words plus a space:

```
textnew = text
textnew = textnew.replace(text[loc[0]:loc[1]],text[loc[0]:pivot]+' '+text[pivot:loc[1]])
```

If we print this new text, we can see that it has correctly inserted a space into the misspelling *oneperfectly*, though it hasn't yet inserted spaces in the rest of the misspellings.

```
The one perfectly divine thing, the oneglimpse of God's paradisegiven on
earth, is to fight a losingbattle - and notlose it.
```

We can put all this together into one beautiful function, shown in Listing 8-1. This function will use a for loop to insert spaces into every instance of two valid words running together to become an invalid word.

```
def insertspaces(text,word_list):

    locs = list(set([(m.start(),m.end()) for word in word_list for m in re.finditer(word, \
text)]))
```

```
spacestarts = [m.start() for m in re.finditer(' ', text)]
spacestarts.append(-1)
spacestarts.append(len(text))
spacestarts.sort()
spacestarts_affine = [ss + 1 for ss in spacestarts]
spacestarts_affine.sort()
partial_words = [loc for loc in locs if loc[0] in spacestarts_affine and loc[1] not in \
spacestarts]
partial_words_end = [loc for loc in locs if loc[0] not in spacestarts_affine and loc[1] \
in spacestarts]
between_spaces = [(spacestarts[k] + 1,spacestarts[k+1]) for k in \
range(0,len(spacestarts) - 1)]
between_spaces_notvalid = [loc for loc in between_spaces if text[loc[0]:loc[1]] not in \
word_list]
textnew = text
for loc in between_spaces_notvalid:
    endsofbeginnings = [loc2[1] for loc2 in partial_words if loc2[0] == loc[0] and \
(loc2[1] - loc[0]) > 1]
    beginningsofends = [loc2[0] for loc2 in partial_words_end if loc2[1] == loc[1] and \
(loc2[1] - loc[0]) > 1]
    pivot = list(set(endsofbeginnings).intersection(beginningsofends))
    if(len(pivot) > 0):
        pivot = np.min(pivot)
        textnew = textnew.replace(text[loc[0]:loc[1]],text[loc[0]:pivot]+' \
        '+text[pivot:loc[1]])
textnew = textnew.replace('  ',' ')
return(textnew)
```

Listing 8-1: A function that inserts spaces into texts, combining much of the code in the chapter so far

Then we can define any text and call our function as follows:

```
text = "The oneperfectly divine thing, the oneglimpse of God's paradisegiven on earth, is to \
fight a losingbattle - and notlose it."
print(insertspaces(text,word_list))
```

We see the output just as we expect, with spaces inserted perfectly:

```
The one perfectly divine thing, the one glimpse of God's paradise given on earth, is to fight
a losing battle - and not lose it.
```

We've created an algorithm that can correctly insert spaces into English text. One thing to consider is whether you can do the same for other languages. You can—as long as you read in a good, appropriate corpus for the language you're working with to define the word_list, the function we defined and called in this example can correctly insert spaces into text in any language. It can even correct a text in a language you've never studied or even heard of. Try different corpuses, different languages, and different texts to see what kind of results you can get, and you'll get a glimpse of the power of language algorithms.

Phrase Completion

Imagine that you are doing algorithm consulting work for a startup that is trying to add features to a search engine they are building. They want to add phrase completion so that they can provide search suggestions to users. For example, when a user types in peanut butter and, a search suggestion feature might suggest adding the word jelly. When a user types in squash, the search engine could suggest both court and soup.

Building this feature is simple. We'll start with a corpus, just like we did with our space checker. In this case, we're interested not only in the individual words of our corpus but also in how the words fit together, so we'll compile lists of n-grams from our corpus. An *n-gram* is simply a collection of *n* words that appear together. For example, the phrase "Reality is not always probable, or likely" is made up of seven words once spoken by the great Jorge Luis Borges. A 1-gram is an individual word, so the 1-grams of this phrase are *reality, is, not, always, probable, or,* and *likely.* The 2-grams are every string of two words that appear together, including *reality is, is not, not always, always probable,* and so on. The 3-grams are *reality is not, is not always,* and so on.

Tokenizing and Getting N-grams

We'll use a Python module called nltk to make n-gram collection easy. We'll first tokenize our text. *Tokenizing* simply means splitting a string into its component words, ignoring punctuation. For example:

```
from nltk.tokenize import sent_tokenize, word_tokenize
text = "Time forks perpetually toward innumerable futures"
print(word_tokenize(text))
```

The result we see is this:

```
['Time', 'forks', 'perpetually', 'toward', 'innumerable', 'futures']
```

We can tokenize and get the n-grams from our text as follows:

```
import nltk
from nltk.util import ngrams
token = nltk.word_tokenize(text)
bigrams = ngrams(token,2)
trigrams = ngrams(token,3)
fourgrams = ngrams(token,4)
fivegrams = ngrams(token,5)
```

Alternatively, we can put all the n-grams in a list called grams:

```
grams = [ngrams(token,2),ngrams(token,3),ngrams(token,4),ngrams(token,5)]
```

In this case, we have gotten a tokenization and a list of n-grams for a short one-sentence text. However, in order to have an all-purpose phrase completion tool, we'll need a considerably larger corpus. The brown corpus we used for space insertion won't work because it consists of single words and so we can't get its n-grams.

One corpus we could use is a collection of literary texts made available online by Google's Peter Norvig at *http://norvig.com/big.txt*. For the examples in this chapter, I downloaded a file of Shakespeare's complete works, available for free online at *http://www.gutenberg.org/files/100/100-0.txt*, and then removed the Project Gutenberg boilerplate text on the top. You could also use the complete works of Mark Twain, available at *http://www.gutenberg.org/cache/epub/3200/pg3200.txt*. Read a corpus into Python as follows:

```
import requests
file = requests.get('http://www.bradfordtuckfield.com/shakespeare.txt')
file = file.text
text = file.replace('\n', '')
```

Here, we used the requests module to directly read a text file containing the collected works of Shakespeare from a website where it's being hosted, and then read it into our Python session in a variable called text.

After reading in your chosen corpus, rerun the code that created the grams variable. Here it is with the new definition of the text variable:

```
token = nltk.word_tokenize(text)
bigrams = ngrams(token,2)
trigrams = ngrams(token,3)
fourgrams = ngrams(token,4)
fivegrams = ngrams(token,5)
grams = [ngrams(token,2),ngrams(token,3),ngrams(token,4),ngrams(token,5)]
```

Our Strategy

Our strategy for generating search suggestions is simple. When a user types in a search, we check how many words are in their search. In other words, a user enters an n-gram and we determine what n is. When a user searches for an n-gram, we are helping them add to their search, so we will want to suggest an $n + 1$-gram. We'll search our corpus and find all $n + 1$-grams whose first n elements match our n-gram. For example, a user might search for crane, a 1-gram, and our corpus might contain the 2-grams crane feather, crane operator, and crane neck. Each is a potential search suggestion we could offer.

We could stop there, providing every $n + 1$-gram whose first n elements matched the $n + 1$-gram the user had entered. However, not all suggestions are equally good. For example, if we are working for a custom engine that searches through manuals for industrial construction equipment, it's likely that crane operator will be a more relevant, useful suggestion than crane feather. The simplest way to determine which $n + 1$-gram is the best suggestion is to offer the one that appears most often in our corpus.

Thus, our full algorithm: a user searches for an n-gram, we find all $n + 1$-grams whose first n elements match the user's n-gram, and we recommend the matching $n + 1$-gram that appears most frequently in the corpus.

Finding Candidate n + 1-grams

In order to find the $n + 1$-grams that will constitute our search suggestions, we need to know how long the user's search term is. Suppose the search term is life is a, meaning that we're looking for suggestions for how to complete the phrase "life is a . . .". We can use the following simple lines to get the length of our search term:

```
from nltk.tokenize import sent_tokenize, word_tokenize
search_term = 'life is a'
split_term = tuple(search_term.split(' '))
search_term_length = len(search_term.split(' '))
```

Now that we know the length of the search term, we know n—it's 3. Remember that we'll be returning the most frequent $n + 1$-grams (4-grams) to the user. So we need to take into account the different frequencies of different $n + 1$-grams. We'll use a function called Counter(), which will count the number of occurrences of each $n + 1$-gram in our collection.

```
from collections import Counter
counted_grams = Counter(grams[search_term_length - 1])
```

This line has selected only the $n + 1$-grams from our grams variable. Applying the Counter() function creates a list of tuples. Each tuple has an $n + 1$-gram as its first element and the frequency of that $n + 1$-gram in our corpus as its second element. For example, we can print the first element of counted_grams:

```
print(list(counted_grams.items())[0])
```

The output shows us the first $n + 1$-gram in our corpus and tells us that it appears only once in the entire corpus:

```
(('From', 'fairest', 'creatures', 'we'), 1)
```

This n-gram is the beginning of Shakespeare's Sonnet 1. It's fun to look at some of the interesting 4-grams we can randomly find in Shakespeare's works. For example, if you run print(list(counted_grams)[10]), you can see that the 10th 4-gram in Shakespeare's works is "rose might never die." If you run print(list(counted_grams)[240000]), you can see that the 240,000th n-gram is "I shall command all." The 323,002nd is "far more glorious star" and the 328,004th is "crack my arms asunder." But we want to do phrase completion, not just $n + 1$-gram browsing. We need to find the subset of $n + 1$-grams whose first n elements match our search term. We can do that as follows:

```
matching_terms = [element for element in list(counted_grams.items()) if \
element[0][:-1] == tuple(split_term)]
```

This list comprehension iterates over every $n + 1$-gram and calls each element as it does so. For each element, it checks whether element[0][:-1]==tuple(split_term). The left side of this equality, element[0][:-1], simply takes the first *n* elements of each *n* + 1-gram: the [:-1] is a handy way to disregard the last element of a list. The right side of the equality, tuple(split_term), is the n-gram we're searching for ("life is a"). So we're checking for *n* + 1-grams whose first *n* elements are the same as our n-gram of interest. Whichever terms match are stored in our final output, called matching_terms.

Selecting a Phrase Based on Frequency

Our matching_terms list has everything we need to finish the job; it consists of *n* + 1-grams whose first *n* elements match the search term, and it includes their frequencies in our corpus. As long as there is at least one element in the matching terms list, we can find the element that occurs most frequently in the corpus and suggest it to the user as the completed phrase. The following snippet gets the job done:

```
if(len(matching_terms)>0):
    frequencies = [item[1] for item in matching_terms]
    maximum_frequency = np.max(frequencies)
    highest_frequency_term = [item[0] for item in matching_terms if item[1] == \
maximum_frequency][0]
    combined_term = ' '.join(highest_frequency_term)
```

In this snippet, we started by defining frequencies, a list containing the frequency of every *n* + 1-gram in our corpus that matches the search term. Then, we used the numpy module's max() function to find the highest of those frequencies. We used another list comprehension to get the first *n* + 1-gram that occurs with the highest frequency in the corpus, and finally we created a combined_term, a string that puts together all of the words in that search term, with spaces separating the words.

Finally, we can put all of our code together in a function, shown in Listing 8-2.

```
def search_suggestion(search_term, text):
    token = nltk.word_tokenize(text)
    bigrams = ngrams(token,2)
    trigrams = ngrams(token,3)
    fourgrams = ngrams(token,4)
    fivegrams = ngrams(token,5)
    grams = [ngrams(token,2),ngrams(token,3),ngrams(token,4),ngrams(token,5)]
    split_term = tuple(search_term.split(' '))
    search_term_length = len(search_term.split(' '))
    counted_grams = Counter(grams[search_term_length-1])
    combined_term = 'No suggested searches'
    matching_terms = [element for element in list(counted_grams.items()) if \
element[0][:-1] == tuple(split_term)]
    if(len(matching_terms) > 0):
        frequencies = [item[1] for item in matching_terms]
        maximum_frequency = np.max(frequencies)
```

```
        highest_frequency_term = [item[0] for item in matching_terms if item[1] == \
maximum_frequency][0]
        combined_term = ' '.join(highest_frequency_term)
    return(combined_term)
```

Listing 8-2: A function that provides search suggestions by taking an n-gram and returning the most likely n + 1-gram that starts with the input n-gram

When we call our function, we pass an n-gram as the argument, and the function returns an *n* + 1-gram. We call it as follows:

```
file = requests.get('http://www.bradfordtuckfield.com/shakespeare.txt')
file = file=file.text
text = file.replace('\n', '')
print(search_suggestion('life is a', text))
```

And you can see that the suggestion is `life is a tedious`, which is the most common 4-gram that Shakespeare used that started with the words `life is a` (tied with two other 4-grams). Shakespeare used this 4-gram only once, in *Cymbeline*, when Imogen says, "I see a man's life is a tedious one." In *King Lear*, Edgar tells Gloucester "Thy life is a miracle" (or "Thy life's a miracle," depending on which text you use), so that 4-gram would also be a valid completion of our phrase.

We can have some fun by trying a different corpus and seeing how the results differ. Let's use the corpus of Mark Twain's collected works:

```
file = requests.get('http://www.bradfordtuckfield.com/marktwain.txt')
file = file=file.text
text = file.replace('\n', '')
```

With this new corpus, we can check for search suggestions again:

```
print(search_suggestion('life is a',text))
```

In this case, the completed phrase is `life is a failure`, indicating a difference between the two text corpuses, and maybe also a difference between the style and attitude of Shakespeare and those of Mark Twain. You can also try other search terms. For example, `I love` is completed by `you` if we use Mark Twain's corpus, and `thee` if we use Shakespeare's corpus, showing a difference in style across the centuries and ocean, if not a difference in ideas. Try another corpus and some other phrases and see how your phrases get completed. If you use a corpus written in another language, you can do phrase completion for languages you don't even speak using the exact function we just wrote.

Summary

In this chapter, we discussed algorithms that can be used to work with human language. We started with a space insertion algorithm that can correct incorrectly scanned texts, and we continued with a phrase completion algorithm that can add words to input phrases to match the content and style of a text corpus. The approaches we took to these algorithms are similar to the approaches that work for other types of language algorithms, including spell checkers and intent parsers.

In the next chapter, we'll explore machine learning, a powerful and growing field that every good algorithm-smith should be familiar with. We'll focus on a machine learning algorithm called *decision trees*, which are simple, flexible, accurate, and interpretable models that can take you far on your journey through algorithms and life.

9

MACHINE LEARNING

Now that you understand the ideas behind many fundamental algorithms, we can turn to more advanced ideas. In this chapter, we explore machine learning. *Machine learning* refers to a broad range of methods, but they all share the same goal: finding patterns in data and using them to make predictions. We'll discuss a method called *decision trees* and then build one that can predict a person's level of happiness based on some of their personal characteristics.

Decision Trees

Decision trees are diagrams that have a branching structure resembling a tree. We can use decision trees in the same way we use flowcharts—by answering yes/no questions, we are guided along a path that leads to a final decision, prediction, or recommendation. The process of creating a decision tree that leads to optimal decisions is a paradigmatic example of a machine learning algorithm.

Let's consider a real-world scenario in which we might use decision trees. In emergency rooms, an important decision-maker must perform triage for every newly admitted patient. *Triage* simply means assigning priority: someone who is minutes from death but can be saved by a timely operation will be admitted to treatment immediately, whereas someone who has a paper cut or a mild case of sniffles will be asked to wait until more urgent cases can be cleared up.

Triage is difficult because you have to make a reasonably accurate diagnosis with very little information or time. If a 50-year-old woman comes to the emergency room and complains of bad chest pain, the person in charge of triage has to decide whether her pain is more likely to be heartburn or a heart attack. The thought process of a person who makes triage decisions is necessarily complex. They'll take into account a number of factors: the age and sex of the patient, whether they are obese or a smoker, the symptoms they report and the way they talk about them, the expression on their face, how busy the hospital is and what other patients are waiting for treatment, and factors that they may not even be consciously aware of. In order to become good at triage, a person has to learn many patterns.

Understanding the way a triage professional makes a decision is not easy. Figure 9-1 shows a hypothetical, totally made-up triage decision process (not meant as medical advice—don't try this at home!).

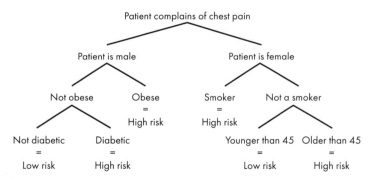

Figure 9-1: A simplified decision tree for heart attack triage

You can read this diagram from top to bottom. At the top, we can see that the heart-attack diagnosis process begins with a patient reporting chest pain. After that, the process branches out depending on the sex of the patient. If the patient is a man, the diagnosis process continues in the left branch and we determine whether he is obese. If the patient is a woman, the process continues in the right branch instead, and we determine whether she is a smoker. At each point in the process, we follow the appropriate branch until we reach the bottom of the tree, where we find the tree's classification of whether the patient is at high risk or low risk for a heart attack. This binary branching process resembles a tree whose trunk branches into smaller offshoots until reaching the ends of the farthest branches. Accordingly, the decision process illustrated in Figure 9-1 is called a decision tree.

Every place you see text in Figure 9-1 is a *node* of the decision tree. A node like "Not obese" is known as a *branching node* because there's at least one more branch to follow before we're able to make a prediction. The "Not diabetic = Low risk" node is a *terminal node* because if we've arrived there, we don't need to branch anymore and we know the decision tree's final classification ("Low risk").

If we could design a thorough, well-researched decision tree that always led to good triage decisions, it's possible that someone without medical training could perform triage of heart attack patients, which would save every emergency room in the world plenty of money because they would no longer need to hire and train judicious, highly educated triage professionals. A sufficiently good decision tree could even make it possible to replace human triage professionals with robots, though whether that's a good goal is debatable. A good decision tree may even lead to better decisions than the average human would make, since it could potentially eliminate the unconscious biases that we fallible humans possess. (And in fact, this has already happened: in 1996 and 2002, separate teams of researchers published papers about their success improving triage results for patients complaining of chest pain by using decision trees.)

The branching decision steps described in a decision tree constitute an algorithm. Executing such an algorithm is very simple: just decide which of the two branches you should be on at every node, and follow the branches to the end. But don't obey the suggestions of every decision tree you encounter. Remember that anyone can make a decision tree that prescribes any conceivable decision process, even if it leads to wrong decisions. The hard part of decision trees is not executing the decision tree algorithm but designing the decision tree so that it leads to the best possible decisions. Creating an optimal decision tree is an application of machine learning, though merely following a decision tree is not. Let's discuss the algorithm that creates an optimal decision tree—an algorithm to generate an algorithm—and proceed through the steps of the process to generate an accurate decision tree.

Building a Decision Tree

Let's build a decision tree that uses information about a person to predict how happy they are. Finding the secret of happiness has preoccupied millions of people for millennia, and social science researchers today spill plenty of ink (and burn through plenty of research grants) pursuing the answers. If we had a decision tree that could use a few pieces of information and reliably predict how happy a person is, it would give us important clues about what determines a person's happiness, and maybe even some ideas about how to achieve it ourselves. By the end of this chapter, you'll know how to build such a decision tree.

Downloading Our Dataset

Machine learning algorithms find useful patterns in data, so they require a good dataset. We'll use data from the European Social Survey (ESS) for our decision tree. You can download the files we'll use from *http://bradfordtuckfield.com/ess.csv* and *http://bradfordtuckfield.com/variables.csv*. (We got our files originally from *https://www.kaggle.com/pascalbliem/european-social-survey-ess-8-ed21-201617*, where they're publicly available for free). The ESS is a large-scale survey of adults across Europe that is conducted every two years. It asks a wide variety of personal questions, including religious affiliation, health status, social life, and level of happiness. The files we'll look at are stored in *CSV* format. The file extension *.csv* is short for *comma-separated* values, and it's a very common and simple way to store datasets so that they can be opened by Microsoft Excel, LibreOffice Calc, text editors, and some Python modules.

The file *variables.csv* contains a detailed description of each question recorded in the survey. For example, in line 103 of *variables.csv*, we can see a description of a variable called happy. This variable records a survey-taker's answer to the question "Taking all things together, how happy would you say you are?" The answers to this question range from 1 (not happy at all) to 10 (extremely happy). Look at the other variables in *variables.csv* to see the variety of information available to us. For example, the variable sclmeet records how often respondents meet socially with friends, relatives, or colleagues. The variable health records subjective general health. The variable rlgdgr records a subjective rating of how religious respondents are, and so on.

After seeing our data, we can start to think of hypotheses related to happiness predictions. We might reasonably suppose that people who have active social lives and good health are happier than others. Other variables—like gender, household size, and age—may be less easy to hypothesize about.

Looking at the Data

Let's start by reading in the data. Download the data from the link and save it locally as *ess.csv*. Then we can use the pandas module to work with it, storing it in our Python session in a variable called ess:

```
import pandas as pd
ess = pd.read_csv('ess.csv')
```

Remember, in order to read the CSV file, you'll have to be storing it in the same place as you're running Python from, or you'll have to change 'ess.csv' in the previous snippet to reflect the exact filepath where you're storing the CSV file. We can use the shape attribute of a pandas dataframe to see how many rows and columns are in our data:

```
print(ess.shape)
```

The output should be (44387, 534), indicating that our dataset has 44,387 rows (one for each respondent) and 534 columns (one for each question in the survey). We can look more closely at some of the columns that interest us by using the pandas module's slicing functions. For example, here's how we look at the first five answers to the "happy" question:

```
print(ess.loc[:,'happy'].head())
```

Our dataset, ess, has 534 columns, one for each question in the survey. For some purposes, we may want to work with all 534 columns at once. Here, we want to look only at the happy column, not the other 533. That's why we used the loc() function. Here, the loc() function has sliced the variable called happy from the pandas dataframe. In other words, it takes out only that column and ignores the other 533. Then, the head() function shows us the first five rows of that column. You can see that the first five responses are 5, 5, 8, 8, and 5. We can do the same with the sclmeet variable:

```
print(ess.loc[:,'sclmeet'].head())
```

The result should be 6, 4, 4, 4, and 6. The happy responses and the sclmeet responses will line up in order. For example, the 134th element of sclmeet is a response given by the same person who gave the response in the 134th element of happy.

The ESS staff strives to get a complete set of responses from every survey participant. However, there are some cases where responses to some survey questions are missing, sometimes because a participant either refuses to answer or doesn't know how to answer. Missing responses in the ESS dataset are assigned codes that are much higher than the possible range of real responses. For example, on a question that asks a respondent to choose a number on a scale from 1 to 10, the ESS records a 77 response if the respondent refuses to answer. For our analysis, we'll consider only responses that are complete, with no missing values for variables that interest us. We can restrict the ess data so that it contains only full responses for the variables we care about as follows:

```
ess = ess.loc[ess['sclmeet'] <= 10,:].copy()
ess = ess.loc[ess['rlgdgr'] <= 10,:].copy()
ess = ess.loc[ess['hhmmb'] <= 50,:].copy()
ess = ess.loc[ess['netusoft'] <= 5,:].copy()
ess = ess.loc[ess['agea'] <= 200,:].copy()
ess = ess.loc[ess['health'] <= 5,:].copy()
ess = ess.loc[ess['happy'] <= 10,:].copy()
ess = ess.loc[ess['eduyrs'] <= 100,:].copy().reset_index(drop=True)
```

Splitting Our Data

There are many ways we could use this data to explore the relationship between someone's social life and their happiness. One of the simplest approaches is a binary split: we compare the happiness levels of people with highly active social lives to those of people with less active social lives (Listing 9-1).

```
import numpy as np
social = list(ess.loc[:,'sclmeet'])
happy = list(ess.loc[:,'happy'])
low_social_happiness = [hap for soc,hap in zip(social,happy) if soc <= 5]
high_social_happiness = [hap for soc,hap in zip(social,happy) if soc > 5]

meanlower = np.mean(low_social_happiness)
meanhigher = np.mean(high_social_happiness)
```

Listing 9-1: Calculating the mean happiness levels of people with inactive and active social lives

In Listing 9-1, we imported the numpy module in order to calculate means. We defined two new variables, social and happy, by slicing them from the ess dataframe. Then, we used list comprehensions to find the happiness levels of all people with lower ratings of social activity (which we saved in the variable low_social_happiness) and the happiness levels of all people with higher ratings of social activity (which we saved in the variable high_social_happiness). Finally, we calculated the mean happiness rating of unsocial people (meanlower) and the mean happiness rating of highly social people (meanhigher). If you run print(meanlower) and print(meanhigher), you should see that people who rated themselves as highly social also rated themselves as slightly happier than their less socially active peers: about 7.8 was the mean happiness level reported by the socially active, and about 7.2 was the mean happiness level for the socially inactive.

We can draw a simple diagram of what we just did, as in Figure 9-2.

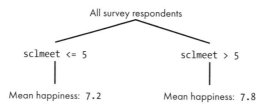

Figure 9-2: A simple decision tree predicting happiness based on frequency of social outings

This diagram of our simple binary split has already started to resemble a decision tree. This is not a coincidence: making a binary split in a dataset and comparing outcomes in each half is exactly the process at the heart of the decision tree generation algorithm. In fact, Figure 9-2 can rightfully be called a decision tree, albeit one that has only one branching node. We can use Figure 9-2 as a very simple predictor of happiness: we find out how often someone goes out socially. If their sclmeet value is 5 or less, then we can predict that their happiness is 7.2. If it is higher than 5, then we can predict that their happiness is 7.8. It will not be a perfect prediction, but it's a start and it's more accurate than random guessing.

We can try to use our decision tree to draw conclusions about the impact of various characteristics and lifestyle choices. For example, we see that the difference between low social happiness and high social happiness is about 0.6, and we conclude that increasing one's level of social activity from low to high could lead to a predicted increase in happiness of about 0.6 on a 10-point scale. Of course, trying to draw these sorts of conclusions is fraught with difficulties. It could be that social activity does not cause happiness, but rather that happiness causes social activity; maybe happy people are more often in the jovial mood that leads to ccalling their friends and arranging social meetings. Disentangling correlation from causation is beyond the scope of this chapter, but regardless of the direction of causation, our simple decision tree has at least given us the fact of the association, which we can investigate further if we care to. As cartoonist Randall Munroe put it, "Correlation doesn't imply causation, but it does waggle its eyebrows suggestively and gesture furtively while mouthing 'look over there.'"

We know how to make a simple decision tree with two branches. Now we just need to perfect how we create branches and then make many of them for a better, more complete decision tree.

Smarter Splitting

When we compared the happiness levels of people with active versus inactive social lives, we used 5 as our *split point*, saying that those who were rated higher than 5 had an active social life and those who were rated at 5 or below had an inactive social life. We chose 5 because it is a natural middle point for ratings that go from 1 to 10. However, remember that our goal is to build an accurate predictor of happiness. Rather than splitting based on intuitions about what a natural midpoint is or what seems like an active social life, it would be best to make our binary split in some place that leads to the best possible accuracy.

In machine learning problems, there are a few different ways to measure accuracy. The most natural way is to find the sum of our errors. In our case, the error that interests us is the difference between our prediction of someone's happiness rating and their actual happiness rating. If our decision tree predicts that your happiness is 6 but it's actually 8, then that tree's error for your rating is 2. If we add up the prediction errors for every respondent in some group, we can get an error sum that measures the decision tree's accuracy for predicting the happiness of members of that group. The closer we can get our error sum to zero, the better our tree is (but please see "The Problem of Overfitting" on page 179 for important caveats). This snippet shows a simple way to find the error sum:

```
lowererrors = [abs(lowhappy - meanlower) for lowhappy in low_social_happiness]
highererrors = [abs(highhappy - meanhigher) for highhappy in high_social_happiness]

total_error = sum(lowererrors) + sum(highererrors)
```

This code takes the sum of all prediction errors for all respondents. It defines lowererrors, a list containing the prediction error for each less social respondent, and highererrors, a list containing the prediction error for each more social respondent. Notice that we took the absolute value so that we're adding only non-negative numbers to calculate the error sum. When we run this code, we find that our total error is about 60224. This number is much higher than zero, but if you consider that this is a sum of errors for more than 40,000 respondents whose happiness we predicted using a tree with only two branches, suddenly it doesn't seem so bad.

We can try different split points to see if our error improves. For example, we can classify everyone with a social rating higher than 4 as high social and everyone with a social rating of 4 or lower as low social, and compare the resulting error rates. Or we could use 6 as our split point instead. In order to get the highest possible accuracy, we should check every possible split point in order, and choose the split point that leads to the lowest possible error. Listing 9-2 contains a function that accomplishes this.

```
def get_splitpoint(allvalues,predictedvalues):
    lowest_error = float('inf')
    best_split = None
    best_lowermean = np.mean(predictedvalues)
    best_highermean = np.mean(predictedvalues)
    for pctl in range(0,100):
        split_candidate = np.percentile(allvalues, pctl)

        loweroutcomes = [outcome for value,outcome in zip(allvalues,predictedvalues) if \
value <= split_candidate]
        higheroutcomes = [outcome for value,outcome in zip(allvalues,predictedvalues) if \
value > split_candidate]

        if np.min([len(loweroutcomes),len(higheroutcomes)]) > 0:
            meanlower = np.mean(loweroutcomes)
            meanhigher = np.mean(higheroutcomes)

            lowererrors = [abs(outcome - meanlower) for outcome in loweroutcomes]
            highererrors = [abs(outcome - meanhigher) for outcome in higheroutcomes]

            total_error = sum(lowererrors) + sum(highererrors)

            if total_error < lowest_error:
                best_split = split_candidate
                lowest_error = total_error
                best_lowermean = meanlower
                best_highermean = meanhigher
    return(best_split,lowest_error,best_lowermean,best_highermean)
```

Listing 9-2: A function that finds the best point at which to split a variable for a branch point of a decision tree

In this function, we use a variable called pctl (short for *percentile*) to loop through every number from 0 to 100. In the first line of the loop, we define a new split_candidate variable, which is the pctl-th percentile of the data. After that, we go through the same process we used in Listing 9-2. We create a list of the happiness levels of people whose sclmeet values are less than or equal to the split candidate, and the happiness levels of people whose `sclmeet` values are greater than the split candidate, and we check the errors that come from using that split candidate. If the error sum from using that split candidate is smaller than any of the error sums from using any previous split candidate, then we redefine the `best_split` variable to be equal to `split_candidate`. After the loop completes, the `best_split` variable is equal to the split point that led to the highest accuracy.

We can run this function for any variable, as in the following example where we run it for `hhmmb`, the variable recording the respondent's number of household members.

```
allvalues = list(ess.loc[:,'hhmmb'])
predictedvalues = list(ess.loc[:,'happy'])
print(get_splitpoint(allvalues,predictedvalues))
```

The output here shows us the correct split point as well as the predicted happiness level for the groups defined by that split point:

```
(1.0, 60860.029867951016, 6.839403436723225, 7.620055170794695)
```

We interpret this output to mean that the best place to split the `hhmmb` variable is at `1.0`; we split the survey respondents into people who live alone (one household member) and those who live with others (more than one household member). We can also see the average happiness levels for those two groups: about `6.84` and about `7.62`, respectively.

Choosing Splitting Variables

For any variable we choose in our data, we can find the optimal place to put our split point. However, remember that in a decision tree like the one in Figure 9-1, we are not finding split points for only one variable. We split men from women, the obese from the non-obese, smokers from nonsmokers, and so on. A natural question is, how we should know which variable to split at each branching node? We could reorder the nodes in Figure 9-1 so that we split by weight first and sex second, or sex only on the left branch or not at all. Deciding which variable to split at each branch point is a crucial part of generating an optimal decision tree, so we should write code for that part of the process.

We'll use the same principle we used to get optimal split points to decide the best split variable: the best way to split is the one that leads to the smallest error. In order to determine that, we need to iterate over each available variable and check whether splitting on that variable leads to the smallest error. We then determine which variable leads to the split with the lowest error. We can accomplish this by using Listing 9-3.

```
def getsplit(data,variables,outcome_variable):
    best_var = ''
    lowest_error = float('inf')
    best_split = None
    predictedvalues = list(data.loc[:,outcome_variable])
```

```
best_lowermean = -1
best_highermean = -1
for var in variables:
    allvalues = list(data.loc[:,var])
    splitted = get_splitpoint(allvalues,predictedvalues)

    if(splitted[1] < lowest_error):
        best_split = splitted[0]
        lowest_error = splitted[1]
        best_var = var
        best_lowermean = splitted[2]
        best_highermean = splitted[3]

generated_tree = [[best_var,float('-inf'),best_split,best_lowermean],[best_var,best_split,\
float('inf'),best_highermean]]

return(generated_tree)
```

Listing 9-3: A function that iterates over every variable and finds the best variable to split on

In Listing 9-3, we've defined a function with a for loop that iterates over all the variables in a list of variables. For each of those variables, it finds the best split point by calling the get_splitpoint() function. Each variable, split at its best split point, will lead to a certain error sum for our predictions. If a particular variable has a lower error sum than any previous variable we considered, we'll store that variable name as best_var. After looping through every variable name, it has found the variable with the lowest error sum, stored in best_var. We can run this code on a set of variables other than sclmeet as follows:

```
variables = ['rlgdgr','hhmmb','netusoft','agea','eduyrs']
outcome_variable = 'happy'
print(getsplit(ess,variables,outcome_variable))
```

In this case, we see the following output:

```
[['netusoft', -inf, 4.0, 7.041597337770383], ['netusoft', 4.0, inf,
7.73042471042471]]
```

Our getsplit() function has output a very simple "tree" in the form of a nested list. This tree has only two branches. The first branch is represented by the first nested list, and the second branch is represented by the second nested list. Each element of both nested lists tells us something about their respective branches. The first list tells us that we're looking at a branch based on a respondent's value of netusoft (frequency of internet usage). Specifically, the first branch corresponds to people whose value of netusoft is between -inf and 4.0, where inf stands for infinity. In other words, people in this branch report their internet usage as 4 or less on a 5-point scale. The last element of each list shows an estimated happiness rating: about 7.0 for those who are not highly active internet users. We can draw a plot of this simple tree in Figure 9-3.

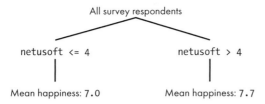

All survey respondents

netusoft <= 4   netusoft > 4

Mean happiness: 7.0   Mean happiness: 7.7

Figure 9-3: The tree generated by our first call to the getsplit() *function*

Our function so far is telling us that people with relatively low internet use report themselves as feeling less happy, with a mean happiness rating of about 7.0, whereas people who report the highest level of internet use report happiness levels at about 7.7 on average. Again, we need to be careful about how we draw conclusions from this single fact: internet use may not be a true driver of happiness, but it may instead be correlated to happiness levels because of its strong correlations with age, wealth, health, education, and other characteristics. Machine learning alone doesn't usually allow us to determine complex causal links with certainty, but, as it has with the simple tree in Figure 9-3, it enables us to make accurate predictions.

Adding Depth

We've completed everything we need to make the best possible split at each branch point and generate a tree with two branches. Next, we need to grow the tree beyond just one branching node and two terminal nodes. Look at Figure 9-1 and notice that it has more than two branches. It has what we call a *depth* of three because there are up to three successive branches you have to follow in order to get the final diagnosis. The final step of our decision tree generation process is to specify a depth that we want to reach, and build new branches until we reach that depth. The way we accomplish this is by making the additions to our getsplit() function shown in Listing 9-4.

```
maxdepth = 3
def getsplit(depth,data,variables,outcome_variable):
    --snip--
    generated_tree = [[best_var,float('-inf'),best_split,[]],[best_var,\
best_split,float('inf'),[]]]

    if depth < maxdepth:
        splitdata1=data.loc[data[best_var] <= best_split,:]
        splitdata2=data.loc[data[best_var] > best_split,:]
        if len(splitdata1.index) > 10 and len(splitdata2.index) > 10:
            generated_tree[0][3] = getsplit(depth + 1,splitdata1,variables,outcome_variable)
            generated_tree[1][3] = getsplit(depth + 1,splitdata2,variables,outcome_variable)
        else:
            depth = maxdepth + 1
            generated_tree[0][3] = best_lowermean
            generated_tree[1][3] = best_highermean
```

```
        else:
            generated_tree[0][3] = best_lowermean
            generated_tree[1][3] = best_highermean
        return(generated_tree)
```

Listing 9-4: A function that can generate a tree of a specified depth

In this updated function, when we define the generated_tree variable, we now add empty lists to it, instead of means. We insert means only in terminal nodes, but if we want a tree that has greater depth, we need to insert other branches within each branch (that's what the empty lists will contain). We also added an if statement with a long chunk of code at the end of the function. If the depth of the current branch is less than the maximum depth we want in a tree, this section will recursively call the get_split() function again to fill in another branch inside it. This process continues until the maximum depth is reached.

We can run this code to find the decision tree that leads to the lowest error in happiness predictions for our dataset:

```
variables = ['rlgdgr','hhmmb','netusoft','agea','eduyrs']
outcome_variable = 'happy'
maxdepth = 2
print(getsplit(0,ess,variables,outcome_variable))
```

When we do so, we should get the following output, which represents a tree with a depth of two:

```
[[['netusoft', -inf, 4.0, [['hhmmb', -inf, 4.0, [['agea', -inf, 15.0, 8.035714285714286],
['agea', 15.0, inf, 6.997666564322997]]], ['hhmmb', 4.0, inf, [['eduyrs', -inf, 11.0,
7.263969171483622], ['eduyrs', 11.0, inf, 8.0]]]]], ['netusoft', 4.0, inf, [['hhmmb', -inf,
1.0, [['agea', -inf, 66.0, 7.135361428970136], ['agea', 66.0, inf, 7.621993127147766]]],
['hhmmb', 1.0, inf, [['rlgdgr', -inf, 5.0, 7.743893678160919], ['rlgdgr', 5.0, inf,
7.9873320537428025]]]]]]]]
```

Listing 9-5. A representation of a decision tree using nested lists

What you see here is a collection of lists nested within each other. These nested lists represent our full decision tree, though it's not as easy to read as Figure 9-1. In each level of nesting, we find a variable name and its range, just like we saw with the simple tree illustrated in Figure 9-3. The first level of nesting shows us the same branch we found in Figure 9-3: a branch that represents respondents whose value of netusoft was less than or equal to 4.0. The next list, nested within the first, begins with hhmmb, -inf, 4.0. This is another branch of our decision tree that branches from the branch we just examined, and consists of people whose self-reported household size is 4 or less. If we drew the portion of a decision tree that we've looked at in our nested list so far, it would look like Figure 9-4.

We can continue to look at the nested lists to fill in more branches of our decision tree. Lists that are nested within other lists correspond to branches that are lower on the tree. A nested list branches from the list that contains it. The terminal nodes, instead of containing more nested lists, have an estimated happiness score.

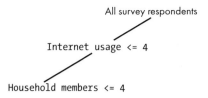

All survey respondents

Internet usage <= 4

Household members <= 4

Figure 9-4: A selection of branches from the decision tree

We've successfully created a decision tree that enables us to predict happiness levels with relatively low error. You can examine the output to see the relative determinants of happiness, and the happiness levels associated with each branch.

There is more exploring we can do with decision trees and our dataset. For example, we can try to run the same code but with a different or larger set of variables. We can also create a tree with a different maximum depth. Here is an example of running the code with a different variable list and depth:

```
variables = ['sclmeet','rlgdgr','hhmmb','netusoft','agea','eduyrs','health']
outcome_variable = 'happy'
maxdepth = 3
print(getsplit(0,ess,variables,outcome_variable))
```

When we run it with these parameters, we find a very different decision tree. You can see the output here:

```
[['health', -inf, 2.0, [['sclmeet', -inf, 4.0, [['health', -inf, 1.0, [['rlgdgr', -inf,
9.0, 7.9919636617749825], ['rlgdgr', 9.0, inf, 8.713414634146341]]], ['health', 1.0, inf,
[['netusoft', -inf, 4.0, 7.195121951219512], ['netusoft', 4.0, inf, 7.565659008464329]]]]],
['sclmeet', 4.0, inf, [['eduyrs', -inf, 25.0, [['eduyrs', -inf, 8.0, 7.9411764705882355],
['eduyrs', 8.0, inf, 7.999169779991698]]], ['eduyrs', 25.0, inf, [['hhmmb', -inf, 1.0,
7.297872340425532], ['hhmmb', 1.0, inf, 7.9603174603174605]]]]]]], ['health', 2.0, inf,
[['sclmeet', -inf, 3.0, [['health', -inf, 3.0, [['sclmeet', -inf, 2.0, 6.049427365883062],
['sclmeet', 2.0, inf, 6.70435393258427]]], ['health', 3.0, inf, [['sclmeet', -inf, 1.0,
4.135036496350365], ['sclmeet', 1.0, inf, 5.407051282051282]]]]], ['sclmeet', 3.0, inf,
[['health', -inf, 4.0, [['rlgdgr', -inf, 9.0, 6.992227707173616], ['rlgdgr', 9.0, inf,
7.434662998624484]]], ['health', 4.0, inf, [['hhmmb', -inf, 1.0, 4.948717948717949], ['hhmmb',
1.0, inf, 6.132075471698113]]]]]]]]]
```

In particular, notice that the first branch is split on the variable health instead of the variable netusoft. Other branches at lower depths are split at different points and for different variables. The flexibility of the decision tree method means that starting with the same dataset and the same end goal, two researchers can potentially reach very different conclusions, depending on the parameters they use and decisions they make about how to work with the data. This is a common characteristic of machine learning methods, and part of what makes them so difficult to master.

Evaluating Our Decision Tree

In order to generate our decision tree, we compared error rates for each potential split point and each potential splitting variable, and we always chose the variable and split point that led to the lowest error rate for a particular branch. Now that we've successfully generated a decision tree, it makes sense to do similar error calculations, not just for a particular branch but for the whole tree. Evaluating the error rate for the whole tree can give us a sense of how well we've accomplished our prediction task, and how well we're likely to perform on future tasks (for example, future hospital patients complaining of chest pain).

If you look at the decision tree output that we've generated so far, you'll notice that it's a little hard to read all the nested lists, and there's no natural way to determine how happy we predict someone is without painstakingly reading through the nested branches and finding the right terminal node. It will be helpful for us to write code that can determine the predicted level of happiness for a person based on what we know about them from their ESS answers. The following function, get_prediction(), can accomplish this for us:

```
def get_prediction(observation,tree):
    j = 0
    keepgoing = True
    prediction = - 1
    while(keepgoing):
        j = j + 1
        variable_tocheck = tree[0][0]
        bound1 = tree[0][1]
        bound2 = tree[0][2]
        bound3 = tree[1][2]
        if observation.loc[variable_tocheck] < bound2:
            tree = tree[0][3]
        else:
            tree = tree[1][3]
        if isinstance(tree,float):
            keepgoing = False
            prediction = tree
    return(prediction)
```

Next, we can create a loop that goes through any portion of our dataset and gets any tree's happiness prediction for that portion. In this case, let's try a tree with a maximum depth of four:

```
predictions=[]
outcome_variable = 'happy'
maxdepth = 4
thetree = getsplit(0,ess,variables,outcome_variable)
for k in range(0,30):
    observation = ess.loc[k,:]
    predictions.append(get_prediction(observation,thetree))

print(predictions)
```

This code just repeatedly calls the get_prediction() function and appends the result to our predictions list. In this case, we made predictions only for the first 30 observations.

Finally, we can check how these predictions compare to the actual happiness ratings, to see what our total error rate is. Here, we'll make predictions for our entire dataset, and calculate the absolute differences between our predictions and the recorded happiness values:

```
predictions = []


for k in range(0,len(ess.index)):
    observation = ess.loc[k,:]
    predictions.append(get_prediction(observation,thetree))

ess.loc[:,'predicted'] = predictions
errors = abs(ess.loc[:,'predicted'] - ess.loc[:,'happy'])

print(np.mean(errors))
```

When we run this, we find that the mean error made by predictions in our decision tree is 1.369. This is higher than zero but lower than it might be if we used a worse prediction method. Our decision tree seems to make reasonably good predictions so far.

The Problem of Overfitting

You may have noticed one very important way that our method for evaluating our decision tree doesn't resemble how predictions work in real life. Remember what we did: we used the full set of survey respondents to generate our decision tree, and then we used that same set of respondents to judge the accuracy of our tree's predictions. But it's redundant to predict the happiness ratings of respondents who already took the survey—they took the survey, so we already know their happiness ratings and don't need to predict them at all! This would be like getting a dataset of past heart attack patients, meticulously studying their pretreatment symptoms, and building a machine learning model that told us whether someone had a heart attack last week. By now, it's already quite clear whether that person had a heart attack last week, and there are better ways to know than by looking at their initial triage diagnosis data. It's easy to predict the past, but remember that true prediction is always about the future. As Wharton professor Joseph Simmons put it, "History is about what happened. Science is about what happens *next*."

You may think that this isn't a serious problem. After all, if we can make a decision tree that works well with last week's heart attack patients, it's reasonable to suppose that it will work well with next week's heart attack patients. This is true to some extent. However, there is a danger that if we aren't careful, we can encounter a common, dastardly peril called *overfitting*, the tendency of machine learning models to achieve very low error rates on the datasets used to create them (like data from the past) and then unexpectedly high error rates on other data (like the data that actually matters, from the future).

Consider the example of heart attack predictions. If we observe an emergency room for several days, maybe, by coincidence, every admitted patient who is wearing a blue shirt is suffering from a heart attack and every admitted patient who is wearing a green shirt is healthy. A decision tree model that included shirt color in its prediction variables would pick up this pattern and use it as a branching variable because it has such high diagnostic accuracy in our observations. However, if we then use that decision tree to predict heart attacks in another hospital, or for some future day, we'll find that our predictions are often wrong, as many people in green shirts also suffer heart attacks and many people in blue shirts don't. The observations we used to build our decision tree are called *in-sample observations*, and the observations that we then test our model on, which are not part of our decision tree generation process, are called *out-of-sample observations*. Overfitting means that by zealously seeking low error rates in predictions of our in-sample observations, we have caused our decision tree model to have inordinately high error rates when predicting our out-of-sample observations.

Overfitting is a serious issue in all applications of machine learning, and it trips up even the best machine learning practitioners. To avoid it, we'll take an important step that will make our decision tree creation process better resemble the real-life prediction scenario.

Remember that real-life prediction is about the future, but when we build our decision tree we necessarily have data only from the past. We can't possibly get data from the future, so we'll split our dataset into two subsets: a *training set*, which we'll use only to build our decision tree, and a *test set*, which we'll use only to check the accuracy of our decision tree. Our test set is from the past, just like the rest of our data, but we treat it as if it's the future; we don't use it to create our decision tree (as if it hasn't happened yet), but we do use it—only after completely building the decision tree—to test the accuracy of our decision tree (as if we got it later in the future).

By doing this simple training/test split, we've made our decision tree generation process resemble the real-life problem of predicting the unknown future; the test set is like a simulated future. The error rate that we find on the test set gives us a reasonable expectation of the error rate we'll get from the actual future. We'll know that we're guilty of overfitting if the error on our training set is very low and the error on our test set is very high.

We can define training and test sets as follows:

```
import numpy as np
np.random.seed(518)
ess_shuffled = ess.reindex(np.random.permutation(ess.index)).reset_index(drop = True)
training_data = ess_shuffled.loc[0:37000,:]
test_data = ess_shuffled.loc[37001:,:].reset_index(drop = True)
```

In this snippet, we used the numpy module to shuffle the data—in other words, keeping all the data but moving the rows randomly. We accomplished this with the `reindex()` method of the `pandas` module. The reindexing is done with a random shuffling of the row numbers, which we get by using the `numpy` module's permutation capability. After shuffling the dataset, we select the first 37,000 shuffled rows as a training dataset, and the remainder of the rows as a test dataset. The command `np.random.seed(518)` is not necessary, but if you run it you'll ensure that you'll get the same pseudo-random results that we show here.

After defining our training and test data, we generate a decision tree using only the training data:

```
thetree = getsplit(0,training_data,variables,outcome_variable)
```

Finally, we check the average error rate on the test data, which wasn't used to train our decision tree:

```
predictions = []
for k in range(0,len(test_data.index)):
    observation = test_data.loc[k,:]
    predictions.append(get_prediction(observation,thetree))

test_data.loc[:,'predicted'] = predictions
errors = abs(test_data.loc[:,'predicted'] - test_data.loc[:,'happy'])
print(np.mean(errors))
```

We find that our mean error rate on the test data is 1.371. This is just a hair higher than the 1.369 error rate we found when we used the whole data-set for both training and testing. This indicates that our model doesn't suffer from overfitting: it's good at predicting the past and almost exactly as good at predicting the future. Quite often, instead of getting this good news, we get bad news—that our model is worse than we thought it was—but it's good to get this news because we can still make improvements before we start using our model in a real scenario. In such cases, before our model is ready to be deployed in real life, we'll need to make improvements to it so that its error rate *on the test set* is minimized.

Improvements and Refinements

You may find that you've created a decision tree that has lower accuracy than you would like. For example, you might have worse accuracy than you should because you're guilty of overfitting. Many of the strategies for dealing with overfitting issues boil down to some kind of simplification, since simple machine learning models are less likely to suffer from overfitting than are complex models.

The first and easiest way to simplify our decision tree models is to limit their maximum depth; since depth is a variable that we can redefine in one short line, this is easy to do. To determine the right depth, we have to check the error rates on out-of-sample data for different depths. If the depth is too high, it's likely to cause high error because of overfitting. If the depth is too low, it is likely to cause high error because of *underfitting*. You can think of underfitting as something like the mirror image of overfitting.

Overfitting consists of attempting to learn from patterns that are arbitrary or irrelevant—in other words, learning "too much" from noise in our training data, like whether someone is wearing a green shirt. Underfitting consists of failing to learn enough—creating models that miss crucial patterns in the data, like whether someone is obese or uses tobacco.

Overfitting tends to result from models that have too many variables or too much depth, whereas underfitting tends to result from models that have too few variables or too little depth. Just as with many situations in algorithm design, the right place to be is a happy medium between too high and too low. Choosing the right parameters for a machine learning model, including the depth of a decision tree, is often referred to as *tuning*, because fixing the tightness of a string on a guitar or violin also relies on finding a happy medium between a pitch that's too high and one that's too low.

Another way to simplify our decision tree model is to do what's called *pruning*. For this, we grow a decision tree to its full depth and then find branches that we can remove from the tree without increasing our error rate by much.

Another refinement worth mentioning is using different measures to choose the right split point and the right splitting variable. In this chapter, we introduced the idea of using the classification error sum to decide where to put the split point; the right split point is one that minimizes our error sum. But there are other ways to decide on the right split point for a decision tree, including Gini impurity, entropy, information gain, and variance reduction. In practice, these other measures, especially Gini impurity and information gain, are almost always used rather than classification error rate, because some mathematical properties make them better in many cases. Experiment with different ways to choose a split point and splitting variable to find one that seems to perform the best for your data and your decision problem.

Everything we do in machine learning is meant to enable us to make accurate predictions on new data. When you're trying to improve a machine learning model, you can always judge whether an action is worthwhile by checking how much it improves your error rate on test data. And feel free to be creative to find improvements—anything that improves your error rate on test data is probably worth trying.

Random Forests

Decision trees are useful and valuable, but they are not regarded as the best machine learning method by professionals. This is in part because of their reputation for overfitting and relatively high error rates, and in part because of the invention of a method called *random forests*, which has become popular recently and provides an unequivocal performance improvement over decision trees.

As its name suggests, a random forest model consists of a collection of decision tree models. Each decision tree in the random forest depends on some randomization. Using randomization, we get a diverse forest with many trees instead of a forest that is just one tree repeated over and over. The randomization occurs in two places. First, the training dataset is randomized: each tree is built considering only a subset of the training set, which is randomly selected and will be different for every tree. (The test set is randomly selected at the beginning of the process, but it's not rerandomized or reselected for every tree.) Second, the variables used to build the tree are randomized: only a subset of the full set of variables is used for each tree, and the subset could be different every time as well.

After building a collection of these different, randomized trees, we have a whole random forest. To make a prediction about a particular observation, we have to find what each of these different decision trees predicts, and then take the average of the prediction for every individual decision tree. Since the decision trees are randomized in both their data and their variables, taking an average of all of them helps avoid the problem of overfitting and often leads to more accurate predictions.

Our code in this chapter creates decision trees "from scratch," by directly manipulating datasets and lists and loops. When you work with decision trees and random forests in the future, you can rely on existing Python modules that do much of that heavy lifting for you. But don't let these modules become a crutch: if you understand every step of these important algorithms well enough to code them from scratch yourself, you can be much more effective in your machine learning efforts.

Summary

This chapter introduced machine learning and explored decision tree learning, a fundamental, simple, and useful machine learning method. Decision trees constitute a type of algorithm, and the generation of a decision tree is itself an algorithm, so this chapter contained an algorithm for generating an algorithm. By learning decision trees and the fundamental ideas of random forests, you have taken a big step toward becoming a machine learning expert. The knowledge you've gained in this chapter will be a solid foundation for other machine learning algorithms you may choose to learn, including advanced ones like neural networks. All machine learning methods attempt the type of task we tried here: prediction based on patterns in a dataset. In the next chapter, we explore artificial intelligence, one of the most advanced undertakings of our adventure.

10

ARTIFICIAL INTELLIGENCE

Throughout this book, we've noted the capacity of the human mind to do remarkable things, whether it be catching baseballs, proofreading texts, or deciding whether someone is having a heart attack. We explored the ways we can translate these abilities into algorithms, and the challenges therein. In this chapter, we face these challenges once more and build an algorithm for artificial intelligence (AI). The AI algorithm we'll discuss will be applicable not only to one narrow task, like catching a baseball, but to a wide range of competitive scenarios. This broad applicability is what excites people about artificial intelligence—just as a human can learn new skills throughout life, the best AI can apply itself to domains it's never seen before with only minimal reconfiguration.

The term *artificial intelligence* has an aura about it that can make people think that it's mysterious and highly advanced. Some believe that AI enables computers to think, feel, and experience conscious thought in the same way that humans do; whether computers will ever be able to do so is an open, difficult question that is far beyond the scope of this chapter. The AI that we'll build is much simpler and will be capable of playing a game well, but not of writing sincerely felt love poems or feeling despondency or desire (as far as I can tell!).

Our AI will be able to play *dots and boxes*, a simple but nontrivial game played worldwide. We'll start by drawing the game board. Then we'll build functions to keep score as games are in progress. Next, we'll generate game trees that represent all possible combinations of moves that can be played in a given game. Finally, we'll introduce the minimax algorithm, an elegant way to implement AI in just a few lines.

La Pipopipette

Dots and boxes was invented by the French mathematician Édouard Lucas, who named it *la pipopipette*. It starts with a *lattice*, or grid of points, like the one shown in Figure 10-1.

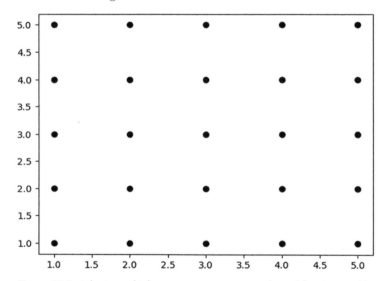

Figure 10-1: A lattice, which we can use as a game board for dots and boxes

The lattice is usually a rectangle but can be any shape. Two players play against each other, taking turns. On each turn, a player is allowed to draw a line segment that connects two adjacent points in the lattice. If they use different colors to draw their line segments, we can see who has drawn what, though that's not required. As they proceed through the game, line segments fill the lattice until every possible segment connecting adjacent points is drawn. You can see an example game in progress in Figure 10-2.

A player's goal in dots and boxes is to draw line segments that complete squares. In Figure 10-2, you can see that in the bottom left of the game board, one square has been completed. Whichever player drew the line segment that completed that square will have earned one point from doing so.

In the top-right section, you can see that three sides of another square have been drawn. It's player one's turn, and if they use their turn to draw a line segment between (4,4) and (4,3), they'll earn one point for that. If instead they draw another line segment, like a line segment from (4,1) to (5,1), then they'll give they'll give player two a chance to finish the square and earn a point. Players only earn points for completing the smallest possible squares on the board: those with a side length of 1. The player who's earned the most points when the lattice is completely filled in with line segments wins the game. There are some variations on the game, including different board shapes and more advanced rules, but the simple AI we'll build in this chapter will work with the rules we've described here.

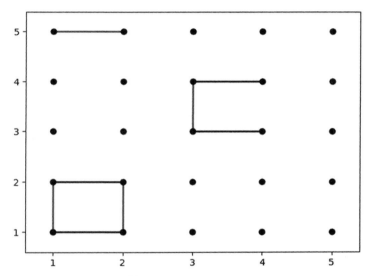

Figure 10-2: A dots and boxes game in progress

Drawing the Board

Though not strictly necessary for our algorithmic purposes, drawing the board can make it easier to visualize the ideas we're discussing. A very simple plotting function can make an $n \times n$ lattice by looping over x and y coordinates and using the plot() function in Python's matplotlib module:

```
import matplotlib.pyplot as plt
from matplotlib import collections as mc
def drawlattice(n,name):
    for i in range(1,n + 1):
        for j in range(1,n + 1):
            plt.plot(i,j,'o',c = 'black')
    plt.savefig(name)
```

In this code, n represents the size of each side of our lattice, and we use the `name` argument for the filepath where we want to save the output. The `c = 'black'` argument specifies the color of the points in our lattice. We can create a 5×5 black lattice and save it with the following command:

```
drawlattice(5,'lattice.png')
```

This is exactly the command that was used to create Figure 10-1.

Representing Games

Since a game of dots and boxes consists of successively drawn line segments, we can record a game as a list of ordered lines. Just as we did in previous chapters, we can represent a line (one move) as a list consisting of two ordered pairs (the ends of the line segment). For example, we can represent the line between (1,2) and (1,1) as this list:

```
[(1,2),(1,1)]
```

A game will be an ordered list of such lines, like the following example:

```
game = [[(1,2),(1,1)],[(3,3),(4,3)],[(1,5),(2,5)],[(1,2),(2,2)],[(2,2),(2,1)],[(1,1),(2,1)], \
[(3,4),(3,3)],[(3,4),(4,4)]]
```

This game is the one illustrated in Figure 10-2. We can tell it must still be in progress, since not all of the possible line segments have been drawn to fill in the lattice.

We can add to our `drawlattice()` function to create a `drawgame()` function. This function should draw the points of the game board as well as all line segments that have been drawn between them in the game so far. The function in Listing 10-1 will do the trick.

```python
def drawgame(n,name,game):
    colors2 = []
    for k in range(0,len(game)):
        if k%2 == 0:
            colors2.append('red')
        else:
            colors2.append('blue')
    lc = mc.LineCollection(game, colors = colors2, linewidths = 2)
    fig, ax = plt.subplots()
    for i in range(1,n + 1):
        for j in range(1,n + 1):
            plt.plot(i,j,'o',c = 'black')
    ax.add_collection(lc)
    ax.autoscale()
    ax.margins(0.1)
    plt.savefig(name)
```

Listing 10-1: A function that draws a game board for dots and boxes

This function takes n and name as arguments, just as drawlattice() did. It also includes exactly the same nested loops we used to draw lattice points in drawlattice(). The first addition you can see is the colors2 list, which starts out empty, and we fill it up with the colors we assign to the line segments that we'll draw. In dots and boxes, turns alternate between the two players, so we'll alternate the colors of the line segments that we assign to the players—in this case, red for the first player and blue for the second player. The for loop after the definition of the colors2 list fills it up with alternating instances of 'red' and 'blue' until there are as many color assignments as there are moves in the game. The other lines of code we've added create a collection of lines out of our game moves and draw them, in the same way we've drawn collections of lines in previous chapters.

NOTE   *This book is not printed in color, and it's not totally necessary to have any colors when you play dots and boxes. But the code for colors is included anyway so you can see them when you run the code at home.*

We can call our drawgame() function in one line as follows:

```
drawgame(5,'gameinprogress.png',game)
```

This is exactly how we created Figure 10-2.

Scoring Games

Next, we'll create a function that can keep score for a dots and boxes game. We start with a function that can take any given game and find the completed squares that have been drawn, and then we create a function that will calculate the score. Our function will count completed squares by iterating over every line segment in the game. If a line is a horizontal line, we determine whether it is the top of a completely drawn square by checking whether the parallel line below it has also been drawn in the game, and also whether the left and right sides of the square have been drawn. The function in Listing 10-2 accomplishes this:

```
def squarefinder(game):
    countofsquares = 0
    for line in game:
        parallel = False
        left=False
        right=False
        if line[0][1]==line[1][1]:
            if [(line[0][0],line[0][1]-1),(line[1][0],line[1][1] - 1)] in game:
                parallel=True
            if [(line[0][0],line[0][1]),(line[1][0]-1,line[1][1] - 1)] in game:
                left=True
            if [(line[0][0]+1,line[0][1]),(line[1][0],line[1][1] - 1)] in game:
                right=True
```

```
        if parallel and left and right:
            countofsquares += 1
return(countofsquares)
```

Listing 10-2: A function that counts the number of squares that appear in a dots and boxes game board

You can see that the function returns the value of countofsquares, which we initialized with a 0 value at the beginning of the function. The function's for loop iterates over every line segment in a game. We start out assuming that neither the parallel line below this line nor the left and right lines that would connect these parallel lines have been played in the game so far. If a given line is a horizontal line, we check for the existence of those parallel, left, and right lines. If all four lines of the square we've checked are listed in the game, then we increment the countofsquares variable by 1. In this way, countofsquares records the total number of squares that have been completely drawn in the game so far.

Now we can write a short function to calculate the score of a game. The score will be recorded as a list with two elements, like [2,1]. The first element of the score list represents the score of the first player, and the second element represents the score of the second player. Listing 10-3 has our scoring function.

```
def score(game):
    score = [0,0]
    progress = []
    squares = 0
    for line in game:
        progress.append(line)
        newsquares = squarefinder(progress)
        if newsquares > squares:
            if len(progress)%2 == 0:
                score[1] = score[1] + 1
            else:
                score[0] = score[0] + 1
            squares=newsquares
    return(score)
```

Listing 10-3: A function that finds the score of an in-progress dots and boxes game

Our scoring function proceeds through every line segment in a game in order, and considers the partial game consisting of every line drawn up to that turn. If the total number of squares drawn in a partial game is higher than the number of squares that had been drawn one turn previously, then we know that the player whose turn it was scored that turn, and we increment their score by 1. You can run print(score(game)) to see the score of the game illustrated in Figure 10-2.

Game Trees and How to Win a Game

Now that you've seen how to draw and score dots and boxes, let's consider how to win it. You may not be particularly interested in dots and boxes as a game, but the way to win at it is the same as the way to win at chess or checkers or tic-tac-toe, and an algorithm for winning all those games can give you a new way to think about every competitive situation you encounter in life. The essence of a winning strategy is simply to systematically analyze the future consequences of our current actions, and to choose the action that will lead to the best possible future. This may sound tautological, but the way we accomplish it will rely on careful, systematic analysis; this can take the form of a tree, similar to the trees we constructed in Chapter 9.

Consider the possible future outcomes illustrated in Figure 10-3.

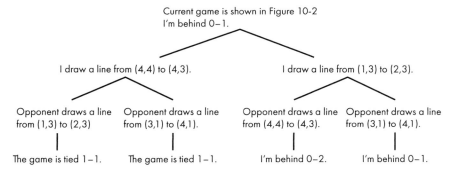

Figure 10-3: A tree of some possible continuations of our game

We start at the top of the tree, considering the current situation: we're behind 0–1 and it's our turn to move. One move we consider is the move in the left branch: drawing a line from (4,4) to (4,3). This move will complete a square and give us one point. No matter what move our opponent makes (see the possibilities listed in the two branches in the bottom left of Figure 10-3), the game will be tied after our opponent's next move. By contrast, if we use our current turn to draw a line from (1,3) to (2,3), as described in Figure 10-3's right branch, our opponent then has a choice between drawing a line from (4,4) to (4,3) and completing a square and earning a point, or drawing another line like one connecting (3,1) and (4,1), and leaving the score at 0–1.

Considering these possibilities, within two moves the game could be at any of three different scores: 1–1, 0–2, or 0–1. In this tree, it's clear that we should choose the left branch, because every possibility that grows from that branch leads to a better score for us than do the possibilities growing from the right branch. This style of reasoning is the essence of how our AI will decide on the best move. It will build a game tree, check the outcomes at all terminal nodes of the game tree, and then use simple recursive reasoning to decide what move to make, in light of the possible futures that decision will open up.

You probably noticed that the game tree in Figure 10-3 is woefully incomplete. It appears that there are only two possible moves (the left branch and the right branch), and that after each of those possible moves, our opponent has only two possible moves. Of course, this is incorrect; there are many choices available to both players. Remember that they can connect any two adjacent points in the lattice. The true game tree representing this moment in our game would have many branches, one for each possible move for each player. This is true at every level of the tree: not only do I have many moves to choose from, but so does my opponent, and each of those moves will have its own branch at every point in the tree where it's playable. Only near the end of the game, when nearly all the line segments have already been drawn, will the number of possible moves shrink to two and one. We didn't draw every branch of the game tree in Figure 10-3, because there's not enough space on the page—we only had space to include a couple of moves, just to illustrate the idea of the game tree and our thought process.

You can imagine a game tree extending to any possible depth—we should consider not only our move and the opponent's response, but also our response to that response, and our opponent's response to that response, and so on as far as we care to continue the tree-building.

Building Our Tree

The game trees we're building here are different in important ways from the decision trees of Chapter 9. The most important difference is the goal: decision trees enable classifications and predictions based on characteristics, while game trees simply describe every possible future. Since the goal is different, so will be the way we build it. Remember that in Chapter 9 we had to select a variable and a split point to decide every branch in the tree. Here, knowing what branches will come next is easy, since there will be exactly one branch for every possible move. All we need to do is generate a list of every possible move in our game. We can do this with a couple of nested loops that consider every possible connection between points in our lattice:

```
allpossible = []

gamesize = 5

for i in range(1,gamesize + 1):
    for j in range(2,gamesize + 1):
        allpossible.append([(i,j),(i,j - 1)])

for i in range(1,gamesize):
    for j in range(1,gamesize + 1):
        allpossible.append([(i,j),(i + 1,j)])
```

This snippet starts by defining an empty list, called allpossible, and a gamesize variable, which is the length of each side of our lattice. Then, we have two loops. The first is meant to add vertical moves to our list of possible moves. Notice that for every possible value of i and j, this first loop appends the move represented by [(i,j),(i,j - 1)] to our list of possible moves. This will always be a vertical line. Our second loop is similar, but for every possible combination of i and j, it appends the horizontal move [(i,j),(i + 1,j)] to our list of possible moves. At the end, our allpossible list will be populated with every possible move.

If you think about a game that's in progress, like the game illustrated in Figure 10-2, you'll realize that not every move is always possible. If a player has already played a particular move during a game, no player can play that same move again for the rest of the game. We'll need a way to remove all moves that have already been played from the list of all possible moves, resulting in a list of all possible moves remaining for any particular in-progress game. This is easy enough:

```
for move in allpossible:
    if move in game:
        allpossible.remove(move)
```

As you can see, we iterate over every move in our list of possible moves, and if it's already been played, we remove it from our list. In the end, we have a list of only moves that are possible in this particular game. You can run print(allpossible) to see all of these moves and check that they're correct.

Now that we have a list of every possible move, we can construct the game tree. We'll record a game tree as a nested list of moves. Remember that each move can be recorded as a list of ordered pairs, like [(4,4),(4,3)], the first move in the left branch of Figure 10-3. If we wanted to express a tree that consisted of only the top two moves in Figure 10-3, we could write it as follows:

```
simple_tree = [[(4,4),(4,3)],[(1,3),(2,3)]]
```

This tree contains only two moves: the ones we're considering playing in the current state of the game in Figure 10-3. If we want to include the opponent's potential responses, we'll have to add another layer of nesting. We do this by putting each move in a list together with its *children*, the moves that branch out from the original move. Let's start by adding empty lists representing a move's children:

```
simple_tree_with_children = [[[(4,4),(4,3)],[]],[[(1,3),(2,3)],[]]]
```

Take a moment to make sure you see all the nesting we've done. Each move is a list itself, as well as the first element of a list that will also contain the list's children. Then, all of those lists together are stored in a master list that is our full tree.

We can express the entire game tree from Figure 10-3, including the opponent's responses, with this nested list structure:

```
full_tree = [[[(4,4),(4,3)],[[(1,3),(2,3)],[(3,1),(4,1)]]],[[(1,3),(2,3)],[[(4,4),(4,3)],\
[(3,1),(4,1)]]]]
```

The square brackets quickly get unwieldy, but we need the nested structure so we can correctly keep track of which moves are which moves' children.

Instead of writing out game trees manually, we can build a function that will create them for us. It will take our list of possible moves as an input and then append each move to the tree (Listing 10-4).

```
def generate_tree(possible_moves,depth,maxdepth):
    tree = []
    for move in possible_moves:
        move_profile = [move]
        if depth < maxdepth:
            possible_moves2 = possible_moves.copy()
            possible_moves2.remove(move)
            move_profile.append(generate_tree(possible_moves2,depth + 1,maxdepth))
        tree.append(move_profile)
    return(tree)
```

Listing 10-4: A function that creates a game tree of a specified depth

This function, **generate_tree()**, starts out by defining an empty list called tree. Then, it iterates over every possible move. For each move, it creates a move_profile. At first, the move_profile consists only of the move itself. But for branches that are not yet at the lowest depth of the tree, we need to add those moves' children. We add children recursively: we call the generate_tree() function again, but now we have removed one move from the possible_moves list. Finally, we append the **move_profile** list to the tree.

We can call this function simply, with a couple of lines:

```
allpossible = [[(4,4),(4,3)],[(4,1),(5,1)]]
thetree = generate_tree(allpossible,0,1)
print(thetree)
```

When we run this, we see the following tree:

```
[[[(4, 4), (4, 3)], [[[(4, 1), (5, 1)]]]], [[(4, 1), (5, 1)], [[[(4, 4), (4, 3)]]]]]
```

Next, we'll make two additions to make our tree more useful: the first records the game score along with the moves, and the second appends a blank list to keep a place for children (Listing 10-5).

```
def generate_tree(possible_moves,depth,maxdepth,game_so_far):
    tree = []
    for move in possible_moves:
        move_profile = [move]
        game2 = game_so_far.copy()
        game2.append(move)
        move_profile.append(score(game2))
        if depth < maxdepth:
            possible_moves2 = possible_moves.copy()
            possible_moves2.remove(move)
            move_profile.append(generate_tree(possible_moves2,depth + 1,maxdepth,game2))
```

```
        else:
            move_profile.append([])
        tree.append(move_profile)
    return(tree)
```

Listing 10-5: A function that generates a game tree, including child moves and game scores

We can call this again as follows:

```
allpossible = [[(4,4),(4,3)],[(4,1),(5,1)]]
thetree = generate_tree(allpossible,0,1,[])
print(thetree)
```

We see the following results:

```
[[[(4, 4), (4, 3)], [0, 0], [[[(4, 1), (5, 1)], [0, 0], []]]], [[(4, 1), (5, 1)], [0, 0], \
[[[(4, 4), (4, 3)], [0, 0], []]]]]
```

You can see that each entry in this tree is a full move profile, consisting of a move (like [(4,4),(4,3)]), a score (like [0,0]), and a (sometimes empty) list of children.

Winning a Game

We're finally ready to create a function that can play dots and boxes well. Before we write the code, let's consider the principles behind it. Specifically, how is it that we, as humans, play dots and boxes well? More generally, how is it that we go about winning any strategic game (like chess or tic-tac-toe)? Every game has unique rules and features, but there's a general way to choose a winning strategy based on an analysis of the game tree.

The algorithm we'll use for choosing a winning strategy is called *minimax* (a combination of the words *minimum* and *maximum*), so called because while we're trying to maximize our score in the game, our opponent is trying to minimize our score. The constant fight between our maximization and our opponent's minimization is what we have to strategically consider as we're choosing the right move.

Let's look closely at the simple game tree in Figure 10-3. In theory, a game tree can grow to be enormous, with a huge depth and many branches at each depth. But any game tree, big or small, consists of the same components: a lot of little nested branches.

At the point we're considering in Figure 10-3, we have two choices. Figure 10-4 shows them.

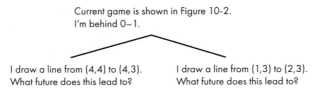

Figure 10-4: Considering which of two moves to choose

Our goal is to maximize our score. To decide between these two moves, we need to know what they will lead to, what future each move brings to pass. To know that, we need to travel farther down the game tree and look at all the possible consequences. Let's start with the move on the right (Figure 10-5).

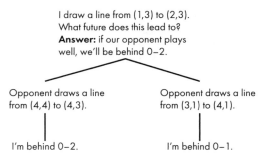

I draw a line from (1,3) to (2,3).
What future does this lead to?
Answer: if our opponent plays well, we'll be behind 0–2.

Opponent draws a line from (4,4) to (4,3).

Opponent draws a line from (3,1) to (4,1).

I'm behind 0–2.

I'm behind 0–1.

Figure 10-5: Assuming that an opponent will try to minimize your score, you can find what future you expect a move to lead to.

This move could bring about either of two possible futures: we could be behind 0–1 at the end of our tree, or we could be behind 0–2. If our opponent is playing well, they will want to maximize their own score, which is the same as minimizing our score. If our opponent wants to minimize our score, they'll choose the move that will put us behind 0–2. By contrast, consider our other option, the left branch of Figure 10-5, whose possible futures we consider in Figure 10-6.

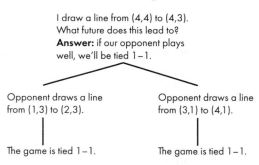

I draw a line from (4,4) to (4,3).
What future does this lead to?
Answer: if our opponent plays well, we'll be tied 1–1.

Opponent draws a line from (1,3) to (2,3).

Opponent draws a line from (3,1) to (4,1).

The game is tied 1–1.

The game is tied 1–1.

Figure 10-6: No matter what the opponent's choice, we expect the same outcome.

In this case, both of our opponent's choices lead to a score of 1–1. Again assuming that our opponent will be acting to minimize our score, we say that this move leads to a future of the game being tied 1–1.

Now we know what future will be brought about by the two moves. Figure 10-7 notes these futures in an updated version of Figure 10-4.

Because we know exactly what future to expect from each of our two moves, we can do a maximization: the move that leads to the maximum, the best score, is the move on the left, so we choose that one.

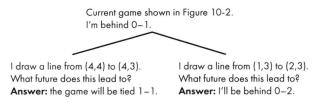

Current game shown in Figure 10-2.
I'm behind 0–1.

I draw a line from (4,4) to (4,3).
What future does this lead to?
Answer: the game will be tied 1–1.

I draw a line from (1,3) to (2,3).
What future does this lead to?
Answer: I'll be behind 0–2.

Figure 10-7: Using Figures 10-5 and 10-6, we can reason about the futures that each move will lead to and then compare them.

The reasoning process we just went through is known as the minimax algorithm. Our decision in the present is about maximizing our score. But in order to maximize our score, we have to consider all the ways that our opponent will try to minimize our score. So the best choice is a maximum of minima.

Note that minimax goes through time in reverse. The game proceeds forward in time, from the present to the future. But in a way, the minimax algorithm proceeds backward in time, because we consider the scores of possible far futures first and then work our way back to the present to find the current choice that will lead to the best future. In the context of our game tree, the minimax code starts at the top of the tree. It calls itself recursively on each of its child branches. The child branches, in turn, call minimax recursively on their own child branches. This recursive calling continues all the way to the terminal nodes, where, instead of calling minimax again, we calculate the game score for each node. So we're calculating the game score for the terminal nodes first; we're starting our game score calculations in the far future. These scores are then passed back to their parent nodes so that the parent nodes can calculate the best moves and corresponding score for their part of the game. These scores and moves are passed back up through the game tree until arriving back at the very top, the parent node, which represents the present.

Listing 10-6 has a function that accomplishes minimax.

```python
import numpy as np
def minimax(max_or_min,tree):
    allscores = []
    for move_profile in tree:
        if move_profile[2] == []:
            allscores.append(move_profile[1][0] - move_profile[1][1])
        else:
            move,score=minimax((-1) * max_or_min,move_profile[2])
            allscores.append(score)
    newlist = [score * max_or_min for score in allscores]
    bestscore = max(newlist)
    bestmove = np.argmax(newlist)
    return(bestmove,max_or_min * bestscore)
```

Listing 10-6: A function that uses minimax to find the best move in a game tree

Our `minimax()` function is relatively short. Most of it is a `for` loop that iterates over every move profile in our tree. If the move profile has no child moves, then we calculate the score associated with that move as the difference between our squares and our opponent's squares. If the move profile does have child moves, then we call `minimax()` on each child to get the score associated with each move. Then all we need to do is find the move associated with the maximum score.

We can call our `minimax()` function to find the best move to play in any turn in any in-progress game. Let's make sure everything is defined correctly before we call `minimax()`. First, let's define the game, and get all possible moves, using exactly the same code we used before:

```
allpossible = []

game = [[(1,2),(1,1)],[(3,3),(4,3)],[(1,5),(2,5)],[(1,2),(2,2)],[(2,2),(2,1)],[(1,1),(2,1)],\
[(3,4),(3,3)],[(3,4),(4,4)]]

gamesize = 5

for i in range(1,gamesize + 1):
    for j in range(2,gamesize + 1):
        allpossible.append([(i,j),(i,j - 1)])

for i in range(1,gamesize):
    for j in range(1,gamesize + 1):
        allpossible.append([(i,j),(i + 1,j)])

for move in allpossible:
    if move in game:
        allpossible.remove(move)
```

Next, we'll generate a complete game tree that extends to a depth of three levels:

```
thetree = generate_tree(allpossible,0,3,game)
```

Now that we have our game tree, we can call our `minimax()` function:

```
move,score = minimax(1,thetree)
```

And finally, we can check the best move as follows:

```
print(thetree[move][0])
```

We see that the best move is [(4, 4), (4, 3)], the move that completes a square and earns us a point. Our AI can play dots and boxes, and choose the best moves! You can try other game board sizes, or different game scenarios, or different tree depths, and check whether our implementation of the minimax algorithm is able to perform well. In a sequel to this book, we'll discuss how to ensure that your AI doesn't become simultaneously self-aware and evil and decide to overthrow humanity.

Adding Enhancements

Now that you can perform minimax, you can use it for any game you happen to be playing. Or you can apply it to life decisions, thinking through the future and maximizing every minimum possibility. (The structure of the minimax algorithm will be the same for any competitive scenario, but in order to use our minimax code for a different game, we would have to write new code for the generation of the game tree, the enumeration of every possible move, and the calculation of game scores.)

The AI we've built here has very modest capabilities. It's only able to play one game, with one simple version of the rules. Depending on what processor you use to run this code, it can probably look only a few moves forward without taking an unreasonable amount of time (a few minutes or more) for each decision. It's natural to want to enhance our AI to make it better.

One thing we'll definitely want to improve is our AI's speed. It's slow because of the large size of the game trees it has to work through. One of the main ways to improve the performance of minimax is by pruning the game tree. Pruning, as you might remember from Chapter 9, is exactly what it sounds like: we remove branches from the tree if we consider them exceptionally poor or if they represent a duplicate of another branch. Pruning is not trivial to implement and requires learning yet more algorithms to do it well. One example is the *alpha–beta pruning algorithm*, which will stop checking particular sub-branches if they are certainly worse than sub-branches elsewhere in the tree.

Another natural improvement to our AI would be to enable it to work with different rules or different games. For example, a commonly used rule in dots and boxes is that after earning a point, a player gets to draw another line. Sometimes this results in a cascade, in which one player completes many boxes in a row in a single turn. This simple change, which was called "make it, take it" on my elementary school playground, changes the game's strategic considerations and will require some changes to our code. You can also try to implement an AI that plays dots and boxes on a lattice that has a cross shape or some other exotic shape that could influence strategy. The beauty of minimax is that it doesn't require subtle strategic understanding; it requires only an ability to look ahead, and that's why a coder who isn't good at chess can write an implementation of minimax that can beat them at chess.

There are some powerful methods that go beyond the scope of this chapter that can improve the performance of computer AI. These methods include reinforcement learning (where a chess program, for example, plays against itself to get better), Monte Carlo methods (where a shogi program generates random future shogi games to help understand possibilities), and neural networks (where a tic-tac-toe program predicts what its opponent will do using a machine learning method similar to what we discussed in Chapter 9). These methods are powerful and remarkable, but they mostly just make our tree search and minimax algorithms more efficient; tree search and minimax remain the humble workhorse core of strategic AI.

Summary

In this chapter, we discussed artificial intelligence. It's a term surrounded by hype, but when you see that it takes only about a dozen lines to write a `minimax()` function, AI suddenly doesn't seem so mysterious and intimidating. But of course, to prepare to write those lines, we had to learn the game rules, draw the game board, construct game trees, and configure our `minimax()` function to calculate game outcomes correctly. Not to mention the rest of the journey of this book, in which we carefully constructed algorithms that prepared us to think algorithmically and to write this function when we needed it.

The next chapter suggests next steps for ambitious algorithmicists who want to continue their journey to the edges of the world of algorithms and push out to further frontiers.

11

FORGING AHEAD

You've made it through the dark forest of searching and sorting, across the frozen river of esoteric mathematics, over the treacherous mountain passes of gradient ascent, past the swamp of geometric despair, and you've conquered the dragon of slow runtimes. Congratulations. If you wish, you're free to return to your comfortable home in a land free from algorithms. This chapter is for those who instead wish to continue the adventure after they close this book.

No single book can contain everything about algorithms. There is too much to know, and more is being discovered all the time. This chapter is about three things: doing more with algorithms, using them in better and faster ways, and solving their deepest mysteries.

In this chapter, we'll build a simple chatbot that can talk to us about previous chapters of the book. Then we'll discuss some of the hardest problems in the world and how we might make progress toward crafting algorithms to solve them. We'll conclude by discussing some of the deepest mysteries of the world of algorithms, including detailed instructions on how to win a million dollars with advanced algorithmic theory.

Doing More with Algorithms

The 10 previous chapters of this book covered algorithms that can perform a variety of tasks in many fields. But algorithms can do even more than we've seen here. If you wish to continue your adventure with algorithms, you should explore other fields and the important algorithms associated with them.

For example, the many algorithms for information compression can store a long book in a coded form that is only a fraction of the size of the original, and they can compress a complex photograph or film file into a manageable size with either minimal or no loss of quality.

Our ability to communicate securely online, including confidently passing our credit card information to third parties, relies on cryptographic algorithms. Cryptography is great fun to study because it comes with a thrilling history of adventurers, spies, betrayals, and triumphant nerds who broke codes to win wars.

Recently, innovative algorithms have been developed to perform parallel distributed computing. Instead of performing one operation at a time, millions of times, distributed computing algorithms split up a dataset into many little parts and then send them to different computers, which perform the needed operation simultaneously and return the results, to be recompiled and presented as the final output. By working on all parts of the data concurrently instead of consecutively, parallel computing saves a huge amount of time. This is extremely useful for applications in machine learning, where there's a need to process datasets that are extremely large or to perform a large number of simple computations simultaneously.

For decades, people have been excited about the potential of quantum computing. Quantum computers, if we can engineer them to work properly, have the potential to perform extremely difficult calculations (including the calculations needed to break state-of-the-art cryptography) in a tiny fraction of the time required on today's nonquantum supercomputers. Since quantum computers are built with different architecture than standard computers, it's possible to design new algorithms that take advantage of their different physical properties to perform tasks with extra speed. For now, this is more or less only an academic concern, since quantum computers are not yet in a state where they are used for practical purposes. But if the technology ever matures, quantum algorithms could become extremely important.

When you learn about algorithms in these or many other fields, you will not be starting from scratch. By mastering the algorithms of this book, you've come to grasp they are, how they tend to function, and how to write code for them. Learning your first algorithm may have felt quite difficult, but learning your 50th or 200th will be much easier, since your brain will be used to the general patterns of how they are constructed and how to think about them.

To prove that you can now understand and code algorithms, we'll explore a few algorithms that work together to provide the functionality of a chatbot. If you can pick up how they work and how to write code for them in the short introduction provided here, then you're on your way to being able to pick up how any algorithm works in any field.

Building a Chatbot

Let's build a simple chatbot that can answer questions about the table of contents of this book. We'll start by importing modules that will be important later:

```
import pandas as pd
from sklearn.feature_extraction.text import TfidfVectorizer
from scipy import spatial
import numpy as np
import nltk, string
```

The next step we'll take to create our chatbot is *text normalization*, the process of converting natural language text to standardized substrings; it enables easy comparison between superficially different texts. We want our bot to understand that *America* and *america* refer to the same thing, that *regeneration* expresses the same idea as *regenerate* (albeit a different part of speech), that *centuries* is the plural of *century*, and that *hello;* is not essentially different from *hello*. We want our chatbot to treat in the same way words that are from the same root, unless there is some reason not to.

Say we have the following query:

```
query = 'I want to learn about geometry algorithms.'
```

The first thing we can do is convert all characters to lowercase. Python's built-in lower() method accomplishes this:

```
print(query.lower())
```

This outputs i want to learn about geometry algorithms.. Another thing we can do is remove punctuation. To do that, first we'll create a Python object called a *dictionary*:

```
remove_punctuation_map = dict((ord(char), None) for char in string.punctuation)
```

This snippet creates a dictionary that maps every standard punctuation mark to the Python object None, and it stores the dictionary in a variable called remove_punctuation_map. We then use this dictionary to remove punctuation like so:

```
print(query.lower().translate(remove_punctuation_map))
```

Here, we've used the translate() method to take all the punctuation marks we find in the query and replace them with nothing—or in other words, remove the punctuation marks. The output we get is the same as we saw before—i want to learn about geometry algorithms—but without the period at the end. Next, we can perform *tokenization*, which converts a text string to a list of coherent substrings:

```
print(nltk.word_tokenize(query.lower().translate(remove_punctuation_map)))
```

We used the nltk's tokenization function to accomplish this, yielding this output: ['i', 'want', 'to', 'learn', 'about', 'geometry', 'algorithms'].

Now we can do what's called *stemming*. In English, we use the words *jump, jumps, jumping, jumped,* and other derived forms that are all different but share a *stem*: the verb *jump*. We don't want our chatbot to be distracted by small differences in word derivation; we want to consider a sentence about jumping to be comparable to a sentence about a jumper, even though they are technically different words. Stemming removes the ends of derived words to convert them into standardized word stems. A function for stemming is available in Python's nltk module, and we can use this function with a list comprehension as follows:

```
stemmer = nltk.stem.porter.PorterStemmer()
def stem_tokens(tokens):
    return [stemmer.stem(item) for item in tokens]
```

In this snippet, we've created a function called stem_tokens(). It takes a list of tokens and calls nltk's stemmer.stem() function to turn them into stems:

```
print(stem_tokens(nltk.word_tokenize(query.lower().translate(remove_punctuation_map))))
```

The output is ['i', 'want', 'to', 'learn', 'about', 'geometri', 'algorithm']. Our stemmer has converted *algorithms* to *algorithm* and *geometry* to *geometri*. It has replaced a word with what it regards as its stem: a singular word or word portion that will make text comparisons easier. Finally, we put our normalization steps together in one function, **normalize()**:

```
def normalize(text):
    return stem_tokens(nltk.word_tokenize(text.lower().translate(remove_punctuation_map)))
```

Text Vectorization

Now you're ready to learn how to convert texts to numeric vectors. It's easier to make quantitative comparisons between numbers and vectors than between words, and we'll need to make quantitative comparisons to make our chatbot work.

We'll use a simple method called *TFIDF*, or *term frequency-inverse document frequency*, which converts documents into numeric vectors. Each document vector has one element for each term in a corpus. Each element is the product of the term frequency for a given term (a raw count of the number of times the term occurs in a particular document) and the inverse document frequency for a given term (a logarithm of a reciprocal of what proportion of documents the term appears in).

For example, imagine that we are creating TFIDF vectors for biographies of US presidents. In the context of creating TFIDF vectors, we'll refer to each biography as a document. In the biography of Abraham Lincoln, the word *representative* will probably appear at least once, since he served in the Illinois House of Representatives and the US House of Representatives. If *representative* appears three times in the biography, then we say its term frequency is 3. More than a dozen presidents have served in the US House of Representatives, so maybe about 20 out of 44 total presidential biographies contain the term *representative*. We can then calculate the inverse document frequency as:

$$\log(\frac{44}{20}) = 0.788$$

The final value we're looking for is the term frequency times the inverse document frequency: $3 \times 0.788 = 2.365$. Now consider the term *Gettysburg*. It may appear twice in Lincoln's biography but never in any other, so the term frequency will be 2 and the inverse document frequency will be the following:

$$\log(\frac{44}{1}) = 3.784$$

The vector element associated with *Gettysburg* will be the term frequency times the inverse document frequency, which is $2 \times 3.784 = 7.568$. The TFIDF value for each term should reflect its importance in a document. Soon, this will be important for our chatbot's ability to determine user intent.

We don't have to calculate TFIDF manually. We can use a function from the scikit-learn module:

```
vctrz = TfidfVectorizer(ngram_range = (1, 1),tokenizer = normalize, stop_words = 'english')
```

This line has created a TfidfVectorizer() function, which is capable of creating TFIDF vectors from sets of documents. To create the vectorizer, we have to specify an ngram_range. This tells the vectorizer what to treat as a term. We specified (1, 1), meaning that our vectorizer will treat only 1-grams (individual words) as terms. If we had specified (1, 3), it would treat 1-grams (single words), 2-grams (two-word phrases), and 3-grams (three-word phrases) as terms and create a TFIDF element for each of them. We also specified a tokenizer, for which we specified the normalize() function we created before. Finally, we have to specify stop_words, the words that we want to filter out because they're not informative. In English, stop words include *the, and, of,* and other extremely common words. By specifying stop_words = 'english', we're telling our vectorizer to filter out the built-in set of English stop words and vectorize only less common, more informative words.

Now, let's configure what our chatbot will be able to talk about. Here, it will be able to talk about the chapters of this book, so we'll create a list that contains very simple descriptions of each chapter. In this context, each string will be one of our *documents*.

```
alldocuments = ['Chapter 1. The algorithmic approach to problem solving, including Galileo and
baseball.',
               'Chapter 2. Algorithms in history, including magic squares, Russian peasant
multiplication, and Egyptian methods.',
               'Chapter 3. Optimization, including maximization, minimization, and the gradient
ascent algorithm.',
               'Chapter 4. Sorting and searching, including merge sort, and algorithm runtime.',
               'Chapter 5. Pure math, including algorithms for continued fractions and random
numbers and other mathematical ideas.',
               'Chapter 6. More advanced optimization, including simulated annealing and how to
use it to solve the traveling salesman problem.',
               'Chapter 7. Geometry, the postmaster problem, and Voronoi triangulations.',
               'Chapter 8. Language, including how to insert spaces and predict phrase
completions.',
               'Chapter 9. Machine learning, focused on decision trees and how to predict
happiness and heart attacks.',
               'Chapter 10. Artificial intelligence, and using the minimax algorithm to win at
dots and boxes.',
               'Chapter 11. Where to go and what to study next, and how to build a chatbot.']
```

We'll continue by *fitting* our TFIDF vectorizer to these chapter descriptions, which will do the document processing to get us ready to create TFIDF vectors whenever we wish. We don't have to do this manually, since there's a fit() method defined in the scikit-learn module:

```
vctrz.fit(alldocuments)
```

Now, we'll create TFIDF vectors for our chapter descriptions and for a new query asking for a chapter about sorting and searching:

```
query = 'I want to read about how to search for items.'
tfidf_reports = vctrz.transform(alldocuments).todense()
tfidf_question = vctrz.transform([query]).todense()
```

Our new query is a natural English language text about searching. The next two lines use the built-in translate() and todense() methods to create the TFIDF vectors for the chapter descriptions and the query.

Now we have converted our chapter descriptions and query into numeric TFIDF vectors. Our simple chatbot will work by comparing the query TFIDF vector to the chapter description TFIDF vectors, concluding that the chapter the user is looking for is the one whose description vector most closely matches the query vector.

Vector Similarity

We'll decide whether any two vectors are similar with a method called *cosine similarity*. If you've studied a lot of geometry, you'll know that for any two numeric vectors, we can calculate the angle between them. The rules of geometry enable us to calculate angles between vectors not only in two and three dimensions, but also in four, five, or any number of dimensions. If the vectors are very similar to each other, the angle between them will be quite small. If the vectors are very different, the angle will be large. It's strange to think that we can compare English language texts by finding the "angle" between them, but this is precisely why we created our numeric TFIDF vectors—so that we can use numeric tools like angle comparison for data that doesn't start out numeric.

In practice, it's easier to calculate the cosine of the angle between two vectors than it is to calculate the angle itself. This is not a problem, since we can conclude that if the cosine of the angle between two vectors is large, then the angle itself is small and vice versa. In Python the scipy module contains a submodule called spatial, which contains a function for calculating the cosines of angles between vectors. We can use the functionality in spatial to calculate cosines between each chapter description vector and query vector, by using a list comprehension:

```
row_similarities = [1 - spatial.distance.cosine(tfidf_reports[x],tfidf_question) for x in \
range(len(tfidf_reports)) ]
```

When we print out the row_similarities variable, we see the following vector:

```
[0.0, 0.0, 0.0, 0.3393118510377361, 0.0, 0.0, 0.0, 0.0, 0.0, 0.0, 0.0]
```

In this case, only the fourth element is greater than zero, meaning that only the fourth chapter description vector has any angular proximity to our query vector. In general, we can automatically find which row has the highest cosine similarity:

```
print(alldocuments[np.argmax(row_similarities)])
```

This gives us the chapter the chatbot thinks we're looking for:

```
Chapter 4. Sorting and searching, including merge sort, and algorithm runtime.
```

Listing 11-1 puts the chatbot's simple functionality into a function.

```
def chatbot(query,allreports):
    clf = TfidfVectorizer(ngram_range = (1, 1),tokenizer = normalize, stop_words = 'english')
    clf.fit(allreports)
    tfidf_reports = clf.transform(allreports).todense()
    tfidf_question = clf.transform([query]).todense()
    row_similarities = [1 - spatial.distance.cosine(tfidf_reports[x],tfidf_question) for x in \
range(len(tfidf_reports)) ]
    return(allreports[np.argmax(row_similarities)])
```

Listing 11-1: A simple chatbot function that takes a query and returns the document that's most similar to it

Listing 11-1 does not contain anything new; all of it is code that we've seen before. Now we can call the chatbot with a query about where to find something:

```
print(chatbot('Please tell me which chapter I can go to if I want to read about mathematics
algorithms.',alldocuments))
```

The output will tell us to go to Chapter 5:

```
Chapter 5. Pure math, including algorithms for continued fractions and random numbers and other
mathematical ideas.
```

Now that you've seen how the whole chatbot works, you can understand why we needed to do the normalization and vectorization. By normalizing and stemming words, we can make sure that the term *mathematics* will prompt the bot to return the Chapter 5 description, even though that exact word does not appear in it. By vectorizing, we enable the cosine similarity metric that tells us which chapter description is the best match.

We've completed our chatbot, which required stitching together a few different smallish algorithms (algorithms for normalizing, stemming, and numerically vectorizing text; an algorithm for calculating cosines of angles between vectors; and the overarching algorithm of providing chatbot answers based on query/document vector similarity). You may have noticed that we didn't manually do many of the calculations—the actual calculation of TFIDF or cosines was done by modules that we imported. In practice, you often don't need to truly understand the guts of an algorithm in order to import it and use it in your programs. This can be a blessing, in that it can accelerate our work and put amazingly sophisticated tools at our command when we need them. It can also be a curse because it causes people to misuse algorithms they don't understand; for example, an article in *Wired* magazine claimed that the misapplication of a particular financial algorithm (a method to use Gaussian copula functions to predict risks) was responsible for "kill[ing] Wall Street" and "swallow[ing] up trillions of dollars" and was a major cause of the Great Recession (*https://www.wired.com/2009/02/wp-quant/*). I encourage you to study the deep theory of algorithms even when the ease of importing a Python module makes such study seem unnecessary; it can always make you a better academic or practitioner.

This is perhaps the simplest possible chatbot, and it answers only questions related to chapters in this book. You could add so many enhancements to improve it: make the chapter descriptions more specific and thus more likely to match a broad range of queries; find a vectorization method that performs better than TFIDF; add more documents so that it could answer more queries. But although our chatbot is not the most advanced, we can be proud of it because it's ours and because we built it ourselves. If you can comfortably build a chatbot, you can consider yourself a competent designer and implementer of algorithms—congratulations for this culminating achievement in your journey through this book.

Becoming Better and Faster

You can do more with algorithms than you could when you started the book. But every serious adventurer will also want to be able to do things better and faster.

Many things can make you better at designing and implementing algorithms. Think about how each algorithm we implemented in this book relied on some understanding of a non-algorithmic topic. Our baseball-catching algorithm relies on an understanding of physics and even a little psychology. Russian peasant multiplication relies on an understanding of exponents and on deep properties of arithmetic, including binary notation. Chapter 7's geometry algorithms rely on insights into how points, lines, and triangles relate and fit together. The deeper your understanding of the field you're trying to write algorithms for, the easier it will be for you to design and implement algorithms. Thus, the way to get better at algorithms is easy: just understand everything perfectly.

Another natural next step for a budding algorithmic adventurer is to polish and repolish your raw programming skills. Remember that Chapter 8 introduced list comprehensions as a Pythonic tool that enables us to write language algorithms that are concise and perform well. As you learn more programming languages and master their features, you'll be able to write code that's better organized, more compact, and more powerful. Even skilled programmers can benefit from going back to the basics and mastering fundamentals until they're second nature. Many talented programmers write disorganized, badly documented, or inefficient code and think they can get away with it because it "works." But remember that code doesn't usually succeed on its own—it is almost always part of a broader program, some team effort or grand business project that relies on cooperation between people and over time. Because of this, even soft skills like planning, oral and written communication, negotiation, and team management can improve your chances of success in the world of algorithms.

If you enjoy creating perfectly optimal algorithms and pushing them to their highest efficiency, you're in luck. For a huge number of computer science problems, there is no known efficient algorithm that runs much faster than brute force. In the next section, we sketch a few of these problems and discuss what's so hard about them. If you, dear adventurer, create an algorithm that solves any of these problems quickly, you could have fame, fortune, and worldwide gratitude for the rest of your life. What are we waiting for? Let's look at some of these challenges for the most courageous among us.

Algorithms for the Ambitious

Let's consider a relatively simple problem related to chess. Chess is played on an 8×8 board, and two opponents take turns moving differently styled pieces. One piece, the queen, can move any number of squares along the row, column, or diagonal where it is placed. Usually, a player possesses only one queen, but it's possible for a player to have up to nine queens in a standard chess game. If a player has more than one queen, it may be that two or more queens "attack" each other—in other words, they are placed on the same row, column, or diagonal. The *eight queens puzzle* challenges us to place eight queens on a standard chessboard such that no pair of queens is on the same row, column, or diagonal. Figure 11-1 shows one solution to the eight queens puzzle.

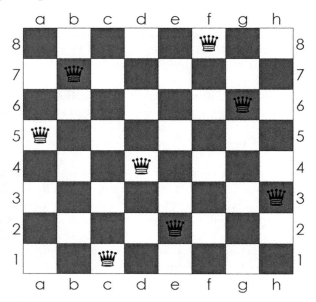

Figure 11-1: A solution to the eight queens puzzle (source: Wikimedia Commons)

None of the queens on this board attacks any of the other queens. The easiest possible way to solve the eight queens puzzle is to simply memorize a solution, like the one in Figure 11-1, and repeat it whenever you're asked to solve the puzzle. However, a couple of extra twists to the puzzle make memorization infeasible. One twist is to increase the number of queens and the size of the board. The *n queens problem* asks us to place *n* queens on an *n×n* chessboard such that no queen attacks any of the others; *n* could be any natural number, no matter how high. Another twist is the *n queens completion problem*: your opponent starts by placing some of the queens, maybe in places that will make it difficult for you to place the rest, and you have to place the rest of the *n* queens so that none attack any others. Can you design an algorithm that will run very quickly and solve this problem? If so, you could earn a million dollars (see "Solving the Deepest Mysteries" on page 212).

Figure 11-1 may remind you of sudoku, since it involves checking for the uniqueness of symbols in rows and columns. In sudoku, the goal is to fill in the numbers 1 through 9 such that each row, column, and 3×3 block contains exactly one instance of each number (Figure 11-2). Sudoku first gained popularity in Japan, and indeed a sudoku puzzle is reminiscent of the Japanese magic squares we explored in Chapter 2.

5	3			7				
6			1	9	5			
	9	8					6	
8				6				3
4			8		3			1
7				2				6
	6					2	8	
			4	1	9			
				8			7	9

Figure 11-2: An uncompleted sudoku grid (source: Wikimedia Commons)

It's an interesting exercise to think about how to write an algorithm that could solve sudoku puzzles. The simplest, slowest possible algorithm would rely on brute force: just try every possible combination of numbers and repeatedly check whether they constitute a correct solution, repeating until the solution is found. This would work, but it lacks elegance, and it could take an extremely long time. It doesn't seem intuitively right that filling in 81 numbers in a grid according to rules that anyone could easily follow should stretch the limits of our world's computing resources. More sophisticated solutions could rely on logic to cut down the required runtime.

The *n* queens completion problem and sudoku share another important trait: solutions are very easy to check. That is, if I show you a chessboard with queens on it, it will probably take you only a few moments to check whether you're looking at a solution to the *n* queens completion problem, and if I show you a grid of 81 numbers, you can easily tell whether you're looking at a correct sudoku solution. The ease with which we can check solutions is, tragically, not matched by the ease of generating solutions—it can take hours to solve a difficult sudoku puzzle that then takes only seconds to verify. This generation/verification effort mismatch is common in many areas of life: I can tell with very little effort whether a meal is delicious, but creating a wonderful meal takes a much greater investment of time and resources. Similarly, I can check whether a painting is beautiful in much less time than it takes to create a beautiful painting, and I can verify whether a plane can fly with much less effort than it takes to build a flying plane.

Problems that are difficult to solve algorithmically but whose solutions are easy to verify are extremely important in theoretical computer science, and they are the deepest and most pressing mystery in the field. Especially courageous adventurers may dare to plunge into these mysteries—but beware the perils awaiting you there.

Solving the Deepest Mysteries

When we say that sudoku solutions are easy to verify but hard to generate, what we mean in more formal terms is that solutions can be verified in *polynomial time*; in other words, the number of steps required for solution verification is some polynomial function of the size of the sudoku board. If you think back to Chapter 4 and our discussion of runtimes, you'll remember that even though polynomials like x^2 and x^3 can grow fast, they are quite slow compared to exponential functions like e^x. If we can verify an algorithmic solution to a problem in polynomial time, we regard that verification as easy, but if the generation of a solution takes exponential time, we regard it as hard.

There's a formal name for the class of problems whose solutions can be verified in polynomial time: the *NP complexity class*. (Here, NP stands for *nondeterministic polynomial time*, for reasons that would require a long digression into theoretical computer science that would not be useful here.) NP is one of the two most fundamental complexity classes in computer science. The second is called *P*, for polynomial time. The P complexity class of problems contains all problems whose solutions can be found by an algorithm that runs in polynomial time. For P problems, we can *find* full solutions in polynomial time, while for NP problems, we can *verify* solutions in polynomial time, but it may take exponential time to find those solutions.

We know that sudoku is an NP problem—it is easy to verify a proposed sudoku solution in polynomial time. Is sudoku also a P problem? That is, is there an algorithm that can solve any sudoku puzzle in polynomial time? No one has ever found one, and no one appears to be close to finding one, but we don't feel certain that it's impossible.

The list of problems that we know are in NP is extremely long. Some versions of the traveling salesman problem are in NP. So is the optimal solution to the Rubik's cube, as well as important mathematical problems like integer linear programming. Just as with sudoku, we wonder whether these problems are also in P—can we find solutions for them in polynomial time? One way to phrase this question is, Does P = NP?

In 2000, the Clay Mathematics Institute published a list called the Millennium Prize Problems. It announced that any person who published a verified solution to one of the problems would receive a million dollars. The list was meant to be seven of the world's most important problems related to mathematics, and the question of whether P = NP is one of them; no one has claimed its prize yet. Will one of the noble adventurers reading these words eventually break the Gordian knot and solve this most crucial of algorithmic problems? I sincerely hope so and wish each of you luck, strength, and joy on the journey.

If there is ever a solution, it will be a proof of one of the following two assertions: either that P = NP or that P ≠ NP. A proof that P = NP could be relatively simple, since all that would be required is a polynomial-time algorithmic solution to an NP-complete problem. *NP-complete* problems are a special type of NP problem defined by the feature that every single NP problem can be quickly reduced to an NP-complete problem; in other words, if you can solve one NP-complete problem, you can solve every NP problem. If you can solve any single NP-complete problem in polynomial time, you can solve every NP problem in polynomial time, which would prove that P = NP. As it happens, sudoku and the n-queens completion problem are both NP-complete. This means that finding a polynomial-time algorithmic solution to either of them would not only solve every existing NP problem but also earn you a million dollars and worldwide, lifelong fame (not to mention the power to beat everyone you know in friendly sudoku competitions).

A proof that P ≠ NP would probably not be as straightforward as a solution to sudoku. The notion that P ≠ NP means that there are NP problems that cannot be solved by any algorithm with polynomial runtime. Proving this amounts to proving a negative, and it is conceptually much harder to prove that something cannot exist than it is to point to an example of something. Making progress in a proof that P ≠ NP will require extended study in theoretical computer science beyond the scope of this book. Though this path is harder, it seems to be the consensus among researchers that P ≠ NP, and that if there is ever a resolution to the P versus NP question, it will probably be a proof that P ≠ NP.

The P versus NP question is not the only deep mystery related to algorithms, although it is the most immediately lucrative one. Every aspect of the field of algorithm design has wide-open fields for adventurers to charge into. There are not only theoretical and academic questions, but also practical ones related to how to implement algorithmically sound practices in business contexts. Waste no time: remember what you have learned here and sally forth anon, carrying your new skills with you to the utmost bounds of knowledge and practice, on your lifelong algorithmic adventure. Friends, adieu.

INDEX

Note: *Italicized page numbers locate definitions of terms.*

findnearest() function, using in
TSP (traveling salesman
problem), 109
float('nan') function, using with
Kurushima's algorithm, 24
floor() function, using for binary
search, 73–74
for loop, using with words and
spaces, 157
fractions to radicals, 88. *See also*
continued fractions
Franklin, Benjamin, 126
Frisbee, trajectory vectors, 6
functions
inverting, 75
recursion, *22*

G

Galilean model, 2–5
game trees. *See also* AI (artificial
intelligence); decision
trees; random forests
building, 192–195
and winning games, 190–192
games. *See also* dots and boxes game
choosing moves, 195–198
minimax algorithm, *195*–198
representing, 188–189
scoring, 189–190
winning, 195–198
Gaussian normal curve, 96
gen_delaunay() function, passing *x*
and *y* values to, 143
generate_tree() function, using with
games, 194
genlines function, using with
triangles, 129
genlines function, TSP (traveling
salesman problem), 104
geometry. *See also* DT (Delaunay
triangulation)
postmaster problem, 126–128
representing points, 128
tangent of angle, 8–9
terminology, 130
triangles, 128–134
get_number() function, using with
continued fractions, 85

get_prediction() function, using with
decision trees, 178–179
get_split() function, using with
decision trees, 174–176
get_splitpoint() function, using with
decision trees, 174
git bisect software, using for binary
search, 75
global variables, defining for
simulated annealing, 122
golden ratio, *78–79*
gradient ascent, *35*
climbing income hill, 44–45
implementing, 40–41
local extrema, 42–44
objections, 41–42
using, 49
gradient descent, *35*, *47*
Gravity's Rainbow, 3
greedy algorithms, TSP (traveling
salesman problem),
112–113
guided search, using in TSP
(traveling salesman
problem), *112*

H

half_double dataframe, RPM (Russian
peasant multiplication), 18
halving column, RPM (Russian
peasant multiplication),
14–20
happiness levels, calculating with
decision trees, 170
hill climbing, 47–48
howfull argument, Kurushima's
algorithm, 31–32

I

if statement
inserting pop() function into,
66–67
using with words and
spaces, 151
imported corpus, using to check for
valid words, 154–155. *See
also* corpus

inner physicist theory, 5–6

in-sample observations, using with decision trees, *180*

`insert()` function, using with bits, 98

insertion sort, 52–55
    comparing to exponential function, 61
    counting steps in, 63–64
    step counter, 58

installing, `matplotlib` module, 3

integers, dividing to get quotient, 84

`inverse_sin(0.9)` function, using for binary search, 75

inverting functions, 75

irrational number, *79*

J

Japanese magic squares. *See also* magic squares; squares
    Kurushima's algorithm in Python, 24–30
    Luo Shu square in Python, 22–23

K

Kepler, Johannes, 78

k-means machine-learning method, 56

k-NN machine-learning method, 56

Kurushima's algorithm
    function, 30–31
    rules, 25–28

L

la pipopipette, *186–187*

language algorithms
    difficulty, 150
    phrase completion, 159–163
    space insertion, 150–158

lattice, using with la pipopipette, *186–187*

LCGs (linear congruential generators), 92–93

`left` and `right` variables, Python, 66

Leibniz, Gottfried Wilhelm, 130–131

LFSRs (linear feedback shift registers), 97–99

lifetime income and education, 42–45

lines of sight, plotting for thrown ball, 7–8

list comprehensions, *149*, 156

list indexing syntax, Python, 68–69

lists, sorting, 153

`loc` functionality, RPM (Russian peasant multiplication), 19

local extrema, problem, 42–45

loops, RPM (Russian peasant multiplication), 18

lower bound, defining for binary search, 73

`lower()` method, using with chatbot, 203

Lucas, Édouard, 186

Luo Shu square, creating in Python, 22–*23*

M

machine learning. *See also* decision trees
    overview, 165
    random forests, 182–183

machine-learning methods, k-means clustering and k-NN, 56

magic eye, 147

magic squares, *22–23*. *See also* Japanese magic squares; squares
    arguments, 31–34
    Kurushima's algorithm, 30–31
    of odd dimension, 24
    patterns, 34
    "walk" through, 28

The Math Instinct: Why You're a Mathematical Genius (Along with Lobsters, Birds, Cats, and Dogs), 5–6

math library, Python, 73–74

mathematical physics, interpretation of, 92

`math.floor()`, RPM (Russian peasant multiplication), 18

perturb search algorithm, *112*. *See also* simulated annealing

phi
  compressing and communicating, 79–80
  and golden ratio, *78*

phrase completion, 159–163

`plot()` function, using with dots and boxes game, 187–188

`plot_triangle()` function
  defining, 129
  improving, 133–134

`plotitinerary()` function, using in TSP (traveling salesman problem), 105

plotting capabilities, Galilean model, 3

.png file, saving to, 129–130

points, representing, 128–130

`points_to_triangle()` function
  defining, 128
  using in triangulation, 134

polynomial, Galilean model, 3

polynomial time, verifying solutions in, 212

`pop()` method
  inserting into `if` statements, 66–67
  using with bits, 98

`pop()` method, sorting via insertion, 55

postmaster problem, 126–128

potential words. *See also* words
  checking for, 153–154
  finding halves of, 156–158

prediction errors, decision trees, 171–172

`print(cities)` function, TSP (traveling salesman problem), 103

`print(lines)` function, TSP (traveling salesman problem), 104

`print(square)` function, using with Kurushima's algorithm, 24–25

PRNGs (pseudorandom number generators), *92*–99

problems, solving with algorithms, 10–11

Project Gutenberg, 160

pruning decision trees, 182, *199*

pseudorandomness, *92*–93

Pynchon, Thomas, 3

Pythagorean theorem
  using, 105
  using with triangles, 130
  using in TSP (traveling salesman problem), 108–109

Python
  creating Luo Shu square, 22–23
  Euclid's algorithm, 20–22
  feedback shift register, 98
  Galilean model, 3
  implementing RPM (Russian peasant multiplication), 18–20
  Kurushima's algorithm, 24
  `left` and `right` variables, 66
  list indexing syntax, 68
  math library, 73–74
  ordered pairs in, 152
  overlapping sums test, *95*–96
  pandas module, 19
  random module, 58–59
  `random.choice()` function, 28
  rules for Kurushima's algorithm, 27–28, 30–31
  square roots in, 90–91
  timeit module, 57
  using tuples with words and spaces, 152

Q

quotient, getting by dividing integers, 84

R

radicals and fractions, 88

radius, returning for triangle, 132–133

Ramanujan, Srinivasa, 88

random forests, 182–183. *See also* decision trees; game trees

random model, Python, 58–59
random number generators
    judging PRNGs
        (pseudorandom number
        generators), 93–95
    LCDs (linear congruential
        generators), 92–93
    LFSRs (linear feedback shift
        registers), 97–99
    overview, 91
random.choice() function, Python, 28
randomness
    Diehard tests for, 95–97
    possibility of, 91–92
random.seed() function, 59
recursion
    of functions, 22
    implementing merge sort
        with, 69
    using with Euclid's algorithm, 85
re.finditer() function, using with
    words, 152
reindex() method, using with
    decision trees, 181
remove() function, using with words
    and spaces, 155
replace() function, using with words
    and spaces, 155
resetthresh variable, adding, 122
revenue
    maximum, 39
    showing for tax rates, 36–37
right and left variables, Python, 66
RPM (Russian peasant
    multiplication), 13–20
rules, applying with Kurushima's
    algorithm, 27, 30–31

S

science, laws of, 130–131
scoring games, 189–190
search suggestions, strategy for
    generating, 160, 162–163
searching versus sorting, 72–75
Shakespeare's works, accessing,
    160–161, 163
siman() function, using for simulated
    annealing, 122–123

Simmons, Joseph, 179
simulated annealing, 115–124. *See
    also* optimization; perturb
    search; TSP (traveling
    salesman problem)
sleep sort, 70–72. *See also* sorting
Smith, David Eugene, 22
solve-for-*x* strategy, *4*–5, 10–11
sorted filing cabinets, merging, 62,
    64–65. *See also* file-sorting
    method
sorting. *See also* merging to sorting;
    sleep sort
    lists, 153
    via insertion, 54–55
    to searching, 72–75
space insertion
    checking for potential words,
        153–154
    checking for valid words,
        154–156
    dealing with compound words,
        152–153
    defining word lists, 151–152
    finding halves of potential
        words, 156–158
    finding words, 151–152
    overview, 150–151
spaces
    getting substrings between,
        153–154
    inserting into texts, 158
    words ending with, 156
split points, choosing for decision
    trees, *171*, 182
splitting variables, choosing for
    decision trees, 182
square brackets ([])
    using with list
        comprehension, 152
    using with loc functionality, 19
square matrix, antidiagonal of, 26–27
square roots, 89–91
squares, filling in, 30–34. *See also*
    Japanese magic squares;
    magic squares
start() function, using with
    words, 153

using with merge sort, 67
using with square roots, 90–91
while loop, RPM (Russian peasant
multiplication), 18
winning games, 195–198
word list, defining, 151–152
words. *See also* compound words;
potential words
checking validity with imported
corpus, 154–156

ending with spaces, 156
finding, 151–152
tokenizing, *159*–160

X

XOR operation, *98*

RESOURCES

Visit *https://nostarch.com/Dive-Into-Algorithms* for errata and more information.